U. S. Presidents: From Awesome to Awful

The Best Three in a Row
And
The Worst Three in a Row

Thomas O. Kelly II and Douglas A. Lonnstrom

Three Lakes Publishing
Clifton Park, NY

Library of Congress Control Number 2013951703

978-0-9843430-3-4   ISBN-13

Printed in the United States of America

Table of Contents

Preface

A preface, dictionaries tell us, is a preliminary, a prelude or introduction. In that context, it seems appropriate to explain how and why the effort began.

This book had its origins in 1980, when the nascent Siena College Research Institute [SRI] began its tracking studies on U. S. Presidents. During the ensuing decades and polls, we noticed that highly successful presidencies rarely succeed each other. It occurred to us that rather than focus on assembling our results in an attempt to examine all American Presidents, we should examine those rare periods of successive, high-achieving presidencies. We would focus not only on individual presidential traits and talents, but on the events, problems and crises that characterized the eras and engaged the intellects, energies and talents of the Presidents involved.

When we examined the responses to our expert opinion tracking studies we saw that they revealed two historic periods in which three consecutive Presidents provided talented leadership to the nation. They also highlighted one mirror-image era, when three consecutive Presidents appear to have been inadequate to the problems that they and the nation faced. It seemed to us that it is probably not coincidental that each triad represents an era of particular significance and/or peril in American history.

Those three eras and nine Presidents form the core of this book. The first group (as determined by the 2002 poll) consists of Franklin D. Roosevelt, Harry S Truman and Dwight D. Eisenhower. The second set focuses on George Washington, John Adams and Thomas Jefferson. The unsuccessful trio includes Millard Fillmore, Franklin Pierce and James Buchanan.

We also noted that the three groups with which we were working dealt with three of the most significant eras in American history. That fact accorded well with our decision to focus on both the period and the Presidents. In the groups isolated, the first came of age in World War I and to mature authority in the period of the Great Depression and World War II. They dealt as well with the origins of the Cold War. The second trio, composed entirely of Founders , directs our attention to three Presidents, all of whom had come to political maturity and authority before and during the American Revolution. Their presidencies were, often consciously, preoccupied with the creation and functioning of republican government. In their minds, that meant a completion of the idea of the American Revolution. They intended to demonstrate a fundamental principle of the Revolution – that men could govern themselves without monarchical or aristocratic establishments.

The third group, the "ineffectives," found itself wrestling with the issues of slavery and territorial expansion and the coming of the Civil War. They came up short.

We determined that the presidency of William J. Clinton, ending at the start of a new century and a new millennium, furnished a logical conclusion, encompassing all American Presidents from George Washington to Bill Clinton.

The determination of rank and place for the Presidents is the result of responses to questionnaires returned to the Siena Research institute by over 200 experts, U. S. college professors of history and political science. Each President was ranked on a scale of 1 to 5 on 20 specific questions, ranging from leadership to integrity. The 20th question, asking each respondent for a current, overall ranking of each President, is resistant to analysis. We simply have appended it at the end of each President's chapter.

We would like to emphasize that the creation of the rankings for each President was not determined by the SRI but by the cumulative weight of the responses of our experts.

Conventional wisdom, based on any number of surveys of college professors of both history and political science and by both academic and commercial polling, tells us that such a sampling will tend to be to the political left of the norm. We think it is more important that it represents a cross section of the profession. Therefore, it undoubtedly represents what American college students are actually being taught, whether in the class lectures and discussions or in scholarly articles and books.

This work is intended for the general reader. We therefore have omitted some of the trappings of academic publication. There are, as a result, a minimal number of footnotes, some of which, where context allows, are included in the text. Some are formal. Any factual item likely to be common knowledge – to appear in a standard text, or to appear in the first page of an internet query – has not been noted.

Issues of space also have caused us to limit analysis of judicial and executive appointments to Supreme Court nominees and members of the President's cabinet.

Over the years, in both general and specific terms, we have, on occasion, found ourselves in less than perfect agreement with the results generated by our respondents. It would then be disingenuous to assume that the reader will necessarily agree with us. Indeed, we invite those who do disagree with us to do so lustily.

Prologue - History of Presidential Polling

Serious expert presidential polling began in 1948 when Arthur Schlesinger Sr., the Harvard historian, asked 58 of his fellow historians to rate presidents in five categories: Great, Near Great, Average, Below Average and Failure. As directors of the Siena College Research Institute, we became concerned about the arbitrariness of his five categories and the self-selection of colleagues. The whole process seemed unduly subjective to us. As a result we designed an instrument that numerically rated Presidents in 20 different categories that were, overall, fair to all – or virtually all – Presidents over the 220 plus years the United States has existed. We then combined those 20 results for each President to create an overall rating.

These rankings represent the combined thinking in 2002 of more than 200 randomly selected experts across the country. They were history and political science professors chosen by their department heads as best qualified to judge presidential history. In summary, we have a ranking for every President in all 20 categories as well as an overall ranking as determined by the experts who, it should be repeated, were not chosen by us. Our method has been widely published and accepted as a standard for rating Presidents. It has been copied by others and our results have been published twice in the prestigious Presidential Studies Quarterly. [A complete discussion of our methodology will be found in the appendix.].

The twenty categories are as follows:

1. Background (family, education, experience)
2. Party Leadership (political)
3. Communication Ability (speak, write)
4. Relationship with Congress
5. Court Appointments
6. Handling of U. S. Economy

7. Luck
8. Ability to Compromise
9. Willing to Take Risks
10. Executive Appointments
11. Overall Ability
12. Imagination
13. Domestic Accomplishments
14. Integrity
15. Executive Ability
16. Foreign Policy   Accomplishments
17. Leadership Ability
18. Intelligence
19. Avoid Crucial Mistakes
20. Present Overall View

The following is the overall ranking of America's Presidents based on their combined rating on the above 20 categories, in the 2002 survey.

1. Franklin Delano Roosevelt
2. Abraham Lincoln
3. Theodore Roosevelt
4. George Washington
5. Thomas Jefferson
6. Woodrow Wilson
7. Harry S Truman
8. James Monroe
9. James Madison
10. Dwight D. Eisenhower
11. James K. Polk
12. John Adams
13. Andrew Jackson
14. John F. Kennedy
15. Lyndon B. Johnson
16. Ronald Reagan
17. John Quincy Adams
18. William J. Clinton
19. William McKinley
20. Grover Cleveland
21. William Howard Taft
22. George H. W. Bush

23. Martin Van Buren
24. Jimmy Carter
25. Richard M. Nixon
26. Rutherford B. Hayes
27. Gerald R. Ford
28. Calvin Coolidge
29. Chester Alan Arthur
30. Herbert Hoover
31. Benjamin Harrison
32. James A. Garfield
33. Zachary Taylor
34. Ulysses S. Grant
35. William Henry Harrison
36. John Tyler
37. Millard Fillmore
38. Franklin Pierce
39. Warren G. Harding
40. James Buchanan
41. Andrew Johnson

The list below is in chronological order. The number in the column to the right of each president is his rank.

1. George Washington	4
2. John Adams	12
3. Thomas Jefferson	5
4. James Madison	9
5. James Monroe	8
6. John Quincy Adams	17
7. Andrew Jackson	13
8. Martin Van Buren	24
9. William Henry Harrison	36
10. John Tyler	37
11. James K. Polk	11
12. Zachary Taylor	34
13. Millard Fillmore	38
14. Franklin Pierce	39
15. James Buchanan	41
16. Abraham Lincoln	2
17. Andrew Johnson	42

18. Ulysses S. Grant	35
19. Rutherford B. Hayes	27
20. James A. Garfield	33
21. Chester Alan Arthur	30
22. Grover Cleveland	20
23. Benjamin Harrison	32
24. William McKinley	19
25. Theodore Roosevelt	3
26. William Howard Taft	21
27. Woodrow Wilson	6
28. Warren G. Harding	40
29. Calvin Coolidge	29
30. Herbert Hoover	31
31. Franklin Delano Roosevelt	1
32. Harry S Truman	7
33. Dwight D. Eisenhower	10
34. John F. Kennedy	14
35. Lyndon B. Johnson	15
36. Richard M. Nixon	26
37. Gerald R. Ford	28
38. Jimmy Carter	25
39. Ronald Reagan	16
40. George H. W. Bush	22
41. William J. Clinton	18

An examination of this list suggests that our experts believe the best Presidents to serve consecutive terms were Franklin Roosevelt, Harry Truman and Dwight Eisenhower. (They also happen to have served for the longest period of time of any three Presidents – 28 years.) They rank 1, 7 and 10 for a combined score of 18, which is dominant in a case, like golf, where low total wins. They form Book I. The next lowest score, of 21 would be George Washington, John Adams and Thomas Jefferson, 4, 12 and 5 for a combined 21. Their service totaled 20 years and constitutes Book II.

This type of comparison seems to necessitate the next step, when and who were the worst. The bottom set, Book III, consists of Millard Fillmore, Franklin Pierce and James Buchanan, the three Presidents immediately preceding the Civil War. Their respective ranks were 38, 39 and 41 for a total of 118, over six and a half times the top three. Their combined terms were just over 10 ½ years. Few, if any, historians would find it possible to argue many points in their favor.

Finally, it seemed logical, indeed virtually necessary, to consider and contrast Abraham Lincoln with his immediate predecessors. Having briefly done this, we decided, somewhat arbitrarily, to equally briefly examine Theodore Roosevelt's presidency. That enabled us to include all of the Presidents who have constituted the top five in all SRI surveys. As we will stipulate, the top five presidents differ in ranking and quality very much from all other Presidents, even the other members of the top ten. Those two presidents constitute Book IV.

In Book V, we have provided a rather skeletal look at the recent Presidents – those from John F. Kennedy through William J. Clinton. In these instances, we have merely indicated the President, his years of service and his ranking, in both individual categories and overall, in the 2002 SRI survey. We have also provided a quotation from each, usually one quite frequently associated with a significant moment or idea of his presidency.

Let us now return to the numerical top of our list and proceed to an examination of the rank and standing of our first group, FDR, Truman and Eisenhower.

Book I

Our calculations indicate that there have been only two periods in American history when three highly competent Presidents have served successive terms in office. The 20th Century three were President Franklin Roosevelt, succeeded by President Harry Truman, and he, in turn, by President Dwight D. Eisenhower.

The second group, where the use of that number is justified only arithmetically, consists of America's first three Presidents – George Washington, John Adams and Thomas Jefferson.

Focusing on the first trio, we might note a very tight chronological grouping. Among them, FDR the oldest, was born in 1882. Harry Truman was born only two years later, in 1884 and Dwight Eisenhower was last, born in 1890. Only eight years separate their births. They are also closely related by history. Each of them, to a greater or lesser degree, was marked by the events and circumstances of World War I and, of course, World War II. Franklin Roosevelt served as Woodrow Wilson's assistant secretary of the navy during World War I, a probably not unconscious parallel with the service of his cousin Theodore in McKinley's time. In those years, (1917-1918) Harry Truman helped raise and then led in combat Battery D of the Missouri National Guard Field Artillery. Dwight Eisenhower, a graduate of the Class of 1915 at West Point, saw non-combat service at Gettysburg, Pa., then called Camp Colt, where the United States Army instituted its early training in the use of armor (tanks) in war.

Finally, during the inter-war years, each man underwent significant personal testing – Roosevelt, most famously, when, in the summer of 1921, only a year after his selection as the vice-presidential nominee of the Democratic Party, he was stricken with polio. The story of Truman's business problems and the near bankruptcy of his haberdashery shop has been told often. It represented a low point in his personal life. However, in a left-handed way, it may have assisted him by shifting his life's work in the direction of politics. Probably less well known is the story of Eisenhower in the 1920s and early

1930s. Like most young officers of that time, his career languished in an army severely underfunded and viewed in many circles as at least a highly dubious career choice. He and Mrs. Eisenhower also lost a dearly beloved child during that era.

What was to transpire, of course, was that these three men – of the same generation and of old stock, Northern European heritage, three men largely formed by very similar historical experiences though of widely different backgrounds and personal experience – would man the helm of American government from March of 1933 until January of 1961 when, as President Kennedy would point out, the torch would be passed to a new generation.

Since academic experts have accorded these three men the highest marks of any three successive Presidents, let us now turn, President by President, to an examination of the categories and the ranking awarded each man in every category that produced that result. In first place, we find President Franklin Delano Roosevelt.

Chapter 1 - Franklin Roosevelt – March 4, 1933- April 12, 1945

"The only thing we have to fear is fear itself."
 – First Inaugural Address, March 4, 1933.

"December 7, a day that will live in infamy."
 – Speech to Congress asking for a Declaration of War against Japan, December 8, 1941.

1. Background (family, education, experience)

FDR ranked fifth in this category, placing him in the top 12 per cent of American presidents. John Quincy Adams ranked first, followed by Thomas Jefferson, John Adams, James Madison and Franklin Roosevelt – three Harvard men, one Princeton alumnus, Madison and Jefferson of William and Mary. We believe that John Quincy Adams is ranked first because, in addition to his formal education at Harvard, he had the richly rewarding experience of accompanying his father to Europe during the American Revolution. There he could watch and marginally assist his father as he negotiated for Dutch loans, represented American interests, jousted with Benjamin Franklin and, finally, assisted in the working out the Treaty of Paris, ending the war and establishing the independence of the nation. Obviously, his extensive government service, up to and including his service as secretary of state under President James Monroe, would also be a part of the equation.

The Hyde Park Roosevelts (Franklin's branch of the family) were the Roosevelts of the Democratic Party. The Oyster Bay Roosevelts (TR's branch) constituted the Republican wing of the family. Both branches were old family in every sense of the phrase – chronology, wealth and status. As early as the middle of the 17th Century, the Roosevelts had acquired extensive land holdings in what is now Manhattan, and they never looked back. Franklin's cousin, Theodore, had led the nation into the 20th Century as President and Franklin's inauguration would take place only 25 years after Teddy left office. Like both Presidents Adams and TR, FDR had the benefit of a Harvard education. Born at Hyde Park on January 30, 1882, Franklin had attended the elite Groton School and, after Harvard, the Law School of Columbia University. In experience, also Franklin's career tended to parallel Theodore's. Each man had served in the New York State Legislature, Franklin in the Senate. Each went on to serve as assistant secretary of the navy. In Franklin's case the post was probably deliberately chosen for political resonance. In addition, like his cousin in 1900, FDR had been his party's vice-presidential nominee in 1920, though the effort had fallen short. Also, like his cousin, he had served as governor of New York. As he accepted his party's nomination for the presidency in 1932, FDR brought with him advantages of family status and connections, broad political and campaigning experience and service in both the legislative and executive branches of government. It would then seem clear that all of these factors resulted in his being the highest ranked modern President in this category.

2. Party Leadership (political)

Here, Franklin Roosevelt is absolutely dominant, ranking first among all Presidents. It seems abundantly clear that from his ascension to the governor's chair in Albany in 1929 until his death in 1945, FDR was guilty of very few political errors. Among the nation's governors, he was fortunate in being able to draw upon the well-established legacy of his predecessor, Alfred E. Smith, in aligning New York on the progressive side of the political spectrum. That, along with New York's then extensive political power, based on the state's huge percentage of the national population, positioned him well for the Democratic nomination in 1932.

At the time, the strength of the Democratic Party was found in the long standing alliance between the urban political machines of the North and the old "Solid South," which had characterized the party since the end of Reconstruction, if not from the days of Jefferson. FDR, with his long standing connections to New York City politics and his residence and retreat in Warm Springs, Ga., after he was stricken with polio, was well placed even geographically in that structure.

There were also to be new sources of strength for the party and the President to develop. Prior to the Great Depression, African-American voters, while few in number, were a reliable source of strength for the Republican Party. From 1936 onward, those voters, assisted by New Deal programs and courted by the party – Eleanor Roosevelt in particular – moved relentlessly into the Democratic Party and became a party bulwark. Similarly, the increasingly powerful and growing industrial unions would find comfort in linkage with the Democrats. The President, the party and the policies of the New Deal all contributed to that end.

Notably, as all this played out, the southern political "Barons" would never find their segregated, white supremacist world challenged. From 1933 to 1945, the nation's chief executive never found it expedient even to propose a federal anti-lynch law in an era when the lynching of African-Americans was an all too common experience.

Whatever else may be said, the years of the Roosevelt Administration (1933-1945) saw both growth and consolidation in the strength of the Democratic Party as it moved past the Republicans to become the nation's majority party. As symbol, as leader, communicator and political evangelist, the President could rightly claim the lion's share of the credit.

3. Communication Ability (speak, write)

Another triumph for Franklin Roosevelt. The man who told his "fellow Americans" that they had "nothing to fear but fear itself," who said that too many Americans were "ill fed, ill clothed, ill housed," who in the wake of a "day of infamy" promised them that they would "gain the inevitable triumph, so help us God," once again emerges at the top of the category.

FDR was a master of communications, not just oral and written, but symbolic as well. He greeted his nomination for the presidency in 1932 by flying to the Chicago convention to accept the nomination in person. He was the first presidential nominee to take such a step. The act combined energy, modernism (flying) and urgency in one package.

That resonated to a nation in the third year of the Depression as a symbol of vigor and of determination to "get on with the job." The somewhat frenetic pace of what came to be known as the "First Hundred Days" seemed to further illustrate energy, determination and a pragmatic willingness to act without regard to political or economic ideology, but to act. Perhaps the best illustration of the dramatic bent was the so-called "Bank Holiday" that seemed to take place almost at the moment that the inaugural parade ended. Banks were closed by executive order, followed by rapid examinations of the banks and then re-openings, with assurances that the opened banks were sound and that Americans were safer. This was perhaps the epitome of the new spirit that FDR seemed to bring to Washington with him.

Similarly, his use of radio, particularly the "fireside chats," seemed to take the American people into his confidence. He was the first American president to take full advantage of the then new medium. It gave him a modern, dynamic means of communication in which he could remain low-key, even folksy, while he proposed and lobbied for new ideas and programs. Nevertheless, the format itself, because of its ready availability, lack of expense and relative unfamiliarity as a political tool, registered emotionally higher on the political scale than anything previous Presidents had done.

4. Relationship With Congress

Here, once again, Franklin Roosevelt leads all other Presidents. In that regard, we must note that the circumstances under which he came to office were unusual. When Herbert Hoover was inaugurated in 1929, the Senate consisted of 56 Republicans, 39 Democrats and one "other." The House was composed of 267 Republicans, 163 Democrats, one "other" and four vacant seats. Two years later, after the stock market crash of October, 1929, Republicans still controlled both houses, but the margins were negligible – 48-47-1 in the Senate and 218-216-1 in the House.

When FDR took his oath of office, members of his party controlled both houses by healthy margins – 59 to 36 and 1 in the Senate and, in the House, 313 to 117 and 5. The new President had led his party to a great victory in the 1932 election. Still, not every Democrat felt a debt of gratitude to the President; many had arrived in Washington under their own steam in 1931.

The question of gratitude to a successful presidential candidate, usually a politically significant one, would, however, be moot for the next few years. That would be especially true during the so-called "Hundred Days of the New Deal." We might note that the American new media more than three-quarters of a century after FDR's first term still trots out that phrase the "Hundred Days" with each change of administration. In the economic crisis of 1933, Congress was less prepared to debate proposals from the executive branch than they were to bow in their direction as they passed over their desks. The Republicans who remained were too stunned for the most part to seriously oppose any New Deal proposals.

At the same time, perhaps as no other President had ever done, FDR was prepared to assume a significant role for the executive branch in the preparation, introduction and management of legislation. This certainly reflected some debt to Woodrow Wilson's World War I efforts to control the economy. To achieve that end, FDR also courted influential members of both houses of Congress. It was the Roosevelt administration, for example, that instituted the practice of providing pens used by the President to sign legislation to the member who had sponsored the bill. That, of course, provided both a memento of the occasion and an opportunity for a photo with the President, which just might be useful in the next campaign.

Nor was the quid pro quo neglected; indeed, it was carefully managed. If, for example, a member sought an appointment for a constituent, it might be suggested to him that a certain bill needed a sponsor, or perhaps ought not to come out of committee. He might from time to time receive gentle reminders of the incipient "log roll" – the exchange of political favors in passing legislation – but few needed to be reminded that the quid was not likely to precede the pro quo.

Franklin Roosevelt also sought to keep Congress conscious of his own power. Before his presidency was half over, he had used the veto close to one-third as many times as all of the preceding Presidents. Possibly apocryphal stories were told of his seeking out items that he might veto. It all reminded Congress that the President could be a good friend but also a bad enemy.

To say the President managed Congress might be seen as an exaggeration. To say that he seems to have influenced it more than any previous President would certainly not.

In 1936, amid some signs of economic improvement, FDR swept into a second term in a genuine landslide. The President carried every state except Maine and Vermont. The Democratic Party now had won more than three-quarters of all seats in the Senate, 75 of 96, to 17 Republicans and four "others." In the House, the proportions were much the same, 333 Democrats faced 89 Republicans and 13 others. To use a cliché, in terms of the American political scene Franklin Delano Roosevelt stood astride his world like a Colossus.

At that point, whether from ideology, arrogance or simple miscalculation, he overplayed his hand. When, in 1937, Roosevelt took his second inaugural oath, the New Deal was legislatively triumphant. The Supreme Court, on the other hand, had proven less malleable than Congress. In a number of cases, perhaps most notably the National Industrial Recovery Act that authorized the President to regulate industry prices, and allowed him to suspend portions of the anti-trust laws the Court had ruled the enabling legislation for New Deal programs unconstitutional. Rankled by those decisions and so recently triumphant with the people, he proposed to "reform" the judicial system. The administration sponsored the Judiciary Reorganization Bill of 1937, which came to be popularly known as the "Court Packing" scheme. The gist of the bill was that federal judges (perhaps especially the members of the Supreme Court?) who failed to retire at 70 should be given assistance in the conduct of their duties. It is a truism to point out that 70 in 1937 was "older" than it is now. In each such case the President could then appoint an additional justice to the Court, to a maximum of six. In theory, this might increase the number of justices from nine to 15. It also, assuming the President chose wisely, was likely to guarantee clear sailing for all New Deal legislation.

In a blizzard of rhetoric, much of it centered on the idea that allowing the President to pack the court with his adherents in this fashion would violate the principle of the separation of powers and destroy the independence of the judiciary, the Senate revolted. FDR was dealt a stunning blow when the idea was buried in the Senate on a 70 to 20 vote even though the President's party commanded 75 votes out of 96.

A furious President set out to defeat many of the opponents he held responsible. For example, in the 1938 election he personally campaigned in Georgia against Senator Walter George in the Democratic primary, an unprecedented step. The President's angry response and dramatic actions had no effect in the Senate and changed no more than one seat in the House. It did, however, alter the political landscape.

In the wake of these events, the Democratic congressional coalition began to show cracks. Republicans were now able to begin the construction of a political coalition of Republicans and Democrats, many southern, which would complicate if not derail liberal political plans for years to come. Indeed, some would say that the post-1937 years, showing little successful legislative action, marked the end of the New Deal.

It should, however, also be noted that from that same period of time the world was sliding into World War II. By 1937, the Spanish Civil War (1936-1939) was in its second year and the Japanese had invaded China, marking the beginning of a conflict that would continue until 1945. The game was changing even as the economic events of 1937 dealt a blow to hopes of a sustained economic recovery. Increasingly, the President would be focusing on foreign policy, though not until 1943 would he stipulate that "Dr. Win the War" had displaced "Dr. New Deal." Hitler, Japan, rearmament, isolationism – all increasingly would be on the lips and minds of both the American people and their leaders. So, too, as Europe prepared for war and placed industrial orders with American business, the economy would show increasing signs of resurgence. However, it was not until after the draft began to put men into the military after 1940 that unemployment problems really begin to disappear.

As these events moved to the forefront, FDR's relations with Congress would ebb and flow with regard to both issues and individuals. The President, however, would continue to display both initiative and vigor in working with and influencing the Congress of the United States. Overall it is difficult to give those efforts anything but high marks, as our experts have done. He did, indeed, have an excellent relationship with Congress, and he was the dominant partner.

5. Court Appointments

This also is an area where the experts have seen President Roosevelt as setting an exemplary record. Once again they responded by according him first place.

Interestingly enough, after a first term during which he never had an opportunity to appoint a single justice and at the end of which he was pressing the Court Packing scheme, the floodgates opened for FDR during his second term. Some have seen the changes, both in the voting records of individual members of the Supreme Court and in the tendering of retirements as a result of the attempt at Court Packing. In this interpretation, a tacit bargain was struck between the Court and the administration.

Implicitly, the interpretation maintains, the Court yielded some ground to the President while the President backed away from further draconian proposals. Cynics, then and since, have rather cavalierly summed it up in the phrase, "A switch in time saves nine."

Be that as it may, he went on to appoint eight members of the Supreme Court – nine if we count his nomination of Justice Harlan Stone as Chief Justice. Only George Washington appointed more members. FDR's designees, in chronological order, were Hugo Black of Alabama, Stanley Reed of Kentucky, Felix Frankfurter of Massachusetts, William O. Douglas of Connecticut, Frank Murphy of Michigan, James Byrnes of South Carolina, Robert Jackson of New York and Wiley Rutledge of Iowa.

Black, Douglas, Jackson and Frankfurter are certainly the best known. Frankfurter served for nearly a quarter of a century and Black and Douglas each for more than 30 years. All three were still on the Court and part of the unanimous decision in Brown v. Board of Education in 1954. Black wrote the unanimous opinion in Gideon v. Wainwright in 1963 and, famously, Douglas was the author of the opinion in Griswold v. Connecticut, 1965, in which he discovered the modern right to privacy that underlies the opinion of the Court rendered six years later in Roe v. Wade (1973). Jackson, of course, served as the American chief prosecutor at the post-World War II Nuremburg War crimes trials.

In short, a significant number of his appointees proved to be major influences in the history of the Supreme Court and of the United States. That influence was rendered more extensive by their long service on the Court and the fact that they were still writing significant opinions on important elements of constitutional law some 30 years after their initial appointments. We would be remiss not to point out that there were hundreds of appointments to the lower Courts and that many of those judges would play significant roles as trial and appellate judges. They too, would write significant opinions that still influence our lives.

6. Handling of U. S. Economy

In this, the sixth category of questions, Franklin Roosevelt again occupies first place.

In 1936, as we have seen, he swept to reelection as a tsunami sweeps over a beach. The New Deal, which began with unemployment hovering around 25 per cent, seemed to have turned the tide. Whether programs such as the CCC, March 1933, the TVA, May, 1933, the PWA, June 1933 or the WPA, March, 1935 (the first three all part of the famed Hundred Days), were, as enemies insisted, merely "make work" projects, or not, they seemed effectual. They did put people to work, though perhaps only marginally, and thereby they reduced unemployment. They employed overwhelmingly male workers, and some men found a bit of their human dignity restored. The acts did not, however, restore capital spending nor boost industrial activity to any substantial degree. Nevertheless, the prospects in 1936 seemed much improved and the election results that fall reflected that perception.

Unfortunately, amidst the political euphoria and political rancor of early 1937 the economy once again turned sour. By 1938, the unemployment figures were again hovering around 20 per cent. The term "doldrums" would characterize the economic climate for the next few years. Indeed, it would require first the threat, and then the fact, of war, and the placement of war orders originally from Europe and then from the United States as it moved toward its own rearmament to genuinely increase employment. Along with that came the resurgent use of America's surplus industrial capacity.

Proponents of Keynesian economic theory, then and now, have frequently blamed FDR because of his efforts after his 1936 re-election to move toward balancing the budget. These critics maintain that he should have sustained the New Deal's "priming the pump" policies which, they aver, would have seen continued progress.

Certainly, the President and the President's men, notably Secretary of the Interior Harold Ickes, embarked on a vigorous and rather angry "populist" posture after 1937. The goal of that posture seems to have been the demonization of capitalists, especially bankers, while inveighing against oligarchs and even decrying "industrial fascism."

Opponents of the administration have maintained that taxation policy, heavy deficits and constantly changing regulatory policies made it impossible for business to plan rationally and spurred a consequent reluctance to invest. In the last decade or so, a spate of publications like Jim Powell's FDR's Folly, NY, 2003, have criticized FDR's policies. The thrust of each publication has been that the policies of the Roosevelt administration did not, and could not, solve the economic problems that the nation faced. Instead, the thesis stipulates, those policies needlessly prolonged those problems and intensified the era's suffering.

Despite this revisionism, the eight decades since the start of the New Deal have been characterized by an enormous volume of writing, both scholarly and popular, which promulgated the idea that the New Deal met and overcame gigantic economic problems, saved the economy and perhaps even saved capitalism. It might not be hyperbole if it were suggested that the last two generations of scholars had, from their youth, effectively been taught that Franklin Roosevelt was the guiding light who enabled the American people to find their way out of the economic wilderness. Obviously, they find little or nothing in their own research to challenge that view.

However it may be seen or discussed, the fact is that the academic community has no doubt that Franklin Roosevelt was the most effective chief executive in history in handling the American economy.

7. Luck

A story has long been told of the Emperor Napoleon, who was being urged to promote a general to the rank of field marshal. The general's intelligence, courage and military skills were all offered into evidence of his worthiness for the promotion. The emperor raised his hand for silence and, as the story goes, asked, "Who cares about all of that? Is he lucky?" It is in this sense that we conceived of luck as a category – "Luck as the residue of design."

We do not think that our experts conceived of luck as pure chance. Chance is the factor that determines whether one wins a lottery. Nothing can be done about it. They would not, we are sure, deny its existence or ignore it, but rather envision chance, supplemented by vision. In this formulation, luck may be influenced. So, it is said, a Hollywood producer once said, "The harder I work, the luckier I get." In short, if one is prepared and the right circumstances occur one may rise to the occasion. In this category, despite his contraction of polio and his early death, FDR ranks fourth overall. How is it that, despite these events, he ranks so high? A number of hypotheses may be risked. For some respondents, the polio, hidden as well as possible, may have brought him a slight degree of sympathy. More importantly, though, it may have given him a degree of empathy. In another formulation, the ordeal of polio finished the formation of FDR's temperament and personality. It made him stronger and more thoughtful and created what some would call presidential timber. Or, perhaps it underlay Justice Holmes' idea that the President had a "first class temperament."

Good fortune also came his way when his predecessor as governor of New York, Alfred E. Smith, was chosen as the Democratic presidential nominee in 1928, and lost. That opened the gubernatorial chair to FDR in 1928 and, thereby, the presidential nomination in 1932. Had Smith still been in Albany in 1932 few possibilities would have been available to FDR.

We have previously written that for a President to come to be perceived as "great" he must meet and overcome a crisis. In the old cliché, "The man and the era, or events, must meet." Roosevelt would confront two crises during his presidency – the Depression and World War II. The great economic crisis was central to his first six or so years in office. It was his first challenge. As it slowly faded into foreign policy concerns and crises, it merged into his second challenge, the peril of World War II. The latter rose to the front of the consciousness of the administration and the American people from 1938 onward.

By the time Roosevelt died in 1945, the economic power of the United States was supreme beyond dispute, and the war was near its end. It lasted one more month in Europe and four more in the Pacific. The end was a political and military triumph – a complete victory over enemies who were clearly evil. It was a total defeat for totalitarianism in what has been called, "The last good war."

On a smaller scale, in April of 1945, the tensions and actions of what would come to be called the Cold War were at most dimly seen on the horizon by the people of the United States. Few, if any, suspected that less than five years after V-J Day (Victory over Japan), American soldiers would again be on troop ships, crossing the Pacific to fight another war, in Korea. That, too, may be seen as fortune favoring the President. World War II was seen as an unalloyed victory, unmarred by future threats of war, hot or cold.

8. Ability to Compromise

This is another category in which Franklin Roosevelt excites the imagination of our experts. It marks the sixth of the eight categories so far addressed in which he is ranked in first place.

It appears to us that compromise seems to have been exercised by the President mainly in the later 1930s and the very early 1940s when he sought to support the European nations against Hitler. He was prepared to make the kinds of compromises necessary to gain support for his efforts to make the United States the "Arsenal of Democracy" and to provide weapons to England to keep her in the war against Germany. These compromises seem not to have been difficult for him. They seemed urgent as the United States began to prepare for war. By 1940, Army National Guard units were being called up, and America's first-ever peacetime conscription began. Men were called to report for duty, albeit with inadequate equipment. The Navy and Army Air Corps were also better funded, perhaps most notably in the Administration's "Two Ocean Navy" bill.

It would not seem that there was an equivalent penchant for compromise present during the first New Deal, except perhaps with the southern barons on the issues of white supremacy and segregation. Nor was there evidence of a compromising disposition during the struggle over Court Packing. In that instance the President seems to have been unbending until his plan was crushed in the Senate.

Certainly, in the case of foreign policy and war or the potential for war, circumstances were very different. Recollections, real or imagined, of the "Great War" combined to produce intense emotions, primarily as a result of the idea that the American role in World War I had been unnecessary and was a result of America having been slyly maneuvered into that war.

By 1933, it was almost a given in western intellectual circles that the Versailles Treaty, which had ended World War I – then still written and spoken of as "The Great War" – had been unjust to Germany. It was a theme that Hitler as politician and as chancellor of Germany played upon frequently. A corollary suggested that the 10 million or more dead from the Great War had recklessly been sacrificed by the old men who controlled the belligerent governments – a generation of politicians who, while using power, had risked nothing in person. When Neville Chamberlain danced to Hitler's tune at Munich in 1938 and yielded the Czech Sudetenland to Germany, one of the factors in his thinking was that he did not wish to be one of the old men who would send the young men off to be slaughtered by the thousands in another war.

Many actions by American isolationists from the mid-1930s onward were designed to prevent just that. Some of those proposals were perfectly designed to preclude the events of 1915-1917 which, it was believed, had deluded America into joining World War I. This type of activity is not unusual. A case can be made that the actions of Presidents Kennedy and Johnson in Vietnam were aimed at preventing another Munich – of avoiding strengthening dictators who would then be harder to control later.

As President Roosevelt was drawn more to foreign policy issues, which tended to revolve around the expansion or threatened expansion of the Axis powers – Germany, Italy and Japan – he had to deal with large isolationist elements in the population. German-Americans were not happy to see their government pursuing anti-German policies. Irish-Americans were not opposed to anything that disconcerted Britain. Still others – intellectuals, proponents of a "Fortress America" policy, anti-Semites, Communists, until June, 1941 when Nazi Germany invaded Russia – all made common cause against an activist American foreign policy.

These citizens were aided by popular politicians and public personalities like Senators Gerald Nye and Burton K. Wheeler and the aviator, Charles Lindbergh. Nye had led a Senate Committee in the early 1930s in pursuit of what he called the "Merchants of Death." These were defined as capitalists and industrialists centered on the munitions industry and financiers arranging loans to England and other allied powers. These men, Nye averred, had been responsible for America's entry into World War I and must never be allowed to do it again. Nye was a Republican, Wheeler a Democrat. The pro-Allied policy carried out by the administration in the late 1930s must have appeared to some to lend credibility to the positions of Wheeler and Nye.

Out of this, and much more, arose a large, popular movement called "America First." This group preached and defended a sort of "Fortress America" notion – the vision of an America standing strong and resolute behind her oceanic moats and insisting that Europe, in particular, solve its own problems. Lindbergh, perhaps the most popular figure of his day, was a prominent leader and spokesman for America First. Like most isolationist groups, America First would not escape at least some elements of anti-Semitism.

All this formed a popular political mix that Franklin Roosevelt could not ignore. Congress, for example, stirred by Nye and others, passed no fewer than four Neutrality Acts between 1935 and 1939.

In the same period, Huey Long of Louisiana, governor of that state and then a U. S. senator – and one of America's historically talented demagogues – was building a personal political machine that potentially controlled six or more states in the Solid South of the Democratic Party. Long's success did not escape the President's notice, nor did his very effective use of radio. Certainly FDR did not wish to provide political fodder for a man like Long.

These events, and others, individually and collectively, would appear to be the source of FDR's need to compromise during the period. They defined as well the areas in which he did compromise. It was not the New Deal, not the Supreme Court, nor such things as his unilateral announcement at the Casablanca Conference that the only terms available for surrender for the Axis powers were unconditional surrender. On none of these was he prepared to compromise.

However, there can be little doubt of FDR's ability to compromise. In the years from 1935 to Pearl Harbor he was called upon with some frequency to compromise. Whether he was fine tuning neutrality acts or negotiating procurement acts for weapons, a strong case can be made that he did so. Whether that represented accommodation or recognition of popular elective power might well be debated.

9. Willingness to Take Risks

A slight change appears here, with Lincoln leading the category and Roosevelt appearing in second place. We believe that the respondents took the idea of risk to mean, primarily, risking one's political capital. This analysis reflects that.

It would be a truism to suggest that Franklin Delano Roosevelt was risk averse, which does not mean that he never took risks. During the so-called first New Deal there was little or no risk to be confronted. Even the most experimental plans were perceived by Congress and the people as, at worst, steps designed to deal with the crisis. Try them; if they worked, fine; if not, discard them and try something else. Before the involvement of the Supreme Court the New Deal showed little concern for constitutional niceties. The Second New Deal saw the President take real risks in his court reform, or Court Packing, plan. The result was a political blow to the President's prestige and, with the emergence of the outline of a conservative coalition, a potential threat to his power.

On foreign policy issues the President would prove, at least on occasion, willing to take risks, though he chose his battles with care and usually was prudent in his choices. It seems clear to us that the experts saw his strength in this category in the macro area of overall policy and rearmament and not in the micro area of specific pieces of legislation. He would, for example, negotiate and nibble at the Neutrality Acts that limited U. S. ability to aid countries in conflict with the Axis powers but would make no real effort to destroy them.

The political stakes were, indeed, high and the political rhetoric often low. Senator Burton K. Wheeler, Democrat of Montana, had been among the earliest figures in the Democratic Party to endorse FDR for president. Throughout the first term, he was a reliable work horse in the Senate on the administration's behalf. He broke with the President first on the Court Packing scheme and then again, over preparedness and foreign policy issues. When, in March of 1941, the Lend-Lease Act was passed, Wheeler, an America First member and a bitter opponent of Lend-Lease, combined those acts and the passage of the first peacetime draft in 1940. He then melded it rhetorically with the New Deal's Agricultural Adjustment Act. The AAA had been designed to raise agricultural prices by creating artificial scarcity and thereby promote farm prosperity. If it was deemed necessary, crops might be plowed under in the field prior to harvest. In that context, Wheeler attacked the President, saying that FDR was prepared to "plow under every fourth American boy."

If a more scathing attack has ever been launched in American political circles, we have missed it. That kind of opposition from within the Democratic Party, as well as the overall strength of the isolationist movement, would virtually force any President to compromise. From time to time, Roosevelt did compromise.

In some areas, we can only speculate on the administration's reasoning. For example, in an era when thousands of European Jews sought refuge in the United States, the President was unwilling to gamble his personal prestige to assist legislation designed to facilitate the immigration of European Jews. Mrs. Roosevelt was induced to approach her husband personally and through his friend, Undersecretary of State Sumner Welles, in the summer of 1939. She was informed that under current circumstances, which included letters to Congress favoring further restrictions on immigration to keep refugees out, it was not felt wise that the administration lend public support to the bill.

Certainly, anti-Semitism was more prevalent and more overt in that period than it is today. Equally clearly, the impact of the Depression as well as anti-Semitism intensified opposition to immigration. Astute politicians were well aware of the results of a Fortune magazine poll of 1938 that showed that two-thirds of the country favored barring refugees from entering the United States. It would, we think, be fair to suggest that the Roosevelt administration was as alert to polling information as any other contemporary group.

Considering all those circumstances, it seems to us that our experts honor Franklin Roosevelt as much as they do primarily for his focus on policies designed to restrict Nazi expansion, to aid Western Europe – specifically England after the fall of France – and to prepare the United States for forthcoming, active, military engagement. In those areas, it is abundantly clear that the President was willing to take prudent risks.

10. Executive Appointments

Once again, we find Franklin Roosevelt occupying second place, this time behind George Washington. A look at the cabinet members who served his administration provides a most impressive list. We omit any mention of FDR's so-called "Brain Trust" or FDR's friend and general factotum, Harry Hopkins, or other members of the executive branch.

There were, in those days, 10 cabinet posts. They were occupied by the secretaries of the U. S. Departments of State, Treasury, War, Justice, Postal Service, Navy, Interior, Agriculture, Commerce and Labor. Unlike our own time, there were then few institutionally recognized advisors other than the cabinet secretaries. There was, for example, no national security advisor or apparatus. The cabinet was therefore much more influential and politically powerful than it is today. Regardless, Roosevelt had a way of using extra-constitutional advisors when he felt it useful. In this, he was not unlike Andrew Jackson, who was famed for his use of non-institutional advisors – his so-called "Kitchen Cabinet."

The first notable point about FDR's primary executive appointments, like his judicial ones, was simply how long they served. Secretary of State Cordell Hull served from the beginning until late November, 1944, after the fourth election, before departing because of his health. A veteran of the Spanish American War, he had served in the House for more than 20 years and was the author of the Federal Income Tax Act of 1913. He had been a long-time leader of the ongoing Democratic Party drive for lower tariffs and a stalwart voice for the party on the House Ways and Means Committee. He also had served a term as chairman of the Democratic National Committee and had been elected to the Senate in 1930. Just two years later, FDR nominated him to be secretary of state. When he resigned, he had served longer than any other secretary of state before or since.

Hull was particularly effective in negotiations with Latin America, providing credible leadership in such talks. He often is credited with the development of FDR's "Good Neighbor Policy." Beginning in1934, he negotiated many reciprocal trade and tariff agreements. True to his years in the House, these agreements generally were designed to lower tariffs and increase trade volume. In most instances, the Latin American states regarded Hull as an honest and trustworthy statesman.

As was true for all cabinet members, Hull too, found it necessary to adjust to the President's habit of by-passing standard authority and lines of control whenever the spirit moved him. FDR was neither the first nor the last President who often made his own foreign policy, though he did it perhaps more frequently and covertly than others.

Hull and the President rarely disagreed on foreign policy issues. That was also true in regard to preparedness and rearmament. Hull, like Roosevelt, was a partisan of collective security agreements. His state department prepared a draft of a "Charter for the United Nations" that became the United States blueprint in the early negotiations to establish that body. Following Hull's resignation, FDR nominated him for the Nobel Peace Prize, which Hull was awarded in 1945. Fortunately, even though he could not attend the

17

ceremony, he lived long enough to accept the laurel.

Secretary of the Treasury Henry Morgenthau, Jr. succeeded his predecessor, William H. Woodin, in 1934. Like Hull, Morgenthau also served the administration to the end, resigning in 1945. A personal friend of Roosevelt's, Morgenthau worked to stabilize the dollar with such success that it became the strongest monetary unit in the world. He also pursued policies making it easier for the Allies in the wake of the Neutrality Acts – and despite isolationist sentiments – to purchase war materiel from the United States.

Before discussing the service secretaries, we should note that the armed services were not unified until after World War II. The army and its air corps, later the U. S. Air Force, came under the war department. The navy existed as the U. S. Department of the Navy with the Marine Corps as an integral part of the naval establishment.

Republican Henry L. Stimson was one of the most experienced cabinet officers in history. He had been secretary of war under President Taft and secretary of state under Herbert Hoover. Stimson was Franklin Roosevelt's third appointee as secretary of war, in 1940. His predecessor, Henry H. Woodring, was an isolationist and, as a result, was seen as an increasingly bad fit for the administration. Despite his then being already over 40 years of age, Stimson had volunteered and served on active duty in France in World War I, in the field artillery.

At virtually the same moment, another Republican, Frank Knox, who had received some consideration for the GOP presidential nomination in 1936 and had received the vice presidential nod, was appointed secretary of the navy. Knox had served in both the Spanish American War and again, like Stimson, in World War I.

A long-time newspaperman, he had at one time been the general manager of all of the daily newspapers in the Hearst chain and, later, publisher of the Chicago Daily News, from which vantage point he regularly assaulted the New Deal's domestic policies. When the President reached out to him, Knox was reluctant to accept. In essence, his decision was based on patriotism. Just as he had joined the Rough Riders in 1898 and reenlisted in the army in his 40s for World War I, he found it hard to resist the call of duty in 1940.

As secretary he would preside over the largest and most rapid expansion of the United States Navy in history. Congress had passed the "Two Ocean Navy" Act just as Knox was being confirmed, and he would preside over its development and fruition. Knox also played a role in the Anglo-American "destroyers for bases" exchange that set the precedent for the Lend-Lease Acts that were to come.

Clearly, by 1940, Franklin Delano Roosevelt had calculated that appointing prominent Republican administrators of impeccable reputation, known ability and a reasonable amount of fame might bring at least some Republicans on board. He had calculated that such appointments would certainly diminish criticism and would enhance his own reputation for bi-partisanship and, perhaps, lead to greater national unity. Cynics might also suggest that if a great deal went wrong with programs and plans then scapegoats who were not members of the President's party might prove convenient.

Harold L. Ickes was FDR's only secretary of the interior and often served as the administration's gadfly and scold. He too served as secretary longer than any other individual to date. Ickes, a former Republican and Progressive, also served as director of the PWA (Public Works Administration), and its projects – Grand Coulee Dam, the Lincoln Tunnel, and others. Ickes' personal probity was evident in his careful management and in his meticulous attention to preventing corruption and graft in those projects. In matters relating to civil rights, he, as a member of the NAACP, was foremost among the members of the cabinet.

Frances Perkins is probably best remembered for her role in the development of the Social Security Act, as well as being the first woman to serve in the cabinet. She also, like Ickes, served at the labor department post longer than any other individual to date.

This listing could certainly go on. We have not yet mentioned Henry A. Wallace, who was FDR's secretary of agriculture for eight years, then vice president for four more and when the President died, was again entering the cabinet as secretary of commerce. The point, though, we think has been made. The executive appointments of the Roosevelt administration provided continuity, exhibited a high degree of ability, served with energy and efficiency and set a high standard.

11. Overall Ability

We find Franklin Roosevelt returning to first place in this difficult-to-define category.

When Alexander Hamilton and Thomas Jefferson sat in a room with George Washington, though each was probably more brilliant and perhaps more imaginative and certainly better credentialed than the President, there was no doubt in anybody's mind as to who was the greatest man in the room.

When Justice Oliver Wendell Holmes, Jr. met Franklin Roosevelt, he famously said that he possessed "a second class intellect but a first class temperament." That raises the question of whether a President, to be considered able, has to be the smartest person in the room. If he can induce bright, talented and imaginative people to enter his service, provide him with ideas and initiatives, offer him their skills at planning and execution and is capable of effectively managing and directing them, is he not, perhaps brilliantly, displaying ability?

We are not certain that our experts would agree with Holmes, but even if they do, they would seem to accept the notion stated above. In any event, Franklin Roosevelt – whether in creating his "Brain Trust" of private advisors, mostly lawyers or academics, or directing the cabinet or in wheedling, cajoling and arm twisting the Congress – appears to satisfy that formula.

If a President can preside over a period like the Hundred Days with its rapid creation of new ideas, its engineering of the replacement of a relatively small government with an increasingly big government, its conjuring up of agencies and bureaus, with aplomb, while "selling" the concepts to the electorate via fireside chats, then surely, he radiates ability. If a President can create a cabinet that even three quarters of a century later still seems to be an exceptionally talented one and largely keep it together for up to a dozen years of service then, must we not acknowledge his ability?

Forty per cent of the members of the cabinet – Hull at state, Morgenthau at the treasury, Ickes at interior and Perkins at labor – served for all, or virtually all of the period. Wallace had two terms at agriculture, one as vice president and had just returned to the cabinet, at commerce, when FDR died. Three others, James Farley as postmaster general, Homer Cummings, the first attorney general and Claude Swanson, Roosevelt's first secretary of the navy, served at least half of FDR's presidency. Knox and Stimson also rendered yeoman service.

If a President can seemingly seamlessly segue from a political agenda tightly focused on a large economic crisis to an even tighter focus on a foreign policy and military crisis while continuing, rain or shine, to present at least an outward façade of optimism and ebullience, that too seems to us to illustrate ability.

Franklin Delano Roosevelt was, and is, many things to many people. He may not have been a textbook model for CEO or COO for the American government, but not even his worst enemies can deny that he possessed ability. Certainly, the SRI's expert respondents hold him in high esteem.

12. Imagination

Once again, only Lincoln surpasses President Roosevelt. The historical record is rife with arguments as to whether FDR came to office with a specific plan in mind to deal with the Depression. Was he awash in a sea of Keynesian ideas? Was he merely reflecting his World War I experience in the Wilson administration as it called not only America's young men to service but "drafted" its economy as well? Was the multiplicity of bureaus and agencies the New Deal spun off simply the 1933 equivalent of the Railroad Administration and "Meatless Tuesday" and "Wheatless Wednesday" of Wilson's wartime administration? However these questions may be answered, it seems clear to us that there was no shortage of innovation, and that innovation is frequently and properly conflated with imagination.

The marshaling of the economy to confront a national crisis was certainly a hallmark of Wilson's policies during the Great War. In Wilson's day, eminent Americans such as Herbert Hoover and Bernard Baruch, who was later publicly perceived as an informal advisor to President Franklin Roosevelt, administered significant portions of the economy to promote more efficient production and distribution of everything from shoes to suits, from boxcars to bread. Many Democrats who came to Washington with Roosevelt in 1933 were returning for the first time since 1921, as was the President-elect. It certainly would have been understandable if they seized upon the precedents created the last time they had been in power.

Assuming that as a likelihood, what followed certainly far outstripped any Wilsonian experience. A torrent of legislation swept a multitude of bureaus and agencies into being. Those agencies dealt not only with areas traditional to federal oversight, but with those which heretofore had been administered only by state and local governments.

In the wake of the Bank Holiday and the Emergency Banking Act, public confidence in banks was restored, and new deposits outstripped withdrawals. Before the end of 1933, legislation was passed to employ men and advance the cause of conservation. The Civilian Conservation Corps was dedicated to these ends. The Agricultural Adjustment Administration, later ruled unconstitutional, was designed to improve commodity prices, if necessary by destroying crops before harvest, but it had mixed success. It tended to aid large-scale farming, drove up food prices and resulted in the actual importation of food stocks. The Tennessee Valley Authority brought electricity and flood control to an area among the most economically blighted in the United States. The Public Works Administration, a portion of the NRA, was meant to boost recovery by providing employment on major projects like the Lincoln Tunnel and the Grand Coulee Dam. The prolonged nature of the Depression saw private charitable institutions and state welfare agencies running out of money. The Federal Emergency Relief Administration under Harry Hopkins provided the states with new, federal, monies for relief. Hopkins sought to tie the funds to employment. Those receiving benefits, it was believed, should work for their money. The years from 1933 through 1936 saw not only these programs and agencies but also additional levels of government participation and change and/or reform in many areas of economic life.

As attention turned to foreign policy, rearmament and war, other imaginative ideas emerged. FDR traded 50 obsolescent World War I American destroyers to Britain in return for leases on British Caribbean island bases for United States defense purposes. This aided Britain militarily, at least in morale. It also technically avoided violating America's responsibilities as a neutral power – or so it was argued. That initiative, in turn, would lead to the establishment of Lend-Lease, which was a godsend for England, which was running out of hard money to purchase American war materiel. FDR described Lend-Lease as having a neighbor whose house was on fire, so you loaned him your garden hose. When the fire was out, he would return the hose. Republican Senator Robert Taft of Ohio rejected that homely analogy. Rather, he suggested, it was like loaning a stick of chewing gum. After the crisis was over, you really didn't want it back.

Certainly, however, and whether one agrees with any or all of it, it all speaks of imagination.

13. Domestic Accomplishments

Again, Abraham Lincoln leads the category and, again, Franklin Roosevelt is second. This is an area where the controversy that so often surrounds the New Deal is very prominent. One person's "handout" is another person's "helping hand." We will try to keep these divergent views in mind, as we think our respondents did. First of all, we think, is the persona of Franklin Delano Roosevelt. If Americans had "nothing to fear but fear itself," then it was bracing to have a President who clearly seemed fearless. He was a jovial, reassuring, immensely self-confident leader who was prepared to try virtually anything to resolve the crisis. He was to many, for all intents and purposes, hope personified.

The month prior to his inauguration had seen another round of bank failures and runs on banks. Almost immediately after his inauguration, FDR declared a nationwide Bank Holiday and called Congress into emergency session. In the first of the famous Fireside Chats, the President explained the plan. All banks were to be examined. Those in good financial shape, with adequate assets, would quickly be allowed to reopen. Those beyond salvation would be closed. Those that were salvageable would reorganize and reopen. As the process played itself out, Americans began to redeposit significant amounts of money. By the summer of 1933, the Federal Deposit Insurance

Corporation was created and funds made available to protect small depositors from bank failures. To oversimplify, confidence in the banking system was restored.

Millions of people were out of work, and the sheer need that gripped the country had overwhelmed the resources of both private charities and state welfare operations. To address these problems, the Federal Emergency Relief Administration was created to directly funnel federal money to the various states for relief operations. At virtually the same instant, the short-lived Civil Works Administration and the Civilian Conservation Corps began to make some jobs available, ranging from road construction for the former, to planting trees for the latter. But they put some people to work. So did the Public Works Administration of the NIRA and various other New Deal Programs.

Farmers and rural regions were addressed by the Agricultural Adjustment Act the Tennessee Valley Authority and the Rural Electrification Act. The TVA brought to one of the poorest areas of the nation electrification, flood control and the promise of development and employment. The REA brought electric power to isolated rural areas and, with it, many of the amenities long available to urban and suburban areas. It substantially altered for the better the daily lives of rural housewives, who could now draw water from a spigot in the kitchen sink instead of using a bucket in a well a hundred feet deep. Other substantial labor-saving improvements also were made possible.

The second New Deal, c. 1935, saw the coming of the Works Progress Administration, the Social Security Act and the Wagner Act. The WPA, administered by Hopkins, was designed to provide economic relief through employment rather than through welfare. WPA workers would help build projects from the Orange Bowl in Miami to LaGuardia Airport in New York City. It would also employ artists, actors and intellectuals. In addition to brick and mortar projects, the WPA also produced plays, post office murals and state tourism guide books.

The Wagner Act is sometimes still referred to as a bill of rights for organized labor. Labor's enemies have sometimes called it a blank check. Labor now had a legal entitlement to organize and to bargain collectively. The National Labor Relations Board was labor's court of appeals. Longtime practices of business used against labor, such as the blacklist, were now outlawed. Under the beneficent cloak of the Wagner Act union membership would burgeon in the next decade.

Clearly, the Depression was not ended by these agencies, activities and laws. But, the country felt that the President cared and was doing his best. Visible physical evidence ranging from the Lincoln Tunnel to the Golden

Gate Bridge, from Grand Coulee Dam to the road to the Florida Keys, told them that things were happening. Many of those projects are with us still. And so, our respondents indicate, are approving historical memories of and scholarly judgments about Franklin Delano Roosevelt.

14. Integrity

It is interesting and important to note that the more than 200 respondents who collectively have given him the consensus ranking of number one have ranked him only 16th in integrity, just outside of the top third of all Presidents, at 39 per cent.

Perhaps the worst accusation against Roosevelt is the charge of some revisionist historians that he deliberately manipulated America's relations with Japan to bring about war. This, it has been alleged, was a conspiracy designed to bring the United States into World War II, primarily to bring about the defeat of Nazi Germany. One problem with the hypothesis is that, following Pearl Harbor, Hitler was under no obligation to wage war against America. Had Hitler chosen not to wage war against the U. S., then FDR's alleged huge political gamble would clearly have been a failure of the first magnitude. As a plan, created by a calculating and cynical, chief executive, it does not compute. We also should mention that after 70 years there is no independent corroboration of this theory, only speculation. How many secrets has the Washington establishment kept in that same period – even briefly? While, by definition, a conspiracy cannot be disproven, scant support exists for this one. We would stipulate that there seems to be a consensus among practicing historians, not all of them FDR partisans, that simply finds the accusations insupportable. We think they play no role in the ranking.

On other fronts, there does seem to be reasonable cause for doubt about the President's integrity. First among the other areas of concern would probably be the seemingly callous abandonment of African Americans to their fate in the American South during Roosevelt's lengthy presidency. What Roosevelt's rationale may have been is certainly debatable, but there can be no doubt that as their loyalty to the Democratic Party and to the President was being consolidated he was unwilling to seek rewards for them from the southern barons. Of course, few African Americans were permitted to vote in southern states in those days, but surely a federal anti-lynch law might not have seemed excessive. We would be remiss not to point out that at the same time, in the burgeoning defense industries, race was forbidden by executive order as a criterion for hiring.

Similarly, European Jews seeking refuge in America seemed to excite little compassion as late as 1939 at 1600 Pennsylvania Avenue.

In other ways, even among his official family, FDR frequently managed to appear petty, arrogant and vindictive. Certainly he was something less than Aristotle's Magnanimous Man. Like Machiavelli's Prince, no one would be surprised that he was willing to promise rewards for political cooperation even when he had no intention of keeping his part of the bargain. It is also known that he was not averse to at least occasional use of the Internal Revenue Service for political purposes.

Sometimes also, his sense of entitlement could override his judgment. The 1938 attempt to purge what he thought of as the "Disloyal Democrats" surely did him at least as much harm as good, probably more. It is also difficult to conceive of the Court Packing Plan without the thought of arrogance entering the mind. The Supreme Court's adverse decision on the National Industrial Recovery Act, for example, was 9-0. Even six new votes would not have mattered.

In his fear and hatred of Hitler, he was frequently tempted to push the bounds of acceptable conduct. Whether that meant adopting a quasi-belligerent status in Atlantic waters, or the FBI "Black Bag" operations in embassies in the District of Columbia or other dodgy practices, he yielded to temptation on more than one occasion. The actual events of World War II – the totality of evil represented by the Nazi regime in particular and the Axis powers in general, the Holocaust, and the world's suffering from 1937 to 1945 – have to a considerable degree tended to camouflage what was bad conduct by Roosevelt. They do not alter it.

Lest the enumeration become overwhelming, let us just mention two more items to bolster the opinion of our experts. The internment of Japanese Americans by executive order and the decision to seek a fourth term, given what we now know of his physical condition at the time, both seem egregious. The former is generally seen by historians to have been unnecessary and the latter, with its disregard for the common weal, pure pride.

All of these, great and small, seem to show more than a passing allegiance to the principle that the end justifies the means. All, collectively, would seem to explain why in this category he is ranked well below the standings awarded him in most other categories.

15. Executive Ability

Presidents Washington and Lincoln precede Roosevelt in this category.

Roosevelt's White House would not have been an appropriate example as a flow chart for a management text book. He had, for example, a penchant for assigning two or more individuals to perform the same, or at least highly similar functions. J. Edgar Hoover was not simply paranoid when he perceived "Wild Bill" Donovan's Office of War Information, later the Office of Strategic Services, as plowing ground – in Latin America, for example – that once had been the exclusive property of the FBI. Nor was it uncharacteristic of the President to unofficially deputize friends and acquaintances (like Donovan) to dabble in diplomacy and even intelligence gathering without the knowledge of resident ambassadors or even the state department.

However, it seems to us that the category concerns itself less with formal structure and function and more with the style and effectiveness of management. To that end, let us offer a definition:

"Executive skills are those mental abilities that govern complex cognitive or behavioral tasks. They include drive, the initiation of cognitive activity, sustained motivation to perform tasks, the ability to recognize patterns, the ability to perform sequences, the ability to plan and execute a strategy, the ability to complete a complex cognitive task, and synthesis, which is the ability to appreciate metaphoric meaning and monitor cognitive performance. Of particular significance is an individual's ability to learn from errors and to self-correct while performing cognitive tasks."

A brief examination of the components of the definition would seem to us to illustrate why FDR's ranking was third among all American presidents. Certainly, no one has ever suggested that the president lacked drive. Whether in his comeback from polio, his pursuit of the gubernatorial nomination or the presidency – even in ill-considered moments such as the 1938 effort to purge the Disloyal Democrats – drive was a major component of his personality. The multi-faceted programs and policies of the New Deal and the virtually constant tinkering with plans, programs and policies speak directly to the initiation of cognitive activity as well as sustained motivation. The ability to recognize patterns and perform sequences would seem to speak directly to any President's necessary interaction with Congress and its members, with his constituents, with interest and pressure groups, with the states and with foreign nations. Few Presidents have been as diligent and artful in these areas as Franklin Delano Roosevelt. When we speak to the planning and execution of strategy we can perhaps best summarize by simply mentioning the title of James MacGregor Burns' magisterial work, Roosevelt, The Lion and The Fox, 1956. His own use of metaphor, whether in speeches, fireside chats or even the Atlantic Charter, shows not only understanding but virtual mastery of the creation and/or use of metaphor as an instrument of persuasion, if not always a means of clarification.

Whether he learned from error or not, there is considerable evidence of self-correction in his presidential years. Some may raise questions about sincerity, but we do not believe that such questions are relevant to the definition.

In summary, then, there would appear to be more than enough evidence of executive ability to justify the conclusion reached in the SRI poll.

16. Foreign Policy Accomplishments

Once again, we are presented with a category in which Franklin Roosevelt is ranked first. Although clearly an internationalist, initially he disappointed his comrades in that category when upon entering office he unilaterally withdrew from the gold standard and effectively renounced international co-operation on monetary stabilization at the London Economic Conference of 1933. Without doubt, he wanted to play a free hand in fiscal and economic matters, and the possible use of monetary policy was just such an area. He would bring the United States into monetary stabilization agreements with Britain and France in the next few years. Nevertheless, it is clear that his own goals, national and political, at least temporarily, trumped internationalism.

The enunciation of the famous Good Neighbor Policy for the Americas promoted better relations with neighbors in the Western Hemisphere. Subsequent lower tariffs and reciprocity agreements, tended to increase trade with those "Good Neighbors."

The primary impact of Rooseveltian foreign policy, however, is to be found in the events leading up to and encompassing World War II. His first initiative, in all probability, came in 1937, with the delivery of his Quarantine the Aggressors speech. At that time, Italy had been in Ethiopia since 1935 and Japan had just initiated the Sino-Japanese War, which would continue until 1945. Germany and Italy were then militarily involved in support of Francisco Franco in his efforts to overthrow the Spanish Republic. It was, in fact, a highly prudent address, so unspecific that it failed to mention any country. In effect, both problem and potential solution were really abstractions, at least on paper. Interestingly enough, only two months later, the Japanese attacked the USS Panay, an American gunboat in China, which resulted in the deaths of more than 30 officers and enlisted men of the United States Navy. Ritual apologies duly followed. Other dictators seemed likewise unintimidated. Within five months, in March of 1938, Germany marched into and annexed Austria in the Anschluss.

Nonetheless, isolationist opinion was furious with Roosevelt and, almost certainly, the vociferous criticism he endured caused him to be even more cautious and hesitant in addressing aggressive behavior. After the Munich Pact of September 1938, and the resulting dissolution of the Czechoslovakian state, additional urgency appeared. The President fought, often rather covertly, to weaken proposed changes in the Neutrality Acts, as seen in his efforts to preserve the "cash and carry" principle. After the German military triumphs in Poland in 1939 and Western Europe in the spring of 1940 – which saw the German conquest of Norway, Denmark, the Low Countries and France – the President was more forward in his efforts to keep Britain in the war. That would weaken Germany by keeping at least one active belligerent in the war against her and, perhaps of greater importance, insure that the Royal Navy did not end up under German command.

Out of those conditions and exigencies would come the destroyers for bases agreement and, ultimately, Lend-Lease. After Germany invaded Russia in June of 1941, the administration at once extended Lend-Lease aid to Stalin and the Soviet Union.

Wartime planning, strategy and policy conferences – particularly, though not exclusively, between the United States and Britain – determined wartime plans, operations and goals. Specifically, that was the determination to put the war against Hitler and Nazi Germany at the head of the list for waging war. The Allied plan was Germany first; then Japan.

True to the ideals of his World War I chief, Woodrow Wilson, Roosevelt had a settled determination, which became a principle of United States foreign policy – collective security and consultation. That would lead to the rebirth of Wilson's League of Nations ideal in somewhat altered form, as the United Nations.

17. Leadership Ability

Here, we find Franklin Delano Roosevelt in a tie for first place with George Washington and, here again, we find a category which is perhaps a bit diffuse.

Our first thought is that our respondents undoubtedly began at the beginning. If the American people elected him President four times – and in particularly dangerous times at that – it is only logical to assume that they must have discerned significant qualities of leadership.

Second, the 1940 election was conducted in a mood of national crisis. By Election Day, Congress had passed and the President had signed the first peacetime conscription act in American history. The first of America's National Guard units had already reported for active duty or had a reporting date assigned. Politically, that meant men from every state in the Union were under orders. Thus, the 26th Infantry Division from Massachusetts, the 27th Infantry Division from New York, the 28th Infantry Division from Pennsylvania, and so on had been "called to the colors." The political impact, added to by the fact that individuals, then called "selectees," would start to be called up in January, 1941, was not yet known. Regardless of the contemporary debate, it was a bold political act.

The Depression, while weakened, was not yet slain. Indeed, like growing industrial demands for war materiel, conscription would greatly help in reducing unemployment, though that was not its intent.

Isolationists were as loudly and vociferously as ever decrying the administration's policies as bringing the country closer to a war that was not America's concern. Let other nations solve their own problems. "It is none of our business," they said.

Finally, largely forgotten now, there was the third term issue. No American President had ever served more than two terms. If it was good enough for George Washington, why wasn't it good enough for Franklin Delano Roosevelt? Was he power mad? If he was, would it be wise to indulge his desire? Today those are really academic questions. In 1940, they were real world, real time questions and were laden with emotion. Voters and politicians who had supported him since 1932, and some even earlier, broke with him in 1940. A third term was just wrong!

The electorate disagreed. As President – whether leading a crusade for reform in the first and second New Deals, attacking the court in 1937, seeking to quarantine the aggressor in 1937, warning of the dangers of the dictatorial states in the late 1930s or leading the nation as its wartime President after December 7, 1941, until his death in April of 1945 – FDR had become a presence. To a large degree, he had come to define the presidency.

18. Intelligence

After careful thought and due deliberation, the experts have given us a consensus ranking of eighth, keeping President Roosevelt just within the top 20 per cent of all presidents through the end of the 20th Century.

First, we think it important to clarify a point. A list of Presidents is not a haphazard list of 40-odd names taken randomly from the phone book in Syracuse, N. Y., or any other town or city. We would stipulate that if, between 1789 and 2001, only 41 men served as President in more than 210 years, then each of them, it must be assumed, had qualities that seemed to separate him from his fellow citizens. Among those possible qualities is, of course, intelligence. By definition, then, to be in the top 20 per cent of such a list strongly suggests more than average intellectual capacity.

We would next point to Roosevelt's high overall rankings. His background includes Harvard University and Columbia University Law. He is clearly recognized as a master of graceful speech and well-wrought prose. These are usually perceived as grace notes which bespeak intelligence. His presidential appointments, judicial and executive, indicate an intellect able to discern talent and intelligence in others and also able to bind those talents to his service. When we addressed his ranking in Overall Ability we wrote that if a President "can induce bright, talented and imaginative people to enter his service, provide him with ideas and initiatives, offer him their skills at planning and execution, and manage and direct them, is he not displaying ability?" And, we would now add, is he not displaying intelligence as well?

He was capable of great charm and wit, as evidenced by his relationship with Winston Churchill. Wit and charm are, not infrequently, conflated with intelligence. We might note, however, that he failed quite conspicuously to charm either Joseph Stalin or Charles de Gaulle.

The breadth of his responsibilities, perhaps particularly post-1936, would seem to make it unlikely that he significantly lacked capacity. However, some might suggest that he was perhaps rather unwilling to seek intellectual depth, other than perhaps in private conversation with trusted advisors.

It seems to us that, subject to the clarifications above, the ranking reflects not only the judgment of the professors but is a reasonable reflection of historical reality.

19. Avoid Crucial Mistakes

Roosevelt is ranked third in this category, once again behind George Washington and Abraham Lincoln. We find this ranking interesting and subtle because, both Washington and Lincoln in this area had much less room to maneuver than did FDR. It was possible for him to plead pragmatism and walk away from a plan or a program. Washington and Lincoln, with an equivalent flaw or failure, might have seen the republic perish. This ranking and judgment seems to us to be mature and sensitive.

Probably the Court Packing Plan in 1937 and the attempted purging of the Democrats who had offended the President in 1938 came closest to potentially crucial mistakes. He was, however, canny enough that by 1938 he was prepared to take what he could get from the Supreme Court, which was quite a bit. So too, he was prepared to cut his losses and almost pretend that there had never been any Disloyal Democrats.

In foreign policy and rearmament, he was almost too cautious. When the chairs of congressional committees told him before the war that they could push through larger naval estimates than the administration had asked for he told them to sustain his requests and not add to them. Some might say that he overestimated the impact, real and potential, of isolationist elements in the Congress and in the country. Nevertheless, he never totally alienated all elements of the isolationists, and he got much of what he sought. The military might have been stronger on December 7, 1941, had he been more aggressive. But it had been strengthened enough, if barely so.

Unlike Churchill, he rarely interfered in direct military operations or command appointments. His conservatism in that regard removed an entire area of war making from the list of possible serious errors.

He could be decisive in military affairs within what he regarded as his purview. A perfect example was the decision to agree with the British chiefs of staff rather than the American and to determine to invade Sicily and Italy in 1943. The alternative was to agree with United States Army Chief of Staff George C. Marshall, who wanted to invade northwest Europe in 1943. Most modern military historians would agree that the Marshall position, given the experience and training of the American Army in 1943, might well have proven a crucial error.

It would be difficult to quarrel with the proposition that he did manage to avoid making crucial errors – which is not to say that mistakes were not made, nor that programs and policies were not tried and found wanting, but only to say that crucial mistakes were avoided.

20. Present Overall View

It is interesting to note that Franklin Roosevelt, who was awarded first place in no fewer than nine of the 19 places we have attempted to analyze, was in this, 20th category, ranked only second, with Abraham Lincoln first.

Chapter 2 - Harry S Truman – April 12, 1945 – January. 20, 1953

The Buck Stops Here
– A motto that President Truman kept on his desk.

1. Background (family, education, experience)

In the first category, President Truman was ranked 32nd, by our historians and political scientists. He was born in LaMar, MO, on May 8, 1884. His family relocated with some frequency, finally settling in Independence, MO in 1890. As a boy, he studied music and took piano lessons for a number of years. He was an avid reader, especially of history, despite his poor eyesight. He was, to date, the last President who did not attend college. He did, however, study law for two years in the early 1920s at the Kansas City Law School.

After he graduated from high school in 1901, he took a number of jobs in succession. He worked for, among others, the Santa Fe Railroad and the Kansas City Star newspaper. Needed by his family, he returned to the family farm around 1906 and worked there until he entered active duty with the United States Army in 1917. He had earlier been a member of the Missouri National Guard, from 1905 to 1911, though barely so. The nearsightedness that had blocked his possible appointment to West Point also threatened to deny him Guard membership. As was not uncommon in the period, he managed to pass the eye examination on the second try. How this was accomplished is not positively known. We do know however, that some potential enlistees resorted to memorizing the eye chart. When America declared war on Germany, Truman reentered the Guard, was selected for a commission and ultimately exercised combat command of Battery D, 129th Field Artillery, 35th Infantry Division. His war record and subsequent reserve status would prove useful in his later political success, as would his long term membership and leadership role in Scottish Rite Masonry in Missouri. He was a Mason for more than 50 years and an officer on a number of occasions, dating from 1909.

Returning to the United States after the war, he married Elizabeth Virginia (Bess)Wallace in June of 1919. He was 35. and she, who had rejected his earlier proposals, was 34. He also opened a haberdashery business in partnership with a friend from his military service, Edward Jacobson. The business failed in 1921.

That failure, while hurting him deeply, certainly was a determining factor in propelling Truman in the direction of a political, as opposed to a commercial, career. A year after the shop closed, Harry Truman was chosen as a candidate for judge of the county court for the Eastern District of Jackson County by Tom Pendergast, boss of the notorious Kansas City Pendergast machine. It should be noted that the term "judge" is an anachronism; the position was administrative, not judicial. It would be reasonable to assume that another friend from World War I service, Lieutenant James M. Pendergast, nephew of the party leader, probably played some sort of role in this decision. With the exception of a single defeat, in 1924, Truman's political career was well and truly launched. It was strictly local until 1934, when, again backed by the Pendergast Machine, he was nominated for and elected to the United States Senate. He occupied that seat until his nomination for vice-president in 1944.

2. Party Leadership (political)

In this category our experts have placed President Truman in the top third of all presidents, at 14th. When Franklin Roosevelt died, President Truman fell heir to virtually all of FDR's fourth term. The length afforded him both benefits and liabilities. Initially he had the benefit of a wave of popular sympathy, including that of his former colleagues in Congress. After all, he had been vice-president for fewer than 90 days when FDR died. On the other hand, the wave ebbed relatively quickly as he faced a myriad of politically tricky decisions and a rapidly changing world – and, perhaps most importantly, because he wasn't Franklin Roosevelt.

The political landscape Harry Truman faced was in nearly constant flux, changing with astonishing rapidity. A kaleidoscope of choices and decisions faced him involving war and peace, domestic and foreign policy, economic and social problems. Difficulty after difficulty, decision after decision confronted the new president, who was required to juggle seemingly dozens of judgments at once.

Less than 30 days after he took the oath of office, the war in Europe came to an end. He proclaimed V-E Day (Victory in Europe) on May 8th. Slightly more than 90 days after that, having made the decision to drop the atomic bomb – the existence of which he had not even been aware before

April 12th, – he was proclaiming V-J Day (Victory over Japan). The Second World War was over.

The end of the war also meant the end of many restraints that the war had imposed, either legally or as a result of agreed-upon patriotic motives. The frustrations of the past three-plus years of war (and in many cases of Depression-necessitated or imposed scarcity) rapidly bubbled to the surface. For example, the "no strike" pledge of the war years disappeared, and latent labor-management antagonism reasserted itself. Troops, some of whom had been in service since before Pearl Harbor, wanted to come home and be discharged immediately. The Depression and the war had caused housing to lag for nearly 15 years. Housing was in very short supply. Returning veterans, eager to marry and start families, created intense demands. Consumer goods, either non-existent or in short supply "for the duration," were now being demanded. Manufacturers as well as consumers were anxious to return to normal production. Would there be jobs for veterans? Would the new economy feature prosperity or would the Depression resume? For each question or need or demand, there was a constituency. And for each constituency there was a congressional bloc. Both constituencies and blocs grew rapidly as political pressures were created and as they blossomed. Simultaneously, Congress, which had been fairly well broken to the yoke by FDR and by the constraints of the war, was now feeling more assertive. The executive branch had led through the previous 12 or more years of economic and military emergency. Now the legislative branch was ready to assume its proper role in governance. It was much less disposed to defer to the executive branch.

To compound President Truman's problems, the Democratic Party was on the cusp of recreating itself. The conservative factions were more prepared to ally with Republicans, and the liberal factions were less disposed to compromise. Truman's relations with the Democratic Congress would be strained. After 1946, for two years, the Republicans would control both houses. Truman's relations with Congress were edgy during that period. In this political morass, the President would find greater success in dealing with foreign policy, where he found more substantial Republican cooperation than in matters of domestic policy.

He would enjoy few victories on the domestic front. The Republican-dominated Congress passed the Taft-Hartley Bill, reining in some labor union power, over Truman's veto. His "Fair Deal" proposals would collapse when he proposed national health care, expansion of civil rights for minorities and the growth of Social Security. Even under a Democratic Congress, repeal of the Taft-Hartley Act proved impossible. He was, however, able to bring about the racial integration of the military by Executive Order.

If he found managing Congress difficult, Truman did prove able to manage the Democratic Party. As the party looked to the 1948 election, portions of the old Solid South, the white supremacist wing of the party, at least partly split with the larger party. Strom Thurmond of South Carolina ran on the "Dixiecrat" ticket. At the same time, Henry A. Wallace, FDR's second vice-president and longtime cabinet member, split to the party's left, running as the Progressive Party's candidate. Other elements in the party were reaching out to General Dwight D. Eisenhower as a potential nominee. Eisenhower proved reluctant.

Aided by the advantages of incumbency, despite internal challenges from the left and right of the Democratic Party, Truman wheedled, cajoled, arm-twisted, outwaited and outwitted his opponents and emerged as a combative and energetic Democratic candidate for the presidency in 1948. Of course, he emerged from that campaign with a stunning victory.

It would be difficult to suggest, considering the large number of political problems and complexities he faced, that Harry Truman does not deserve to be ranked at least in the upper third of all presidents in party leadership.

3. Communication Ability (speak, write)

For the second time in a row, our expert respondents have ranked Harry Truman 14th – that is to say, barely outside the upper one-third of America's presidents.

President Truman's speech lacked the aristocratic tones and oratorical sweep of Franklin Roosevelt's. His vocal pattern was a flat, mid-western tonality. He was sometimes emotionally flat as well. On the other hand, from his acceptance speech at the Democratic National Convention in 1948 through his whistle stop campaign of that year he was able to rouse and to energize his base with signal success. The 1948 Democratic National Convention had been, at best, unenthusiastic about its candidate and the party's chances. Indeed, the President did not even get to the microphone until early in the morning. His arrival changed all that as he walked out on the stage, showing confidence in his every gesture and delivering a ringing campaign speech that brought the delegates to life. Throughout his imaginative whistle stop campaign, with a speech from the back of the train at every stop, crowds shouted and applauded the mantra of, "Give 'em hell, Harry," to which he sometimes responded, "I'm doing it," or words to that effect. Nearly a decade later, Truman would say, "I never did give them hell. I just told the truth, and they thought it was hell." While Truman was famed for neither his oratory or prose style he always spoke and wrote clearly. In 1948, when it counted most, he surely rose to the occasion.

4. Relationship with Congress

Our respondents ranked Truman 17th among American Presidents in his relations with the Congress. As we have indicated, Congress, which had been deferential toward, if not subservient to, Franklin Delano Roosevelt, no longer felt either personal or patriotic restraints in its dealing with a new chief executive.

The political universe Truman confronted was also a different place. Where Roosevelt had struggled to jumpstart housing, Truman was faced with a 15-year dearth of home construction. Between the Depression and World War II, between scarcity and wartime priorities, little had been done about new housing between 1930 and 1946. To exacerbate the housing crisis, literally millions of veterans were coming home, being discharged, getting married and starting to raise families. Where and how were they to be housed?

When we look at that new political universe of 1945-1946, it seems fair to suggest that few presidencies have had to be as continually active on as many fronts as did that of Harry S Truman. A partial list of the activities and actions of the period may serve to summarize just how busy the administration would find itself.

When Truman took the oath in April of 1945, what was to be called the "reconversion" of the American economy to peacetime industrial activity had, unbeknown to most Americans, already begun. As it accelerated through the next few years, it would involve inflation, labor unrest, competition for scarce raw materials rather than wartime allocation, strikes and accusations of fraud and price gouging.

More than 10 million men and a few hundred thousand women would have to be processed, discharged and returned to civilian life. The G.I. Bill of Rights would have to be converted from a paper charter to reality with college tuition and benefits provided. Vets also got what were really unemployment benefits paid through what was called the "52-20 Club." Various other benefits, ranging from mortgage loans to small business assistance, went into operation. The 52-20 Club was a grant of $20 a week for 52 weeks to newly discharged veterans under the G.I. Bill. The money served, in essence, as unemployment insurance.

In such an admixture of actions, entitlements and benefits across the entire economy, it was rare for the administration to act without opposition. When, for example, in 1946 the railroad workers threatened to strike, the President responded by threatening to draft them into the army. He won that battle, but it was not productive of friends among labor unions or those who represented them in Congress. Indeed, his irascibility, at least on occasion, impeded his goals.

At the same time, in July, 1945, he attended the Potsdam Conference with Joseph Stalin of the U.S.S.R. and Clement Attlee of Great Britain, who had been chosen to succeed Winston Churchill as prime minister after Britain's first post-War election. The President had also been briefed on the secret of the atomic bomb and had decided to use the weapon. That now-controversial decision was then greeted with virtually universal and unalloyed joy by the troops staging in the Pacific Ocean Area for the invasion of Japan, scheduled for that November.

Truman's support for the foundation of the United Nations was as staunch as FDR's had been. One sign of that was his appointment of Eleanor Roosevelt as a member of the first United States delegation to the General Assembly.

As the policies of Stalin and the Soviet Union seemed to grow increasingly inimical to American interests and ideals, President Truman grew less patient with Soviet adventurism. One obvious result was a flurry of policies and activities between 1947 and 1950 designed to contain such policies. His general policy of containment would become encapsulated as the Truman Doctrine. He formally announced the doctrine in 1947, which was also when Secretary of State George C. Marshall announced the creation of the European Recovery Program (better known as the Marshall Plan) to rebuild the shattered economies of Europe. The first monies were appropriated by Congress in 1948.

The Truman Doctrine had been accompanied by a promised extension of military assistance to Greece and Turkey against the Soviet Union in 1947. A United States military advisory group had been set up in Greece to assist the government in resisting a Communist rebellion. By 1949, the series of actions supporting the Truman Doctrine included the creation of the North Atlantic Treaty Organization. NATO represented a major change in United States foreign policy. It saw America entering into quasi-permanent alliances in the name of collective security against Communism. The United States agreed to assist free governments against the aggressive activities of totalitarian states. That constituted the policy of containment, and that policy remained the strategic doctrine of the United States until the fall of the Soviet Union, a half century later.

Also in 1947, the legal framework for the independent status of the United States Air Force came into being, along with the consolidation of the United States armed forces under the Department of Defense. A Central Intelligence Agency to replace the Office of Strategic Services was established as was the National Security Council. Let us conclude what is a suggestive rather than an exhaustive list of items demanding the time and attention of the President, and various responses from the Congress, by noting that it was, and is, as daunting a list of policies and programs, foreign and domestic, as any American President has been called upon to deal with in a brief period.

As President Truman surveyed the approaching election of 1948, his prospects seemed dim. His party was less than enthusiastic about his plans and his candidacy. As we have already seen, despite the Democratic Party's splintered condition, Truman would be able to retain both his leadership of the party and its nomination for reelection.

Campaigning added still another dimension to his level of activity. Truman's Fair Deal campaign called for the establishment of national health insurance, the expansion of civil rights for minorities and repeal of the Taft-Hartley Law. Of his quite ambitious platform, he would achieve legislative victory only in the 1949 Housing Act. Defeats in Congress in regard to Civil Rights were at least partially offset by his use of additional Executive Orders. As he had used such orders to integrate the armed forces, so he now called for an end to racial discrimination in regard to civil service appointments and issued an order that forbade discrimination against any bidders on contracts for the armed forces.

Truman's surprise reelection in 1948 also saw the return of the Congress to the control of the Democratic Party. That party triumph did not, however, guarantee congressional approval for presidential initiatives in the next few years.

In May of 1948, the President recognized the legitimacy of the new state of Israel, against the objections of his own State Department. Analysis of his motives has run the gamut from altruistic and humanitarian to pragmatic and political. In the first case, it is suggested he did it in spite of real fears about the reaction of the Arab states because it was the right thing to do. In the second instance, he was said to be acutely aware that his action would yield a rich harvest of Jewish votes in 1948. We do not know of a valid and definitive either/or answer. We also know that individuals, even Presidents, often act from mixed motives.

In December of 1949, the defeated Nationalist Chinese armies were driven from the Chinese mainland by the Communist forces of the People's Republic of China. Now, Truman's administration would be accused of "losing China" to the Communist regime of Mao Zedong. That allegation in turn was to play a role in the ongoing political debate about loyalty – loyalty to the United States versus loyalty to Communism, Marxist-Leninist ideology or to the Soviet Union. That bitter quarrel would continue long after Harry Truman left Washington. The rhetoric would involve "reds" and "pinks" and "fellow travelers" and Alger Hiss and Richard Nixon and Senator Joe McCarthy. It would entail discussions of loyalty oaths and treason and pumpkin papers and names and quarrels now forgotten, though perhaps not irrelevant.

It all would seem to flow from what appeared to many, perhaps most, Americans, in and out of Congress, to be an incomprehensible reversal of fortune in a seemingly infinitesimal amount of time. On September 1, 1945, the United States was a political and economic giant that clearly dominated world politics. With her allies, she had defeated, indeed humiliated, the Axis powers, which as recently as 1942 had posed a credible threat to dominate the world. The United States possessed a huge military machine, a dominant air force and the largest navy the world had ever seen. In addition to those attributes she was economically and industrially the only super power in the world, with about 50 per cent of the globe's gross domestic product. And, the United States alone possessed the atomic bomb.

Five years to the day later, the country had been at war in Korea since June. It was about to launch (September 15) a dramatic amphibious landing at Inchon harbor in Korea that might allow the nation to reverse the fortunes of war, which had run against her. The landing force was the 1st Marine Division. At that moment, that division constituted the entire national strategic reserve. If the landings failed, new troops would have to be recruited, trained and transported before other strategies could be attempted. The Navy could not blockade the coasts of North Korea because it was no longer large enough to do so. Soviet Russia now also possessed the bomb. Americans were psychologically stunned. How could this be? There must have been some sort of betrayal. At least misfeasance, malfeasance or nonfeasance! Someone must be responsible! How about the folks in charge?

Each of the problems – economic, political, military, foreign policy or ideological – brought both supporters and detractors to President Truman's cause. Perhaps most notable among his supporters was Senator Arthur Vandenberg, Republican of Michigan, whose assistance was critical on foreign policy issues such as the Truman Doctrine, the Marshall Plan and NATO. On the other hand, detraction and carping would be forthcoming from many other members of Congress. If we accept such attitudes as normal and add to them a fractious Congress seeking to reestablish its own authority plus the immense variety and sheer number of issues on the table, we can perhaps see why President Truman is accorded only a ranking in the top 40 per cent in this category.

5. Court Appointments

Here, Harry Truman is ranked 12th, just behind John Kennedy and just ahead of James Monroe, but still in the upper third of all presidents. Many would consider this a generous ranking.

President Truman had four opportunities to nominate members of the Supreme Court. His nominees were Associate Justice Harold H. Burton, Chief Justice Fred M. Vinson and Associate Justices Tom Clark and Sherman Minton. The respective nominations were in 1945, 1946, and two in 1949.

All were friends of the President. Burton and Minton had served with him in the senate. All were judicial conservatives, akin to the philosophical position of the President who selected them. Truman felt, very strongly, that the judiciary should show deference to the elective branches and avoid making policy from the bench. There seems to be no significant evidence to sustain a stellar position in American legal history for any of them. Truman himself would come to think that Clark's appointment was one of his own significant errors as President. Truman's opinion was certainly colored by the fact that Clark voted against the President (though with the majority) in Youngstown Sheet and Tube Co. v. Sawyer.

In any event, there is no reason to believe that this ranking does the President any injustice.

6. Handling of the U. S. Economy

In this category our experts rank Truman seventh, in the top 20 per cent of American Presidents.

Perhaps mindful of the failure of his own business during the post-World War I boom and bust cycle, the President feared a recurrence of that post-war period of inflation and unemployment and felt a need to act. To combat that cycle, he proposed wage, price and rent controls as well as additional public housing construction. Proposals for the extension of Social Security and an increase in the minimum wage were also made.

Congress was not disposed to acquiesce. Rising prices did lead to labor unrest and to strikes. Though the President was a strong adherent of labor and of unionism, he nevertheless felt it necessary to issue executive orders, seek court injunctions and, even, as we have seen, to issue threats to draft recalcitrant railway workers. Similarly, when faced with coal strikes, he seized control of the mines.

The emerging post-war economy was rather like a river which has just been released from a newly opened dam. There was, as we have stipulated, a pent-up demand for consumer goods caused by the strictures of the Depression and the war. So, too, the demand for housing stock and automobiles was well above the norm. Returning veterans fed the demand, as did the initial stages of what would come to be called the "Baby Boom."

While there were, indeed, inflationary pressures, the economy was not as troubled as it had been post-World War I. Instead, a virtually unparalleled economic boom, to be further fed by the reconstruction of Europe and Japan, the Korean War and the Cold War in general, began. Those prosperous times would endure throughout Truman's presidency and that of Eisenhower as well.

Given the reality of this prosperity, the measurable increase in Gross Domestic Product, successful reconversion, and the rest, it would be difficult to quarrel with the rank awarded to President Truman by our respondents.

7. Luck

Ranking at number 12 Harry Truman again falls within the upper third of American Presidents in this category. Clearly, for vice presidents succeeding after the death of a sitting President, the issue of his "luck" in coming to office in such a fashion is subjective. We have no way of interpreting how or whether that subjectivity entered into the responses we received.

In the realm of luck as happenstance, we may wish to consider good fortune emerging from bad luck. In this sense, Mr. Truman's lack of success with investments and his failure in the retail haberdashery trade may be seen as significantly influencing his political career. We might credibly suggest that had he enjoyed commercial success he might well never have embarked upon a life in politics. Instead, as a newly married man and then father, in the 1920s, the Pendergast machine and political office must have seemed a godsend to him. Politics offered him not only a means to support his family but also a modicum of respect and dignity.

Good fortune continued to flow from politics. In 1934, when the Pendergast machine had no immediate candidate for the United States Senate, Harry Truman emerged as a sort of dark horse, won a three-way primary and then defeated his Republican opponent. While unanswerable questions about election tactics and deceased voters were raised, Truman took his seat in the Senate in 1935.

After winning reelection in another three-way contest in 1940, Truman emerged as a major figure in the Senate. His wartime service as the chairman of the so-called Truman Committee, searching for and finding corruption in war orders and other government contracts, brought him to the attention of the electorate in a positive light. Thus, in 1944, he was "available" when the behind the scenes wise men of the Democratic Party expressed their concerns about the combination of FDR's shaky health and the quite far-left politics of Vice President Henry Wallace. It was decided that Wallace would have to be replaced. FDR appeared indifferent to the matter.

With Wallace on the left and James Byrnes of South Carolina on the right, Senator Truman emerged as the ideal compromise candidate. Truman, who was evidently enjoying his newly elevated senatorial status, was reluctant to agree but was dragooned into acceptance.

On a quite different level of good fortune, in the wake of the North Korean invasion of South Korea in the summer of 1950, President Truman decided that it was necessary to limit the expansion of Communist regimes by militarily opposing that invasion. At that point, Stalin presented the President with a considerable stroke of luck. Truman did not wish to have the world perceive the opposition to be unilateral on the part of the United States. He much preferred that the position be that of the United Nations as a collective. Fortunately for American policy makers, the Soviet Union was at that time boycotting the U. N. Security Council, where, of course, it possessed a veto. With Stalin cutting off his nose to spite his face, the decision to take military action in Korea was taken in the name of the United Nations, with concomitant benefits for the President in both credibility and propaganda.

President Truman was an enthusiastic poker player, but it would be wrong to suggest that the poker table was the only place where luck was with him.

8. Ability to Compromise

A ranking of 15th indicates that our responding scholars do not believe this to be a category in which this President deserves praise.

Truman himself said that the "S" in Harry S Truman stood for no name at all, but represented a family compromise. Each of his grandfathers had a name that began with the letter S. Given that circumstance, one might pardonably expect that he might be predisposed to compromise. Such an expectation would probably be heightened by the fact that, in 1944, he was something of a Democratic Party compromise candidate for Vice President with President Roosevelt. Such expectations would prove to be a weak reed upon which to lean. So, too, when Truman's anxieties about the postwar economy found him at odds with labor or management his resort to threats of drafting strikers or seizing steel mills do not speak to a spirit of sweet reason or compromise.

He certainly could work well with others. The bipartisan foreign policy coalition dominated by Truman and GOP Senator Arthur Vandenberg of Michigan, which played such a large part in establishing the pillars of

Western Cold War policy, demonstrates that. The Marshall Plan and the Truman Doctrine speak well for both men. Clearly, however, it was Senator Vandenberg who was altering his ideas and shifting his stances to the greater degree.

On another front, once he turned his attention to easing the plight of African Americans, Truman never looked back. Even in 1948, faced with an uphill fight for reelection and confronted with the actual revolt of the white supremacist element of the Democratic Party, the Dixiecrats, he remained committed to the more liberal plank of the Democratic Party Platform. There was real political danger, but he did not turn aside; he did not compromise.

These instances and others like them may be why he has relatively poor results in this category. Once he had convinced himself that he was right, Harry Truman had a genuine streak of obstinacy in him. He was known from time to time to compare himself with a Missouri mule.

Whether overruling his own State Department and quarreling with Secretary Marshall about recognizing the state of Israel, continuing personal loyalty to the discredited and disgraced political "Boss" Tom Pendergast or confronting Joseph Stalin, President Truman was reluctant to yield to anyone on anything.

9. Willingness to Take Risks

This is the category in which President Truman receives his highest rank, fifth, just outside the top 10 per cent. Few Presidents have taken as many risks, political and otherwise, in as many areas as consistently as he did. Indeed, perhaps few have needed to.

First, with barely enough time to get his feet under the presidential desk, he made the decision to use the atomic bomb and to indicate to Japan that the United States would continue to do so as long as necessary. The Japanese, of course, were unaware that the Hiroshima and Nagasaki bombs constituted the entire arsenal. The bomb, it should also be remembered, did not then possess the significant symbolic content that it has now, but the decision was still a weighty one.

Second, in a sort of rough chronological order, his concern for the postwar economy led him to risk the anger of an important segment of his political constituency when he potentially alienated the powerful labor movement in his efforts to control the economy and muzzle inflation. Between Truman seizing mines and mills and threatening to draft striking railway men, labor leaders in every segment of the economy had to view him as at least an occasional enemy.

Third, by 1947 he was willing to take considerable risk to limit or contain Soviet expansionism. He began in the eastern Mediterranean with intervention to bolster Greece and Turkey, as the United States found itself replacing England as the guarantor of stability in the region. In 1947, the American government announced the so-called Truman Doctrine. The United States would support those whose freedom was threatened by "armed minorities" and/or "outside pressure." With support from the Congress, the outlines of what would soon be called the policy of containment began to emerge.

On another front, he would try to achieve a delicate balance between the anti-Communist policy of the Truman Doctrine and resistance to demands for purges of Communist influence within his own government. HST was prepared to gamble political capital on those issues.

In the summer of 1948, Stalin and the Soviet Union presented President Truman with yet another crisis. Contrary to the agreed-upon terms for the occupation of Germany, Soviet military forces established a blockade, denying the Western Allies access to Berlin by road and rail. Truman countered with imagination and vigor. The President organized the Berlin Airlift as the western response to the Berlin Blockade. The United States Air Force, with assistance from the Royal Air Force, supplied the physical needs of Berlin's western sectors for food and fuel and other necessities by air. Failure or excessive losses in the airlift would have been likely to produce a significant diminution of the prestige and influence of the United States, as well as invigorating the political elements at home wishing for a more direct response to Stalin. Perhaps it also discouraged further Soviet adventurism. The action was unprecedented and highly successful. Incidentally, it did much to speed the development of the ability of aircraft to fly in hostile weather conditions, to the subsequent advantage of civil aviation. The process continued into the late spring of 1949, when the Soviets backed away.

As the Cold War became a hot war in Korea in 1950, he again took great risks. An American Army, barely a shadow of what had existed five years earlier, was thrown into the breach to stem the North Korean invasion of South Korea. Regardless of what happened later, Truman was successful in stopping and turning back the invasion and guaranteeing the continued existence of the Republic of Korea.

Finally, he was a consistent proponent of civil rights for African Americans. In February of 1948, he sent to the Congress a 10-point Civil Rights Bill upon which no action was taken. On July of 1948 he issued Executive Order # 9981 ending segregation in the armed forces. It was a logical corollary to his February proposals, but as commander-in-chief he did not need congressional cooperation.

He also supported a civil rights platform in the 1948 Democratic Party Presidential Platform, even though it was for many Southern Democrats a sort of last straw. Southerners bolted the party and formed the so-called Dixiecrat party, which siphoned off electoral votes that otherwise would certainly have gone to Harry Truman. He took the risk and paid the consequence. Obviously, it was not sufficient to prevent his 1948 electoral triumph.

10. Executive Appointments

When President Truman took the oath of office in April of 1945, there were, as there had been under President Roosevelt, 10 cabinet positions. When he left office, there were nine. The War and Navy departments had been incorporated under the office of the secretary of defense as a result of the National Security Act of 1947 and its 1949 amendments. That act also created the National Security Council and the office of the National Security Advisor.

At the time of his swearing in, Truman already had 10 cabinet members, all appointed by FDR. By the latter part of 1945, all had been replaced except Henry Wallace at Commerce, Harold Ickes at Interior and James Forrestal at Navy. The first two were gone by 1946. Forrestal stayed on at Navy until 1947, when he was appointed the first Secretary of Defense. Including Forrestal, Harry Truman would appoint 24 cabinet officers to nine cabinet positions in the period between 1946 and 1953. The quality of his appointments seems singularly uneven. Nevertheless, our professorial respondents assess him as ranking eighth among the Presidents in this category.

At the State Department, he replaced FDR's Edward Stettinius with James F. Byrnes, George C. Marshall and Dean Acheson. All were strong figures. Byrnes had been a Senate colleague of Truman's and had his confidence. Only after a period in which he seemingly ignored the President and sought to make policy without consulting him was that confidence shattered. At that point, the President brought in retired Army Chief of Staff George C. Marshall as secretary. Marshall would head the State Department for only a brief period (1947-1949) but he is unquestionably the cabinet star of the administration.

While Truman did not hesitate to overrule Marshall – as he did, for example, on the recognition of Israel – they worked well together. They produced the Cold War policy of containment, the Truman Doctrine and the Marshall Plan, which would be the pillars of American policy with regard to Soviet expansionism throughout the Cold War Era. Marshall would win the Nobel

Peace Prize in 1953, a rare gift for a soldier, even a retired one.

Secretary Marshall was replaced by Dean Acheson. Acheson was a highly controversial figure. Though unquestionably one of the engineers, if not architects, of the containment policy, his refusal "to turn my back" on his friends – notably, Alger Hiss, when he was accused of spying for the Soviet Union – did much to weaken his credibility and to dilute his influence as a spokesman for administration foreign policy. Still, none of these men can be represented as a nonentity or as an incompetent.

At the Department of Defense, Forrestal was also competent. His, however, was a brief term, also 1947-1949, which ended with a nervous breakdown and a presumed suicide. The new department's trials also included the so-called "Revolt of the Admirals," when a group of ranking naval officers and the secretary of the Navy, then as now a subordinate of the secretary of defense, successfully challenged decisions of the Defense Department with regard to procurement. Those decisions had seemed to many to favor the Air Force.

Forrestal's successor, Louis A. Johnson, had been highly supportive of those decisions. Johnson and the President had become convinced that nuclear weapons, of which the United States enjoyed a monopoly until 1949, would inexpensively guarantee America's security. On Johnson's watch, drastic cuts were imposed on all services, though the Air Force was perceived to suffer least. When the early stages of the Korean War exposed the folly of the policies that the President and Secretary Johnson had advocated, politically, the secretary had to go.

Once again, the President turned to George C. Marshall. Marshall agreed to serve for one year to reverse the policies and strengthen the United States military. As agreed, he served as secretary of defense from September of 1950 until September of 1951. Moving quickly, he doubled available military manpower, vastly increased the military budget, tried to get the Congress to introduce universal military training and expanded the age limits and terms of service under the Selective Service Act. Robert A. Lovett, Marshall's Deputy Secretary of Defense, succeeded him. He was fully cognizant of the problems the department faced as well as its culture and how it functioned. He was an able administrator who continued most of his predecessor's policies and initiatives, into many of which he had previously had substantial input.

If we were to assign grades to each, Forrestal might be judged B/B+, Marshall A-/A, and Lovett, perhaps a B+. Johnson, though fully in line with Truman's thinking, gets at best a D.

To look quickly at other cabinet members who served Mr. Truman we might contrast John W. Snyder, secretary of the treasury, 1946-1953, and Attorney General J. Howard McGrath, July, 1949 to April, 1952. Snyder had met Truman during World War I, and they were long-time friends. For good or for evil, Truman was very comfortable with his fellow World War I veterans. Snyder and Truman also had worked together in Washington when Truman was in the Senate and Snyder worked at the Reconstruction Finance Company. Snyder's administration of the Treasury Department was competent and insightful. Truman had seen McGrath appointed as head of the Democratic National Committee (1947-49) and, in that capacity he had energetically overseen the President's successful reelection campaign of 1948. He also had integrated the staff of the Democratic National Committee. That policy may have alienated a number of southerners but it did the President no harm among big city minority voters. In the wake of investigations and the failure of McGrath to fulfill his promises of cooperation with investigators, HST found it necessary to demand his resignation.

Truman's cabinet members would not appear to attain the stature of FDR's, and certainly not the level of stability. On the other hand, his appointments at State and Defense, by far the most important in those years are, with the single exception of Johnson, more than competent.

A rank, eighth, which places him among the top 20 per cent of American Presidents in this category, seems to be at least arguable and sustainable.

11. Overall Ability

Mr. Truman achieves ranking of seventh place in overall ability behind only FDR, Lincoln and Washington, TR, Jefferson and Wilson. It certainly places him in distinguished company. Can we suggest that the ranking reflects the achievements of the administration? We think we can.

His decision to use the atomic bomb, after only a short period of time in office and with no preliminary idea of its existence, is a good illustration of his characteristic decisiveness. So, too, were his decisions to seize the railroads and steel mills and his threats to draft railway men.

Clearly, however, the major issues of his presidency were, and are, irrevocably intertwined with the persona of Joseph Stalin and the issues surrounding the expansionist policies of the Soviet Union, post-World War II. Truman's responses to these policies and provocations were thoughtful, energetic and decisive and are best summarized in the single word "containment." Containment meant the decision to attempt to deny the Soviet Union the opportunity to subvert sovereign states and convert them to puppets of Moscow, like those that had passed behind the Iron Curtain by 1948-1949. That is, subsequent to the coup in Czechoslovakia in 1948 and the success of

Mao's forces over the Kuomintang in China in 1949, a line was drawn that said, "thus far and no farther."

To that end, President Truman proposed and supported the programs and policies we have outlined above. From the Marshall Plan to NATO, from the Berlin Airlift to Korea, the common theme was containment. To the same end, America committed its wealth under the Marshall Plan to the reconstruction of postwar Europe and, through Truman's Point Four funding program, to assistance for the world's underdeveloped nations.

His domestic legislative agenda was much less successful, but he did, via proposed civil rights bills and executive orders, move civil rights issues onto the front burner of American politics. It was an executive branch committee, appointed early in his administration, which sent a number of recommendations to the Congress. Some of those proposals, such as outlawing the poll tax, would not come to fruition for almost 20 years. Clearly, however, Truman presented these issues to the nation much more forcefully than had his predecessor. In that context, he did much to help set that portion of the national agenda for the next several decades.

12. Imagination

The professors who responded obviously did not think of Mr. Truman as a particularly imaginative man. They ranked him only at 14 of 41 presidents.

The record, it seems to us, produces a mixed result. Truman's use of the term "Fair Deal" certainly does not argue imagination. Whatever resonance it may have clearly derives almost entirely from its association with Franklin Roosevelt's "New Deal," perhaps even Theodore Roosevelt's "Square Deal." While not quite a cliché, it was certainly banal.

On the other hand, the 1948 campaign, with its use of whistle stop campaigning, reminiscent of an earlier day, though one still within living memory, and the assumed verities associated with that day, was a striking form of electioneering. It also put Truman in close touch with many voters, not unlike the result he had achieved when he campaigned from his car in his senatorial race of 1940. This tactic of bringing the President to the people – on their doorstep, so to speak – seems also to have been rather prophetic of one element of modern campaigning. It let the people and the local media hear the President, unfiltered by pundits and the national press.

In 1948, HST also sought, with considerable success, to identify the Republican Party with the Republican majorities of the 80th Congress. He always, for campaign purposes, referred to as the "do nothing" 80th Congress. Congressional recalcitrance and obstructionism would be defined as the opponent, more than the GOP candidate, Governor Thomas E. Dewey of

New York.

The masterpiece of the campaign was reached in the summer of 1948, when Truman called Congress back to Washington for a special session and challenged the congressional Republican majority to enact the 1948 Republican Presidential Campaign Platform. When the session ended in bluster and futility, Mr. Truman had achieved a significant public relations victory in an unparalleled manner. Politically, it would appear that HST and his cohorts were not entirely lacking in imagination.

In foreign policy too, many of the Cold War initiatives were highly innovative. The Marshall Plan and Point Four represented new ways of winning support for American policies. Even in the Korean War, the overall strategy of containing and limiting aggression rather than destroying the aggressor represented a departure from past American strategic and operational military planning.

These events, if not imaginative, were certainly new and different.

13. Domestic Accomplishments

In this category, HST comes in just within the top 20 per cent, at eighth. In most traditional areas, it would seem difficult to justify such a ranking. When he succeeded to office, his own Democratic Party had majorities in both houses. After the 1946 elections, the Republicans possessed those majorities, and after 1948 the Democrats regained control and held it until the end of his presidency. That is, he enjoyed the luxury of having his party in the majority throughout three-quarters of his term, though with limited results on his domestic policy proposals.

To majorities of both parties President Truman presented elements of what he called his Fair Deal program. They included a full employment policy and increased minimum wage legislation. He requested executive authority to regulate wages and prices in peacetime, expansion of Social Security coverage, more public housing, additional provision for the federal government to provide public power, (a la TVA), some form of health insurance and a fair employment practices act to ban discrimination.

At no time under either party was there any sign of significant enthusiasm for the program. Forms of fair employment practice acts and full employment acts would pass and, during the Korean War, both price and wage control authority was temporarily provided. In general, though, minus a specific outside force or threat, no element of his domestic agenda seemed to have political appeal.

In addition, the 80th Congress had passed the Taft-Hartley Law, seen by labor and by Truman as union busting legislation, over Truman's veto. Even the return of Democratic majorities was not enough to get it repealed.

Perhaps two elements motivated our respondents to rank him as highly as they did. First, we would, again, refer to his ground-breaking efforts in opposition to racial discrimination. On the eve of the civil rights era, Truman's efforts, whether failed or not, offered a strong sign of leadership. Most dramatically, of course, there was the issuance of Executive Order # 9981 on July 26, 1948, ordering the integration of U. S. armed forces. Other executive orders were also issued forbidding discrimination in awarding Defense Department contracts and in the civil service. Many other initiatives in the form of proposed legislation were defeated, but the issues were kept alive.

That record may have been reinforced for our professors by his relatively liberal attitudes and policies during a period marked conspicuously by McCarthyism and Red Baiting. The Cold War spun off a domestic version of concern about domestic subversion, about spies, "fellow travelers" and "parlor pinks." While Truman was very much an anti-Communist in foreign policy, on the international stage he was much more ambivalent in the area of loyalty oaths, of concern about subversives, of domestic Communists and the like. He was very much a skeptic in these areas, speaking on occasion of "red herrings" being dragged about to confuse the unwary and to interfere with appropriate focus on what was really important. While he certainly had then and now critics from the left who felt he did not do enough, others saw his attitudes and internal policies during a time of blacklists and concerns about parlor pinks as courageous and appropriate. Critics from the right maintained that his domestic course was "soft on Communism." We leave his critics and his supporters to their respective views.

14. Integrity

Here, Mr. Truman ranks at seventh. He is famed for his personal probity, and no ex-president has been more careful of guarding his personal reputation and that of the presidency. He was scrupulously wary during his post-presidential years to avoid even a hint of exploiting the office he had held.

At the same time there can be no question that, as a politician, he was the child, albeit an honest one, of the notorious Pendergast machine. He remained loyal, and gave every evidence of taking pride in that fact. He was true to the Pendergasts even after the boss, Tom Pendergast, had been indicted, convicted and incarcerated. Similarly, when his presidential military aide, Major General Harry Vaughan, a friend from Army days and a machine stalwart, was deeply implicated in charges of influence peddling, including the procuring of a number of then-scarce deep freezers – one of which was sent to Mrs. Truman – the President responded angrily. Truman behaved as though he, personally, had been accused and came to Vaughan's defense. The controversy did not redound to Truman's credit.

In each case, it is arguable that the response represented deep-seated personal loyalty and, therefore, might even be admirable. If that is accurate, we believe such loyalty to be misplaced. The presidential entourage, staff and advisors, not just constitutional officers, must be held to a very high standard.

Mr. Truman certainly held himself to the highest of standards. When he left the White House, he was to all intents and purposes, penniless. There was, as yet, no presidential pension, and the now normal ex-presidential book deal had not emerged as a standard. HST refused to accept lucrative posts with private corporations because it seemed to him it would be tantamount to selling the prestige of the presidency.

Once again, on balance, the ranking appears to be appropriate. It recognizes his individual integrity but also slightly offsets it, allowing for the flaws he displayed in regard to his friends and associates.

15. Executive Ability

Truman is here ranked as seventh among all Presidents, well within the upper fifth.

It seems appropriate once again, to refer here to the definition we offered in our examination of Franklin Roosevelt's ranking in this category. (In this category, italicized words and phrases refer to the definition in Chapter 2, FDR, Executive Ability.)

No one has ever suggested that Harry Truman lacked *drive*. Even a cursory study of his senatorial reelection campaign of 1940 and the storied campaign for the presidency in 1948 would serve well to illustrate his *physical energy and drive*.

The events, plans and policies inherent in HST's management of the closing phases of World War II, his plans for reconversion of the economy and those for coping with Soviet adventurism illustrate not only drive but also the *initiation of cognitive activity*. Such activity is implicitly illustrated in the *initiatives* he undertook and explained to Congress and the nation. Of course, it also indicates *sustained motivation* illustrated in the pursuit of those policies throughout the years of his presidency.

As we pointed out in our analysis of Franklin Roosevelt, the *ability to recognize patterns and perform sequences* seems directly related to normal presidential interaction with Congress and the various presidential constituencies. Whether in the creation of NATO, working with the United Nations to defend South Korea or the formulation of other initiatives, Truman and his surrogates and colleagues seem always to have worked with dynamism, clarity and cogency. The hallmark of the administration was multiple initiatives tending to the same goal.

The planning and execution of strategy were strong points for Truman's administration. By the time he left office, there was little to add to overall United States Cold War strategy. There would, obviously, be later shadings and nuances, but the basic policy of the United States, which would endure until the collapse of the Soviet Union, had been put in place and a strategy for its implementation sketched out.

Other elements of the definition are illustrated by the clarity of the administration's views on both its civil rights policy and its foreign policy. In each area the position was placed on the table, argued and implemented to the best of the President's ability and constitutional authority. Truman was clear, consistent and conscientious in his positions.

Whether he learned from error and/or was able to self-correct is difficult to assess since presidents prefer to at least appear never to have erred. We would assert that evidence of self-correction is obviously present, as with virtually all Presidents, but as is also true of most Presidents, hedged about with quibbles regarding sincerity, political aims and goals. It is our belief that such criticisms are not relevant to the definition. Truman's rating in this category seems apt.

16. Foreign Policy Accomplishments

Along with the category of Willingness to Take Risks, this category represents President Truman's highest ranking, fifth. Few American Presidents have faced foreign policy challenges as daunting as those facing Harry Truman. Between using the atomic bomb to force Japan's surrender in the summer of 1945 and committing American troops to a land war in Asia (Korea) in the summer of 1950, the world seemed to have gone mad. To use the cliché, in September of 1945 the United States bestrode the world like a colossus. Its enemies everywhere lay prostrate. It enjoyed total victory and was the sole possessor of the atomic bomb. America possessed unrivaled armed forces, and its navy and air force were each the greatest in world history. By 1950, on the other hand, its armed forces had dwindled to a shadow of those of 1945, and Stalin and the Soviet Union now also possessed nuclear weapons. In Korea, initially, the United States Army was hard pressed even to cope with the North Korean invasion of South Korea.

Much of that was clearly a result of President Truman's overly optimistic view of nuclear weapons as the primary and a relatively inexpensive guarantor of peace. That, in turn, had led to a drawing down of conventional United States forces to the point that, during the Korean War, a virtual rearmament program became necessary.

Despite those difficulties, and despite the development of what was coming to be called the Iron Curtain and the Cold War, HST continued moving into place the basic elements of the policy of the containment of the Soviet Union. Confronted with the reality of the post-World War II Soviet expansionist policy, the United States was not willing to risk a hot war to drive Russia out of its satellite states, but it was willing to give its aid to prevent any further Soviet expansion.

Given its historical experience with the United States between 1945 and 1951, the U.S.S.R. was unable to realistically predict what American response to further adventurism might be. Absent the ability to predict, the expansionism slowed and virtually stopped. Surrogates might in later years be used to try new approaches, but not the mother country. The policies of containment and the nuclear umbrella – the doctrine of Mutually Assured Destruction – seemed to, and probably did, make the world not a safe, but a safer place.

By and large, containment succeeded, and it ultimately concluded with the collapse of the Soviet Union, the flight of the satellite states and the isolation of the few remaining Communist states. Truman's foreign policy would be, with an occasional wobble, the foreign policy of Eisenhower, Kennedy, Johnson, Nixon, Ford, Carter, Reagan and George H. W. Bush. Such a continuum is surely an otherwise unrecorded feat in American history.

17. Leadership Ability

This is the third category in which President Truman finishes at eighth. One measure of his leadership might be sought in the impact of the major policies of his administration upon the American people. If we recall that the political impact of isolationism in the years before Pearl Harbor was sufficient to give Franklin Roosevelt pause, and then factor in the reality that by 1950 HST had fully engaged the United States in a dramatically interventionist foreign policy – the Truman Doctrine, the Marshall Plan, complete with entangling alliances like NATO and even war, in Korea – Truman's initiatives really represented a massive change. Obviously, the policies and attitudes and the adventurism of Stalin and the U.S.S.R. influenced the thought and reasoning of the American people, as had the events of World War II. However the successful selling of such dramatic policy changes in such a short time – only six or so years – bespeaks significant leadership skills.

In Presidential Leadership: Rating the Best and Worst in the White House, 2004, Terry Eastland, the then publisher of The Evening Standard, wrote the essay on Truman. His point of departure was the emphasis that the authors of The Federalist Papers placed upon energetic, decisive and firm leadership in the presidency. Eastland then stipulates that Truman's presidency "… is a study in 'energy in the executive'; energy that often benefited the nation (p. 160)." The essay then goes on to enumerate administration policies and actions befitting the thesis – the decision to drop the bomb, the development of the containment policy and the concomitant corollaries, the consequent extension of the influence of the American presidency well beyond the nation's geographical boundaries. Other areas would include Truman's open display of support for minority rights. That would include his use of executive orders to implement such support, as well as lesser but still useful actions, such as having the United States Justice Department file friend of the court briefs in the federal courts on behalf of those aggrieved by various aspects of legal segregation at state and local levels.

In short, it seems that Harry Truman not only possessed leadership skills but was prepared to use them with aptitude and gusto. His style was very different from that of his predecessor, but his results, perhaps particularly in foreign policy, seem to have possessed equivalence or near equivalence. The notion of the American President as leader of the free world seems to have continued unimpaired.

In the area of civil rights, he was, indeed, much more advanced in his thinking than FDR. While he was nowhere near being universally successful, he was creating an agenda for what was to come.

18. Intelligence

Our scholarly respondents have awarded Mr. Truman a rank of 17th in intelligence. It is our suspicion that the fact that he is the last President not to have a college degree played a significant role in that ranking.

We feel constrained to note that poverty alone seems to have deprived young Truman of the opportunity to attend college. Or, perhaps it was poverty and poor eyesight, since tradition seems to suggest that it was only his extremely poor vision which kept him from attending West Point. (It might be interesting to note here that had HST gone to West Point at age 18 in 1902 he would have been there when his later political antagonist, Douglas MacArthur, USMA '03, was First Captain of the Corps of Cadets.)

A number of sources attest to Truman's love of reading. Local lore says that the staff of the Independence, MO public library maintained, probably in jest, that he had read every book in the library. In any event, there is no evidence in what we know of his education to suggest anything other than that he was a bright and inquisitive boy and young man.

His family's economic circumstances seem to have kept him at work on the farm well beyond the time he would have wished to strike out on his own. When he finally broke away, there is no record of nostalgia.

We can say that, as he ventured into the political world, there seems to have been little or nothing that he failed to master. Whether in Missouri or Washington D.C., or upon the international stage, he seems to have more than held his own.

We would suggest that it is only in the area of academic credentials that he was in any substantial way disadvantaged. On the other hand, we have no specific evidence to offer to justify a higher ranking, other than his presidency.

19. Avoid Crucial Mistakes

President Truman stands ninth among Presidents in this area. The historical record seems to indicate few major errors.

In hindsight, the policy that he and Secretary of Defense Johnson pursued in the Department of Defense, with its rapid draw-down of American forces in the wake of the end of World War II, was clearly unwise. It was, of course, Secretary Johnson who paid the political price for the error. The President recovered, ironically, aided by the success of MacArthur's strategy at Inchon. That, plus General Marshall's able work at the Department of Defense, amounted to a successful intervention that seemed to successfully restore American military prowess. The Marshall appointment must be said to have been both intelligent and decisive on the President's part. In such fashions are presidential mistakes ameliorated.

Certainly, the world he confronted would have made such errors fraught with peril for the nation. In foreign policy, he found himself performing an elaborately choreographed ballet in a tight rope act with the Soviet Union. If United States foreign policy were overly accommodating, then more of the states of Europe and elsewhere might very well have vanished into the maw of Soviet expansionism. If it were overly adamant, on the other hand, Truman feared the possibility of a hot war and, after 1949, a war with a viable threat of nuclear weapons. Nijinsky himself, probably could not have made the act work much better than did Harry Truman.

Some economists might argue that, had Congress acceded to Truman's requests for wage and price controls early in the post War period, those controls might have strangled the burgeoning economy. As one of our former professors used to say, "There is little to be learned from the 'if' school of history." If it had happened? If it had proved to be a crucial error? If the economy had failed? It didn't, therefore, it wasn't, and it never happened. The issue is not whether Truman was capable of a crucial error; of course he was. Rather it is whether he committed a crucial error with regard to the economy or any other area. The answer is, he did not.

20. Present Overall View

The present overall view of our respondents places President Truman sixth among American presidents.

Chapter 3 - Dwight D. Eisenhower

I Like Ike!
– Campaign Slogan

"Suaviter in modo, fortiter in re"
– "Pleasantly in manner, powerfully in deed."
– A motto President Eisenhower kept on his desk. (National Review, March 5, 2012, p. 43)

Dwight Eisenhower completes our first presidential trio.

1. Background (family, education, experience)

He was born on October 14, 1890, in Texas to David and Ida Eisenhower and named David Dwight. Apparently he was always called Dwight, perhaps to distinguish father and son. When he later entered West Point, he chose to reverse the names, probably to reflect family custom. His early years were not unlike those of Harry Truman. Though his father was better educated than Truman's, he was no more successful financially. Due to economic difficulties the family soon moved back to Abilene, Kansas, where David could count on family assistance and where Dwight grew up.

Like the Roosevelts and the Trumans, the Eisenhowers were "old stock," of northern European Protestant ancestry and with roots here that predated the American Revolution. Another similarity he shared with Truman was an interest in gaining an appointment to one of the military academies, Eisenhower initially favored Annapolis. Ike's interest appears primarily to have been whetted by a desire for a free college education. His mother, whose religious roots were Mennonite and pacifist, seems to have somewhat sadly but pragmatically accepted the military academy as providing an education that would benefit Dwight.

Available evidence seems to indicate that he read quite widely as a youth, with his interests weighted in the direction of history. Indeed, when he graduated from Abilene High School in 1909, the "class prophecy predicted that he would 'wind up as a professor of history at Yale.'"

He entered West Point in 1911 and graduated in 1915. So many men from that class would become general officers that it became known as "the class the stars fell on." A reasonably good student, he did experience some difficulty in accepting disciplinary constraints.

To his regret, after the United States entered World War I in 1917 he would see no combat. On Armistice Day in 1918 he found himself in Gettysburg, PA, at what was then called "Camp Colt," on the Civil War battlefield, supervising early United States Army training in tank warfare. Given the limited availability of equipment, the schooling was long on theory and short on experience.

That duty brought him into contact with then Colonel George S. Patton, Jr., who had commanded American armor in battle in France. Both were early proponents of armored warfare until the hostility of their superiors sent them back to more conventional duties. They did, however, form a bond of friendship.

To all intents and purposes, for the next quarter century Eisenhower's military experience was fundamentally as a staff officer. He may have chafed at the duty, but it certainly helped to form and to prepare him for what lay ahead. His preparation was probably most notably advanced when, from 1922-1924, he served in the Panama Canal Zone under General Fox Conner. Conner seems to have been a genuine mentor to young Eisenhower. Conner assigned Eisenhower readings, demanding analytical exercises, and led him in discussions of military history and theory, effectively preparing Eisenhower for high command. After leaving Conner in 1925, Eisenhower was assigned to the Command and General Staff School during 1925-1926 and then to Fort Benning, GA, where he commanded an infantry battalion until 1927.

He then served in the office of the assistant secretary of war and then on the staff of the Chief of Staff of the United States Army, General Douglas MacArthur. When MacArthur finished his tour of duty, he went to the Philippine Islands as military advisor to the Philippine Commonwealth. He took then-Major Eisenhower with him. MacArthur's task was to create a Philippine Army in preparation for the independence of the islands. The period would strain the relationship between the two men, but it did provide Eisenhower with unusual scope and opportunities for development.

After his return to the United States, he remained a staff officer and came to the attention of the press as chief of staff of the Third Army during the Great Louisiana Maneuvers of 1941. Those maneuvers are still the largest such exercises ever held by the United States Army. Thereafter, General George Marshall, the Army chief of staff, sought him out for increasingly responsible positions until he would emerge as the commander of the largest and most complex military alliance in history.

From 1948-1950, he served as President of Columbia University and then, on leave from Columbia, was called out of retirement to create and lead the military aspects of the new North Atlantic Treaty Organization (NATO). When he ran for president in 1952, Eisenhower presented an all-American resume – from wrong-side-of-the-tracks poverty, through military fame to the confidante of prime ministers and premiers, even of kings.

Our respondents rated him at 14th, which we attribute to his early background, We think it represents an accolade as we think it did for President Truman that one who started with so many obstacles was able to overcome them and to achieve so much – though, as with Truman and Washington, we fear it may not place enough weight on experience.

2. Party Leadership (political)

Eisenhower received a rating of 18th in this category, keeping him in the upper half of all presidents. As with many other elements of his presidency, we are prone to ask how close perception and reality are in his case. We would first note that Ike liked to stay above the fray. It is said, for example, that during the 1952 campaign he never mentioned his opponent's name (Adlai Stevenson) in any but the most formal way. It was, rather, political surrogates who sought to link Stevenson to the Truman administration and the GOP's 1952 mantra, "Communism, Korea and corruption."

Unlike his predecessors in office, Eisenhower would enjoy only two years with Congress under the control of his party, 1953-1955. In addition, both parties were significantly divided during the Eisenhower years. Republicans were split into what Eisenhower liked to call "Modern Republicans" and the "Old Guard." In addition, they were further split by the persona and the issues that swirled around anti-Communism and the figure of Senator Joseph McCarthy. Democrats were largely split over racial and civil rights issues as well as the geographic and cultural divisions between northern, liberal Democrats and the southern Democrats. The southerners often were conservative, older, segregationist and even white supremacist. They were frequently dominant in the House and Senate because of the seniority system controlling committee assignments. These basic divisions, plus occasional factions and splinter groups, formed a sort of political stew from which the President was forced to construct majorities for his proposals, whether foreign or domestic. He did, quite early, achieve a cordial working relationship with the Democratic Speaker of the House, Sam Rayburn of Texas.

It should be stipulated that, while real and vigorous, party politics seems to have been less visceral and vitriolic then than it has since become. We can illustrate the difference by an anecdote, real or apocryphal, involving Speaker Rayburn and his Republican counterpart, Joe Martin of Massachusetts, who was Speaker from 1953-1955. As the story is told, Rayburn was asked one campaign season to travel to Massachusetts and stump for Martin's Democratic opponent. Rayburn supposedly replied, "Speak against Joe? Hell, if I lived up there, I'd vote for him." Whether a literal truth or not, the anecdote seems to us clearly to describe the milder degree of partisanship, with minimum levels of vitriol and personal attack, which then prevailed.

In any event, Eisenhower was, other than by Senator Joe McCarthy, probably less significantly challenged from within his own party than Harry Truman was. Indeed, in that brief period of Republican dominance there is little to suggest that he was not a commanding presence in the party. The 1952 election indicated that Ike had coattails.

The other side of the coin, of course, is that in the absence of semi-public political quarrels there is little evidence to allow an analysis of the force or dominance of his presence.

3. Communications Ability (speak, write)

Here, the returns from the survey find President Eisenhower ranked 21st. It is his lowest ranking and places him just outside the upper half.

As with party leadership, this area presents certain difficulties. We know beyond doubt that Eisenhower could and did create clear, cogent and analytical prose. The documents still exist. We also know – and, again, beyond doubt – that he could move into a sea of reporters at a press conference and deliver a series of remarks replete with non-sequiturs, fractured syntax and seemingly stream of consciousness narratives that could leave even seasoned participants baffled as to his meaning.

It was he, by the way, who introduced the televised (although videotaped) press conference in 1955. There are those who suggest that the famous fog generated by his press conference musings was deliberately created by the President.

Certainly, if we examine his usage as supreme commander of the Allied Expeditionary Force or his 1953 "Atoms for Peace" speech or his valedictory, with its warning about the "Military-Industrial complex," we see an entirely different style.

It is an area of his presidency that has been under review for at least the past 20 years. In that context, we would suggest that the reading of Martin J. Medhurst's Dwight D. Eisenhower: Strategic Communicator and/or his, Eisenhower's War of Words: Rhetoric and Leadership might be rewarding.

4. Relationship with Congress

Professors responding to the survey ranked Ike eighth in this category.

In his first year in office he had an excellent relationship with Senator Robert Taft as majority leader. The Senator had adjusted well to his loss of the nomination to Eisenhower. Regrettably, Taft died in that first summer and his successor, Senator William Knowland, was less well organized and brought less focus and clarity to the leadership. The administration also worked well with Speaker Joseph Martin. Democrats regained control of Congress in the 1954 elections.

Eisenhower won reelection quite handily in 1956, winning by a larger margin than in 1952. His platform of peace and prosperity worked well. This time, however, there had been no coattails.

In the wake of those changes, President Eisenhower managed to work well with the new Senate Majority Leader, Lyndon B. Johnson of Texas, as well as with Speaker Rayburn. Sometimes, there were private, unannounced White House meetings among the three. Joe Martin soldiered on as minority leader in the House, and Knowland continued as the Republican leader in the Senate until 1959, when Everett Dirksen of Illinois became Senate minority leader. In those years, Eisenhower worked with Knowland where feasible but did find it necessary to approach some problems informally through influential members, committee chairs and senior members of committees, often across party lines.

In any event, as we have seen, many significant policy issues of the era required some sort of bipartisan coalition of internationalist Republicans and Democrats on foreign policy issues, or Old Guard Republicans and southern Democrats for efforts at budget balancing or liberal Democrats and "Modern Republicans" for social welfare legislation. In such circumstances, Ike could and did use combinations of personal contact, surrogates and/ or some mixture of congressional leadership to construct the majorities needed. It certainly appears that, from the time of his inauguration, he was conscious of the need for both good communications and amiable personal relations with Congress and that he worked diligently to create and sustain such ties.

Obviously, our experts do not think that such successful bipartisan management entitles him to a higher ranking.

5. Court Appointments

To a great degree, in this category, Presidents are the servants of events. Some have multiple opportunities to appoint judges, particularly, Supreme Court justices. Others have none. Eisenhower would nominate five men who would sit on the Supreme Court. His first was Earl Warren as chief justice. Warren, then the sitting governor of California, was nominated upon the death of Chief Justice Fred M. Vinson in October of 1953. Next, in March of 1955, came the nomination of Associate Justice John Marshall Harlan II. (It seems necessary to note that Harlan was the son of Associate Justice John Marshall Harlan of New York, who was the justice in 1896 who issued the sharp dissent in the case of Plessey v. Ferguson, challenging the segregationist ruling that "separate but equal" was equal.) Third among his nominations was that of William J. Brennan of New Jersey in October of 1956. Charles Evans Whittaker of Missouri was selected in March of 1957 and, finally, Potter Stewart of Ohio in October of 1958. Curiously, all of his appointments occurred in either March or October. These, as well as his other judicial appointments resulted in Eisenhower ranking fifth in this area.

Whether one agrees with their jurisprudence, judicial philosophy or influence, two of the five, Earl Warren and William Brennan, must be recognized as consensus greats in the court's history. If you go to any search engine or other reference for influential members of the court their names inevitably will appear. Since both were significantly more liberal than Eisenhower, there is certainly a note of irony here. Like Truman with Justice Clark, Eisenhower is sometimes said to have regarded his appointment of Warren as an error. In addition, the more conservative John Marshall Harlan II has been assessed as one of the most influential members of the court in the 20th century. Justice Potter Stewart, though more moderate than Warren and Brennan, is certainly also reckoned a heavy hitter in judicial circles. In short, of the five men only Justice Whittaker is likely to be assessed as an average or below average appointment.

In any case, like FDR's appointments, Eisenhower's gave us men who were to serve long years on the bench. Warren and Harlan served 16 years each, Stewart, 23 years, and Brennan, 34 years. Only Whittaker had short service, at 5 years. In addition, one or more would go on to participate in such consequential decisions as Brown v. Board of Education, Gideon v. Wainwright and Roe v. Wade.

It is an impressive and influential list, which would certainly seem to justify his high ranking in this area. Whether, like Eisenhower himself, the reader might find the results occasionally unpalatable, they are still of great historical significance.

6. Handling the U. S. Economy

In this area we find the President ensconced in ninth place. The administration slogan was "Peace and Prosperity." Eisenhower thought, planned and worked to achieve that goal.

The administration, in economic terms, was essentially moderate, believed in a free market and downplayed government planning. This represented a modest shift away from New Deal/Fair Deal attitudes and practices. An overall view shows eight years of consistent economic growth at between 2 and 3 per cent per year, with little inflation and low unemployment. Three minor recessions occurred, none lasting a full year.

Ike strongly believed in balanced budgets and managed to produce three during his eight years in office. After the end of the Korean War, he moved to cut military expenditures, preferring to rely on the "Massive Retaliation" nuclear deterrent, both in terms of policy and as a cost-saving measure. These cuts were less extreme than those of the early Truman years.

The continuing post-World War II economic expansion caused significant growth in America's Gross National Product, which in the Truman and Eisenhower years more than doubled. On Eisenhower's watch, personal income increased by more than 40 per cent. There was a virtual explosion in the acquisition of consumer goods, television sets and the like and the emergence of a new symbol of economic status, the credit card. It was not an accident that the period came to be perceived as an age of affluence, giving rise to the term, "the affluent society."

Affluence was, of course, not evenly distributed. While overall poverty declined in those years, it also spread geographically with the movement of southern blacks into the North. New agricultural machinery, displacing African-American field workers, as well at the desire to escape the worst excesses of Jim Crow laws, spurred significant migration from the South to northern industrial centers. One result of the southern outmigration was a growth in poverty in those centers.

Nevertheless, most Americans, still scarred by the Depression and its memories, reveled in the contemporary economic security and delighted in the continuing boom. The era, in a stereotype, would come to be seen as untroubled and recalled later as "Happy Days."

7.   Luck

This category sees President Eisenhower again at ninth. Looking at Eisenhower's life as a whole, one is unsure how large a role luck played, and we think our respondents' ranking reflects that. His early life would seem bereft of much good fortune while the last 30 years were replete with it.

As a youth, his appointment to West Point – for which, be it noted, he had labored long and hard to prepare himself – must have seemed a stroke of luck for a young man of his background. After he graduated and was commissioned, he was unable to solicit a World War I combat assignment and rarely found himself commanding troops. For 20-plus years, he found himself primarily a junior staff officer. In essence, from 1915 to 1939, that was his career, though he frequently found himself on the staff of brilliant senior officers such as Generals Conner and MacArthur. To an ambitious young officer those years of sterility and the low pay created by service in a weakly supported peacetime army must have seemed awash in bad luck. The preparation for the future, though, was significant. Then, from 1940, in a period of about five years, he rocketed from colonel to brigadier general, to major general, to lieutenant general, to general, and then to the five-star rank of general of the Army, the American equivalent of field marshal. In the next five years he served as chief of staff of the Army, President of Columbia University and the first NATO Supreme Commander. In 1953, he was inaugurated as President of the United States. It was certainly a stretch of success that most men, in most eras, would acknowledge as filled with exceptionally good luck.

Our questions in that regard would be:

A.) Do not most individuals in a lifetime have, or seem to have, alternating periods of good and bad fortune?

B.) Was the 1915-1939 period really bad luck, though at that time it must have seemed so?

Fox Conner certainly helped to create the mature Eisenhower by his mentoring of Ike in Panama. Despite their later antipathy, Eisenhower certainly learned from MacArthur. After all, when MacArthur went to the Philippines after his tour as chief of staff ended, Eisenhower went with him, which he surely did not have to do. It is certainly fortunate that Eisenhower returned by 1939. Had he remained in the Philippines much longer he might very well have been killed or captured by the Japanese in 1941-1942. Nor would he have been as well placed, as he was in 1939-1941 to draw the attention of his superiors. The old general manager of the Brooklyn Dodgers, Branch Rickey, said that "luck is the residue of design." Does that period of learning fit Rickey's definition?

We accept the notion that no one's life or career is unaffected by luck.

Overall, however, we are not sure that luck played quite as large a role in Eisenhower's life and career as it did in those of Harry Truman or FDR.

8. Ability to Compromise

In regard to this question, Eisenhower achieves his highest ranking, fourth, in the top 10 per cent overall. Ike certainly believed in compromise and found it as essential to his presidency as it had been to his World War II commands. He said, "Things are not all black and white. There have to be compromises. The middle of the road is the entire usable surface. The extremes, right and left, are the gutters." His press secretary, James Haggerty, once remarked that persuading people to compromise their separate views without requiring anyone to surrender principle was perhaps Eisenhower's greatest skill.

He did, on occasion, find compromise less than satisfying, as when the southern barons in the Senate forced him to yield on the 1957 Civil Rights Act, designed to secure voting rights for southern blacks. The then majority leader, Lyndon Johnson, persuaded him of the necessity, but the bill was seriously weakened. Ike ultimately accepted it because it would represent the first civil rights legislation to pass Congress since the 19th century and Reconstruction. In any event, something emerged, even though the President had to cajole and arm twist his own party members in the Senate, who furnished the majority of the votes for the legislation. He also cobbled together coalitions in the Congress to extend Social Security benefits to hitherto excluded classes and to authorize the creation and construction of the Saint Lawrence Seaway.

Internal party divisions also meant that Ike not only would have to court and cozy up to members of the House and Senate but to compromise with them as well. We have already alluded to that rather Byzantine process.

Perhaps his most dramatic effort at compromise took place less than a year after his inauguration and on a larger stage than Washington, D.C. In December of 1953, he delivered to the United Nations what is known as his "Atoms for Peace" speech. In it he proposed a sharing, for civilian purposes, of nuclear raw materials for peaceful research into the use of nuclear energy. He then called upon the Soviet Union to join the United States in initiating such an effort. Certainly, at that juncture the United States had more to risk in such a venture than did Russia.

He had hoped, particularly after the death of Stalin, to begin a rapprochement with the Soviet Union. Ancillary to that goal, he had opened an ongoing series of cultural exchanges with the Soviet Union which he hoped would dispel distrust between the two peoples. Nevertheless, it proved impossible to persuade Soviet leaders to join him in a Russo-American summit conference before Nikita Khrushchev came to power in 1960. That meeting was aborted by the Russians after the U-2 incident.

Succinctly put, Ike seems to have believed, virtually always, that problems laid upon the table to analyzed and discussed could be resolved via compromise of one sort or another.

9. Willingness to Take Risks

Ike's ranking in this category is 20th, just within the 50 per cent mark. It seems to us probable, to some degree, that this relatively low ranking owes something to Harry Truman's ranking of fifth place. That is because Truman had run a number of significant risks from 1945-1953, Eisenhower in continuing the policy of containment was not equivalently engaged in potential or actual risk taking. While there is certainly logic to such a contention, we suspect that it might, nevertheless, be arguable.

We would note, for example, that by 1953, the Korean War peace talks had been going on for about a year and a half, since the summer of 1951. Eisenhower, impatient with the progress or lack thereof, passed the word to the Chinese via back-door diplomacy that if progress were not forthcoming he would consider the use of more extreme methods. Since that time, virtually all students of the period have at least assumed that to mean an implicit threat to use nuclear weapons. Whether there was a causal connection cannot be absolutely known. By July, 1953, however, all issues were resolved, and the truce was signed. There were certainly risks implicit in such a course of action. Revisionist authors have pointed to the death of Stalin in March of 1953 as being at least as, if not more, important than nuclear diplomacy in the resolution of the conflict. To the best of our knowledge, no definitive answer is available.

At another level, Ike believed in the use of covert action in foreign affairs. The Central Intelligence Agency was, therefore, used to overthrow anti-American regimes in Iran in 1953 and in Guatemala in 1954. Certainly, these activities had significant risks attached, even though they were successful. All of these actions, at the very least, risked the prestige and credibility of the United States. Had they failed the reputation of the nation and trust in its policies would have been placed in significant jeopardy.

It seems likely that the weakness this rating reflects stems primarily from the administration's response to the uprisings in the Soviet satellite states, which characterized the era. First, in June of 1953 in East Germany and then in October-November, 1956 in Hungary there was significant unrest. Indeed, in the latter, there occurred absolute revolution. Eisenhower's

Secretary of State, John Foster Dulles, had frequently spoken of not just containing Soviet expansionism to the satellite states but also of rolling it back. At the time of the Hungarian Revolution some people felt that United States' failure to assist, or even meaningfully protest the subsequent Soviet military intervention and repression, was hypocritical.

The latter moment represented a particularly full plate for the President because, at virtually the same moment, Britain, France and Israel attacked Egypt and seized the Suez Canal. The United States found itself at once joining the U.S.S.R. in the United Nations in condemning its own allies and forcing their withdrawal from Suez and attempting, simultaneously, to protest the presence of Soviet tanks on the streets of Budapest. In any event, the administration was unwilling, or felt itself unable, to take risks by confronting Soviet intervention in Hungary.

Still other critics may be downgrading Eisenhower for what they perceive to be a failure to act vigorously enough on civil rights issues in the era. Despite the Civil Rights Acts of 1957 and 1960, and the use of the 101st Airborne Division to integrate the schools of Little Rock, those critics perceive him as at best a procrastinator on the issue. Here the complaint would be that he was not willing to risk his political capital in such a quarrel. What other or stronger modalities might have been available at that time is not entirely clear.

Eisenhower is ranked within the top third of his peers, in 13th place in this category.

10. Executive Appointments

In this category, the SRI experts have placed Eisenhower at 13th.

There were nine cabinet posts when Eisenhower was inaugurated, a 10th being added three months later. Uniquely, the President had been authorized to reorganize the executive branch, subject to congressional veto. Eisenhower actually created the U. S. Department of Health, Education and Welfare, which was officially formed in April of 1953. He appointed Oveta Culp Hobby, who had organized and commanded the WAAC (Women's Auxiliary Army Corps) during World War II, as its first Secretary. She also had been an early member of the Texas branch of Democrats for Eisenhower. For the second time in a dozen years, she found herself organizing and staffing a new institution in the American government. The President found himself with a highly credible female cabinet member and at least a titular Democrat, to boot.

Of the many problems that came her way, probably the most stressful was managing the public introduction of the Salk Polio Vaccine, complicated by early, flawed versions. Parents, as terrified of polio as they were in those days, wanted it released at once. Prudence dictated that scientific trials, for the purposes of safety, be allowed to run their course. Hobby managed a program of voluntary distribution. Considering the constituencies involved, that seems to have been a course safely steered between two dangerous reefs.

When she left the cabinet in 1955, Ike held a special press conference, with just Hobby and the President seated at a table, during which he lauded her services. The secretary of the treasury said, in what was then a socially acceptable remark, that she was, "the best 'man' in the cabinet."

With the initial appointments of the cabinet members, it was noted that the cabinet was heavily weighted with successful business leaders, with the exception of the secretary of labor, Martin Durkin, who was head of the plumbers and steamfitters union. In what would now be seen as an inside the beltway comment, they were sometimes referred to as "nine millionaires and a plumber."

The cabinet symbolized the President's belief in capitalism and the free market. It also made it much easier for him when he not only failed to even consider dismantling New Deal and Fair Deal policies but, in fact, modestly expanded them in areas such as Social Security and the creation of the department of health, education and welfare.

Unable to persuade Eisenhower to support the repeal or serious modification of Taft-Hartley, Durkin left the cabinet that summer, to be replaced by James P. Mitchell, a labor relations executive from New York City. (He was also, coincidentally, the nephew of the Academy Award-winning actor Thomas Mitchell.) Mitchell had enjoyed considerable standing with the labor movement since the WPA days and was fortunate enough to serve as secretary in a time of considerable prosperity and relative labor tranquility. If Durkin had the shortest term in history as secretary of labor, Mitchell had the longest, post-World War II tenure in that role.

In Mitchell's time, the minimum wage was increased, and more people were hired to enforce it. There were also improvements in unemployment insurance coverage. Congress authorized the secretary to begin establishing standards for on-the-job health and safety, and he also served as chair of the President's Commission on Migratory Labor. It is probably worth noting that on the occasion of his retirement from office the AFL-CIO chose to host a gala for him.

Stability was a hallmark of the Eisenhower cabinet. With 10 cabinet positions and two terms, Eisenhower had only 20 cabinet members in all.

For the most part, they were functional and efficient. Some were major figures, such as John Foster Dulles at the state department. One, at least, was significantly eccentric, Ezra Taft Benson, who was at the U. S. Department of Agriculture for eight years. Benson was so anti-Communist that, at least once, he questioned Eisenhower on the subject. George M. Humphrey, his first secretary of the treasury was, like Ike, in favor of balanced budgets and opposed to inflation. He favored the reduction of government spending. Humphrey was quite close to Eisenhower, and, to assist the inflation fighting/budget balancing agenda, Eisenhower had the treasury secretary added to the National Security Council so that his view of defense requests would be complete. They both agreed that defense expenditures were logical areas for cutting.

Herbert Brownell was the administration's first attorney general. Another close advisor, Brownell was anathema to many southerners due to his support for minorities. He was influential in the appointment of judges who would favor integration and in crafting the original 1957 Civil Rights Bill, which was so watered down in the Senate.

Charles E. Wilson, head of the General Motors Corporation, became the first Eisenhower secretary of defense. His confirmation hearings were quite contentious because of the very large amount of General Motors stock he held and the lucrative dealings with the department of defense by GM. He is famously quoted as having told a Congressional committee, "What's good for General Motors is good for the country." What he actually said was that he "had long thought that what was good for the country was good for General Motors and vice versa."

In addition to reorganizing the defense department, he and Eisenhower moved to put in place Ike's "New Look" defense program, with the emphasis on nuclear weapons and nuclear deterrence, the policy that came to be called Massive Retaliation. Significant savings in defense expenditures were realized.

John Foster Dulles was the Secretary of State from 1953-1959. To contemporaries, he was certainly the best known member of the cabinet. He seemed almost to have a hereditary right to the post. His grandfather, John Foster had been secretary of state under Benjamin Harrison. John Foster had arranged a post for Dulles at the second Hague peace conference while the grandson was still a Princeton undergraduate. His uncle, Robert Lansing, had been Wilson's secretary of state and, perhaps not coincidentally, John Foster Dulles had been a part of the United States delegation to the Versailles Peace Conference in 1919.

A vehement anti-Communist, he was a proponent of somehow rolling back Soviet expansion, though he achieved no progress in that realm. He also supported collective security arrangements and was always willing to consider such arrangements, as in the case of SEATO (South East Asia Treaty Organization).

Eisenhower used his cabinet in many ways; not infrequently to mask his own control. He was quite willing to allow secretaries to bask in public acclaim while he remained in the background as a sort of bland, avuncular figure. One result of the increased availability of administration documents over the last 30 to 40 years has been to illustrate his real role. Those disclosures have revealed the much more active nature of his involvement. We believe that to be a principal reason why his stature has increased so much in recent decades.

11. Overall Ability

Once again we find Eisenhower within the top third, at 13th. Once again, his elliptical and oblique style makes defining the placement more difficult.

We might begin by recalling an acknowledged but largely overlooked idea. It was a commonplace conviction among contemporary academics and pundits that the actions of the New Deal and the Fair Deal would not be politically secure until a Republican administration had, in effect, ratified them. Eisenhower and his "modern Republicanism" or "dynamic conservatism" did just that, albeit, in Ike's style, quite quietly. Indeed, as we have from time to time mentioned, he even modestly expanded some, as in the area of Social Security and developed others, as in health and safety standards on the job. As was so often the case in his "hidden hand" style of administration, there were few caveats and none directed at the President.

His reorganization of various elements of government, and particularly of the executive branch, may have seemed to many like a housekeeping chore, but it did produce significant improvements in the operating efficiency of government. When he denominated Sherman Adams, his White House assistant, as The Assistant to the President, the definite article announced the birth of the now omnipresent figure of the White House chief of staff. (Ironically, Ike was advised not to use that term as it was "too military"). So too, his creation of the position of assistant to the President for national security sffairs was the birth announcement of the president's national security advisor.

To many, the organizational changes and the seemingly heavy reliance on members of the cabinet represented laxity and drift. Rather, the formal committee structure he created was not only efficient but was bolstered with processes designed to ensure that policy alternatives were sought out and made available for analysis. The President himself was careful to consult a variety of sources from outside the formal structure, and indeed from outside politics and government, to be more fully aware of alternative views.

In an administrative framework he was something of an organizational genius whose very successes tended to mask the key role he played. During his terms in office, pundits spoke of John Foster Dulles or Sherman Adams or other movers and shakers as the gray eminence behind the administration or one another of the administration's policies or actions. Access to the papers of the administration now tells us with what frequency the hidden hand was that of Dwight David Eisenhower.

One of the clearest examples of this would seem to be the internal debate over whether the United States should provide direct military aid to the French in their struggle in French Indo China, now Vietnam. There can be little doubt that the decision against involving American troops was made by the President, himself.

His hand, too, appears in the ultimate downfall of Senator McCarthy. Subtly and slyly he prodded the Senate to deal with its own problem. He was criticized frequently in his own time for not "taking McCarthy on." He felt that direct presidential confrontation with McCarthy would add to McCarthy's stature and credibility, not weaken him. At best, a more direct face-off might have brought the senator down sooner, but that can never be known.

With due deference to his press conference grammar and syntax, we would again call attention to his thoughtful, well-constructed and analytical addresses, the valedictory, "Atoms for Peace" and other speeches, which more than suggest that when he deemed it appropriate and important, he could step to the podium and sell ideas.

In terms of overall ability we might suggest that as the academic world has accessed archival materials of the era Eisenhower has moved from the bottom half of all Presidents, where he was rated in 1962, to the top 10 as the 20th Century ended. Whether his rise will continue remains to be seen, but we doubt that he will fall in rank until the list of other memorable Presidents grows longer.

12. Imagination

This category marks the second time that he is ranked 20th among the Presidents, just within the top half. It would be difficult to objectively quarrel with this rank, though one might reexamine it with greater subtlety.

In a period of "peace and prosperity" there were few reasons to embark upon dramatic or sweeping government programs. Still, within the first decade of the Cold War – and fully accepting the concept of containment wedded to the Truman Doctrine and administering the Marshall plan and its adjuncts – there was also little new to add to the international stage. In essence, there was not only a proclivity toward maintaining the status quo but also cogent reasons for doing so. The defense of what was then known as Formosa (now, Taiwan) and the Pescadores and increased activity in the Middle East seemed to many to be little more than the application of containment to different geographic regions of the world.

Proposals that were, in their own way, sweeping and dramatic – such as the Saint Lawrence Seaway project and the creation of the Interstate Highway System – were masked or obscured by a number of factors. In the first case, there were a number of progenitors. The Interstate Highway System, drawing as it did on the experience of the young Eisenhower leading an army convoy across the United States in 1919 and General Eisenhower recognizing the clear utility of the German autobahn in 1944-1945 to the Allies, tended to indicate perhaps overly vague origins. Finally, in the context of that time and even our own – while very important in the economic and social history of the United States – they just were not politically "sexy" enough to be seen as imaginative, though, of course, they were.

Ike's espousal of space exploration and the creation of NASA was much too obviously a response to the launching of Sputnik by the Soviet Union in 1957. It really was just catch-up and, for Eisenhower, had little meaning. The reality was that the United States had such a significant lead in missiles and in nuclear warheads that it was unassailable, other than in public relations, as in the 1960 campaign's "Missile Gap" rhetoric.

13. Domestic Accomplishments
Survey respondents place Eisenhower 14th here, just outside the upper-third.

As we have seen in a few areas such as Social Security and the minimum wage Ike initiated mild extensions of New Deal or New Deal-type programs. His approval of the creation of on-the-job health and safety regulations for workers through the U. S. Labor Department would be an example. Perhaps his most significant step in this kind of area was the establishment and staffing of the U. S. Department of Health, Education and Welfare.

These steps, while hardly over-dramatic, did establish the fact that both parties now believed that at least some type of social welfare legislation legitimately fell within the purview of the federal government. There would be no rollback of the New Deal.

Of the domestic accomplishments of the Eisenhower administration, the Saint Lawrence Seaway and the Interstate Highway projects probably created the largest economic and social impact. The two together provided an economic stimulus for commercial and industrial activity, both long- and short-range. The highway system, by greatly reducing trucking costs, lowered the price of many goods throughout the nation. The buildup of the system also would have an unforeseen adverse impact upon American railroads and American cities.

Among other unforeseen consequences of the Interstate Highway System, together with the G.I. Bill, was as a spur to urban outmigration, with the parents of the Baby Boomers leaving the central cities, leading to their deterioration and to the inception and development of suburban living and the beginning of urban and suburban sprawl.

The 1950s also saw what we might call the opening act of the civil rights revolution of the 1960s. Eisenhower's record in that regard is better than some would acknowledge, but it cannot be described as displaying full-throated enthusiasm.

In regard to civil rights, in 1957, the President would initiate one activity and be thrust into another. The administration asked Congress that year to pass a civil rights bill that Attorney General Herb Brownell had prepared. Its primary goal was to ensure minority-voting rights in southern states. In the Senate, Majority Leader Lyndon B. Johnson found his southern colleagues up in arms. The senator told the President that the bill could not be passed as drafted and urged the acceptance of amendments which, to all intents and purposes, emasculated the bill. Cynics have suggested ever since that LBJ hoped to garner credit for the passage of a bill while at the same time placating southerner senators because it had been deprived of substance.

In any event, a form of the bill passed, the first new legislation on minority rights in over 80 years. Its purpose, despite the passage of the 1960 Civil Rights Act, also proposed by DDE, would not be fulfilled until the passage of the Civil Rights Act of 1965.

The second activity involved Little Rock, Ark. In the wake of the Supreme Court Decision in Brown v. Board of Education, the high school in Little Rock was scheduled to be integrated in September, 1957. Governor Orval Faubus of Arkansas found the situation ripe for mischief and political gamesmanship. He even used the Arkansas National Guard to prevent integration. Eisenhower met with Faubus and thought he had defused the situation. Upon returning to Arkansas, however, Faubus ramped it up again. Eisenhower, pointing out that the Supreme Court's decision was the law of the land and had to be obeyed, sent in more than 1,000 soldiers of the 101st Airborne Division, which resulted in the restoration of order and the admission of nine children to the high school. To handcuff Faubus,

Eisenhower also federalized the Arkansas National Guard and required it to keep a troop presence in Little Rock for the entire school year.

Critics suggest that Eisenhower failed to act swiftly enough and that his reluctance encouraged those who opposed integration. He should, they insist, have been more aggressive. However, it remains unclear what further steps might have improved the outcome. The criticism may be perfectly correct but reacting positively to it would have required the President to hone a new presidential style. His style was based on apparent ease and on the absence of perceived struggle. He seems to have tried for that here, but the intransigence of Faubus made that effort fail. Faubus understood the political arithmetic of his intractability quite well, as his subsequent terms as governor of Arkansas demonstrate.

Eisenhower's civil rights record, while certainly not the acme of presidential leadership, is not without merit. He introduced and supported the Civil Rights Bills of 1957 and 1960 and, in percentage terms, delivered more affirmative GOP Senate votes than the Democrats provided. He firmly enforced the decrees of the federal courts in all circumstances, and many of the judges he appointed to the lower federal courts proved favorable to minority rights. It was a long way away from a period less than 20 years earlier when it had proved impossible to get a President to sponsor an anti-lynch law.

14. Integrity
Once again at ninth, he immediately follows Harry Truman and is ahead of all of his 20th Century successors except James Earl Carter. Parenthetically, it might be of interest to note that of the 18 American Presidents who held office in the 20th Century only TR, Truman and Carter join Eisenhower in the top 10 in this category.

Eisenhower considered integrity a very important virtue. He once said, in what has since become a virtually ubiquitous quotation, "The supreme quality of leadership is unquestionably, integrity. Without it, no real success is possible, no matter whether it is on a section gang, a football field, in an army or in an office."

Nevertheless, like all administrations, his too felt the breath of scandal. One highly publicized instance would be the so-called Dixon-Yates scandal. Dixon and Yates each represented a power company with a federal contract that was alleged to be improper. More important was the scandal involving Sherman Adams, The Assistant to the President – in current terms, the White House chief of staff.

Dixon-Yates, in 1954-1955, involved a plan to build a power-generating plant to provide more power to a Tennessee Valley region, essentially competing with the TVA. New Deal Democrats in Congress alleged a conflict of interest, and Eisenhower's administration backed away. Though there were many allegations, in 1959 the United States Court of Claims ruled that the contract had been perfectly legitimate. The 3-2 decision seems to have ended any further debate about the issue.

Sherman Adams had been seen as the power behind the throne in the White House. He largely controlled access to the President. He was not an especially affable man. In some Washington circles he was known as "The Abominable 'No' Man." In 1958 it became known that he had accepted favors and gifts from individuals and had then made inquiries of government agencies on their behalf. The activity was perhaps not illegal then, though it almost certainly would be now. The most famous gift was, ostensibly, a highly publicized vicuna coat. (A vicuna is a llama-like creature native to South America.)

Adams' resignation was inevitable, though it hurt Eisenhower personally and probably hurt the GOP, which did badly in the 1958 elections. It also appears to have weakened the conduct of the administration in its last years, since Adams' successor seems to have been less competent.

15. Executive Ability

Once again, we find Eisenhower ranked at ninth and once again, in this group, one of only five 20th Century Presidents who rank between first and 10th.

The executive style of President Eisenhower was, or appears to have been, quite different from those of Presidents Truman and Franklin Roosevelt. Ike's style conformed more closely to what a management text might decree to be appropriate; it was, perhaps, less of a "one man band."

Probably as a result of his military experience, certainly connected with the "invisible hand" style he cultivated in what was undoubtedly an effort to appear to be above the fray, Eisenhower's presidency was run on organizational principles. It was, to a large degree, strongly staffed.

As we have noted, he was far more active and much more of a decision-maker than sometimes appeared to be the case. Virtually all issues were "staffed" en route to ultimate decisions. It seems to have been in this manner that he assured significant opportunity for the tabling of alternative opinions and provision for some opposition to the conventional wisdom of the era. Few within the administration seemed to have had any real doubt as to who was making the decisions.

In foreign affairs as well as in domestic concerns, there seem to be parallels.

Ike's frequent reliance on the CIA and covert action helped to further veil his invisible hand. In such cases, a policy goal was determined, a plan was established and an action carried out. Few, if any, could point to the President or were even likely to be aware of his influence in the matter, often until years later.

In perhaps what is now the best known example, we have previously cited the deliberations about whether to commit troops to support the French in Indo China; Eisenhower's influence is now known to have been determinative. There were arguments in favor, and rational ones, but the President was opposed, and it was certainly he who determined that troops would not be sent.

In the years from 1953-1961, reporters and pundits saw energetic cabinet members hard at work and an avuncular President, golfing and smiling, like an English monarch; reigning but not necessarily ruling. The political reality was a President who effectively directed his administration while publically seeming the personification of American friendliness and good spirits.

16. Foreign Policy Accomplishments

For the third time in succession, Ike is ranked ninth, and also, once again, is one of only five 20th Century Presidents to rank in the top 10.

The first item to be listed certainly should be the ending of the Korean War. As we have pointed out, the peace talks in Korea had been limping along for about a year and a half when he came into office. He had campaigned on ending the conflict, pledging, "I will go to Korea." Once inaugurated and acclimated, DDE seems to have accelerated the process, possibly through back-channel nuclear threats, and the truce was completed in a matter of six months.

Clearly, Eisenhower's policies toward the U.S.S.R. and Red China marched in parallel with those established by Harry Truman. Containment remained the basic foreign policy of the United States despite the somewhat more bellicose rhetoric of rollback favored by Secretary of State John Foster Dulles. Even new initiatives like the Eisenhower Doctrine were thought to some degree to be merely the application of the Truman Doctrine to the Middle East. Obviously, the passage of time and historical events raised additional issues, such as the influence of Egypt's Gamal Abdul Nasser, fears of pan-Arabism and growing concerns about the Arab states and oil reserves.

Conservative Arab states proved, post-Suez, less open to the Eisenhower Doctrine than had been hoped. After the 1958 intervention in Lebanon had ended at the behest of Lebanon's embattled president, the Eisenhower

Doctrine was allowed to fade away. Nasser turned out to be less enthralled by the Soviet Union than had been feared; the Soviets also proved quite capable of significant errors of their own, and the United States moved toward a more complex diplomatic policy with the Arab states.

The "Atoms for Peace" initiative had some favorable impact on world opinion, and American support for NATO continued unabated, coupled with a diplomatic quest for other collective security agreements.

Eisenhower's "New Look" for defense policy, laden with the notion of massive retaliation threatening to escalate any conflict into a potential nuclear clash, tended to intensify Soviet anxiety about possible nuclear war, which may have bridled further adventurism. Certainly, Stalin's death may also have played a role, as large or larger, in what seems to have been a clear diminution in the dynamic of Soviet aggression.

It should be noted that throughout this period America had a significantly larger armory of nuclear weapons and was developing the so-called "triad" of aircraft, missile and submarine-launched nuclear platforms. The United States even developed tactical nuclear weapons – specifically, nuclear artillery. The aura of General Eisenhower, the World War II European Supreme Allied Commander, must have lent credibility to military policy statements emerging from the White House, both in American and foreign circles.

Probably the best quick summary of Ike's record in this area would be Eisenhower's. He liked to say, after he had left office, that on his watch America had lost neither lives nor an inch of ground. Obviously, he was allocating the Korean War casualties of 1953 to the Truman administration.

17. Leadership Ability

Eisenhower is ranked seventh here and third among 20th Century American Presidents.

When President Eisenhower raised his hand to take his oath of office in January of 1953, he probably had better leadership credentials than any newly inaugurated President in history, with the exception of George Washington.

In the preceding decade or so he had, almost literally, moved from triumph to triumph and almost invariably from one degree of responsibility to the next higher. He had ended his World War II experience as the Supreme Commander of the Allied Expeditionary Force in Europe in command of millions of men of disparate nationalities. He dealt, on a daily basis, not only with other Allied commanders, such as Montgomery, who was his subordinate, but with Soviet commanders, like Zhukov, who were not under his command, He also dealt with heads of government and heads of state.

He was one of the very few American soldiers ever to be promoted to five-star rank, General of the Army. He then embarked upon stints as chief of staff of the United States Army and as president of Columbia University.

With the formation of the North Atlantic Treaty Organization, he was asked to leave Columbia and return to active duty as the first NATO supreme commander. In that capacity he created a coalition army for collective security. That task included persuading European governments and parliaments, still reeling from the burdens and devastation of World War II, to participate, including bearing a share of the troops and treasure needed to put flesh onto the coalition army's bones.

As usual, Eisenhower's management style tended to feature layers that obscured the degree of his active leadership. We think it is a tribute to the professionalism of those who participated in the SRI study that they were able to perceive the degree of direction and vigor he provided and to rank him just ahead of Harry Truman.

In our judgment, his willingness to send troops into Little Rock in 1957 and his use of federal authority – deploying federal marshals, as well as troops, to enforce federal court decrees in integration cases – also provides examples of leadership. That firm "laws must be obeyed and the President will ensure that they are" attitude did not end the recalcitrance and the glacial pace of integration, but, it seems to us, it did establish a boundary to what might be tolerated. Similarly, while the "Atoms for Peace" initiative did not achieve its specific ends, it did provide for the possibility of an alternative direction. It was not taken, but it certainly offered possibilities, and redounded to the credit of the nation.

On a different plane, the decision to avoid troop commitments in French Indo China was weighted with meaning, symbolic and otherwise. If a President who was one of America's military heroes felt "the game was not worth the candle," few would argue. Nor did they. The experience of the next administrations might be seen as illuminating the worth of that decision.

18. Intelligence

Here Eisenhower ranks in 18th place just after Truman and eight places below President Carter. Some elements of the ranking we think we can account for. Ike's seemingly halting and often apparently confused grammar and syntax at press conferences would certainly not give the impression of a swift and analytical mind at work. As a society we have always tended to conflate intelligence with the articulate speaker. His rather folksy and somewhat rural usage reflected an earlier time and place, but it also played rather badly when contrasted with, for example, the more sophisticated and urbane style of his immediate successor, John F. Kennedy.

Yet, increasingly, scholars are telling us that many of such usages were quite consciously and deliberately adopted to mask the degree of his active involvement or to obscure the results at which he aimed. There is great irony, but also great significance, in then Vice President Richard Nixon's frequently quoted reflection that Eisenhower was the most devious man he had ever met; which was not intended to be a pejorative.

We know also, that during the years that Douglas MacArthur was chief of staff, most of the reports and speeches which emanated from his office were crafted by a major on his staff, Dwight D. Eisenhower. The same was true for the Philippine years. These documents, like the frequently mentioned farewell address and Atoms for Peace speech, offer an interesting contrast to the examples mentioned above. The Eisenhower of the army years was frequently described as brilliant, though his academic record at the Military Academy was mediocre. His mature efforts, at the Command and General Staff School, for example, where he finished first in his class, were outstanding. It should be mentioned here that members nominated for each class at the Command and General Staff School were preselected as the army's brightest and best.

President Lyndon Johnson once told "… Arthur Krock of the New York Times that … history would 'make a great mistake' if it overlooked Eisenhower's talents, industry and wisdom. He went on to tell Krock that in conferences Eisenhower was the sharpest mind at the table. [It was he] who constantly saw critical points and consequences that eluded 'the whiz kids' in his [Johnson's] administration and Kennedy's."

We might suggest at this juncture that we are not entirely comfortable with this ranking. We suspect, with the passage of time and the emergence of additional information, it might well go higher.

19. Avoid Crucial Mistakes

In this category, our respondents have ranked Eisenhower in sixth place, and in third place in the 20h Century, trailing only the two Roosevelts.

The Eisenhower Doctrine had the potential to be a crucial error. It made inadequate allowance for postcolonial distrust of the West and overestimated the credibility gained by the United States by forcing Britain, France and Israel out of Suez in 1956. It also misjudged the reaction of the conservative Arab states. Fortunately, the problem was recognized relatively quickly. Also, fortunately, the Soviets proved less than agile in diplomacy, and the doctrine, announced in January of 1957, was allowed to lapse after the Lebanese intervention of 1958.

Critics of the Eisenhower administration have taken the President to task for what they perceive to be a dilatory and weak response to the phenomenon of McCarthyism and the persona of Senator McCarthy. Ike's partisans would suggest that the President's response denied the senator additional publicity and allowed his peers in the Senate to reduce him to near oblivion. In any event, they would say, his power was largely gone within two years of the inauguration.

In a similar fashion, the President has been attacked as being wishy-washy at best on civil rights issues, and those who criticize decry what they see as a failure of presidential leadership. His defenders point to the use of federal troops in Little Rock, which was far more innovative and dramatic than it now seems, as well as to the authoritative use of federal authority in other venues. They would go on to cite the Civil Rights Acts of 1957 and 1960 which, while watered down by Congress, were, in fact, the first civil rights legislation to get through Congress in more than 80 years. They might also be seen, in the light of the civil rights legislation of the early 1960's as the "nose of the camel under the tent".

20. Present Overall View

In any event, it would seem that the judgment of our experts in this category could not be too far off the mark. The respondents have awarded Eisenhower ninth place in the overall view category.

Book II

Our second set of Presidents consists of George Washington, John Adams and Thomas Jefferson. As was true with their 20th Century counterparts, they too show marked similarities. Like the first group, though less evenly, they form a fairly tight chronological group by birth, separated by only 11 years, with Washington and Adams less than three years apart. Not surprisingly, they, too, are an exclusively "old stock" group.

By the standards of the day, they were well educated, with Washington having the least formal education. Jefferson had graced the campus of William and Mary, and Adams became the first Harvard graduate to be elected president.

Once again, akin to the first group they are united by the experience of history. All are Founding Fathers. All three were serving in the Second Continental Congress when the American Revolution began. Adams nominated Washington as commander in chief of the Continental Army. Of course, both Adams and Jefferson voted for what proved to be his unanimous selection, in the spring of 1775.

The following summer, Adams and Jefferson, along with Benjamin Franklin, were the dominant members of the drafting committee for the Declaration of Independence, with Jefferson as principal draftsman. It fell to Washington as commander in chief of the Army in New York to have the document formally read to his troops.

All remained active throughout the entire Revolutionary era, though both Adams and Jefferson were out of the country on diplomatic missions when Washington, in 1787, presided over the constitutional convention in Philadelphia.

Once the Constitution was ratified, all assumed significant roles in the new government. Washington, of course, was the first President, and Adams served as vice president during both his terms. On his return from France, Jefferson entered the cabinet as secretary of state. When the General refused a third term, Adams succeeded him as President. Due to an anomaly in the Constitution as it then existed, Jefferson, who had been Adams' electoral rival, became vice president. After one term, Adams was defeated, and

Jefferson became the third President of the United States.

In short, from the pre-Revolutionary years to 1809, these three men exercised significant leadership roles in the events that led to American independence and to the establishment of a new government under the Constitution of the United States.

Like their 20th Century counterparts, they would have significant political differences. So too, they have generally impressed modern American academics with their talents and character.

Chapter 4 - George Washington – April 30, 1789 – March 4, 1797

"First in War, first in peace and first in the hearts of the American people."
-"Light Horse Harry" Lee, on the occasion of Washington's death.

"Washington, however, did not deceive them."
- John Adams

1. Background (family, education, experience)

Since the professors have ranked Washington in seventh place in this category it is our assumption that they have weighted the response rather negatively in the direction of family and education as opposed to experience.

He was born in Westmoreland County, Virginia, in February of 1732, to Augustine Washington and his second wife Mary, née Ball. His education was local. In addition to the three R's, we know that he was introduced to bookkeeping, geography, geometry, trigonometry and, of course, surveying. Unlike his older step brothers, he was not sent to England to further his education. Presumably, the funds were not available. We also know that at his death, he left a personal library of over 700 books, and that, by the standards of his day, he was a keen student of agronomy. Unlike Adams or Jefferson, he was not afforded an opportunity to attend college. His schooling tended to the practical rather than to the academic.

Little is known of his father, who died when he was 11, other than that he was a big man, from whom, it is assumed, Washington inherited his physique. At maturity, the President stood about six feet two or three inches tall. He was a man of great strength and athleticism and, Jefferson averred, was the best horseman in Virginia. He was also, it would seem, an excellent dancer. When the future President was born, his family had been in Virginia for about 75 years and, while not one of the great families of the colony, did rank among the gentry.

At the death of his father, Washington inherited the Ferry Farm, among other properties. There he lived with his mother and those of his siblings born of Mary Ball. His mother lived on as a widow, and a seemingly formidable one, for nearly 50 more years. His older half-brothers perhaps fared better in the will. In Lawrence, he found not only a half-brother but also a mentor and friend until Lawrence's premature death and the subsequent death of his widow. Lawrence, childless, left to George the plantation that the future President loved best, Mount Vernon. Whenever Washington in later years spoke of retiring to his vine and fig trees, it was of Mount Vernon that he spoke.

By the time he was 16, he had embarked upon his first career as a land surveyor. Through Lawrence, who had married Ann Fairfax, young Washington had entrée into the world of the Fairfax family, probably the greatest of the colonial great families of Virginia. A number of his early surveying contracts were done for them. Surveying brought the young man income and enabled him to embark on the quest that almost obsessed him until the Revolution – the quest for land. The acquisition of land would occupy much of his thinking and planning for the next quarter century.

Surveying provided him not only the wherewithal to buy land, but also the opportunity to view the land. Of this group of Presidents, Washington alone seems to have had a natural Western orientation. Jefferson would come to it, perhaps primarily to ensure land for the dominance of his perfect model of humanity, the yeoman farmer. Washington, on the other hand, seems virtually to have been born with a near continental vision.

The task of surveying also required careful observation, accurate calculation and a firm grasp of mapmaking and reading. These skills, and the eye for terrain and able map reading, would stand him in good stead in his second career, that of a soldier.

In 1752, with his brother Lawrence dying, Washington solicited Virginia's Governor Robert Dinwiddie for a post as militia adjutant. Lawrence's death created a vacancy. He also brought the influence of the Fairfax family into play. Perhaps somewhat distasteful today, that constituted acceptable behavior at the time. Suddenly, at 20, with no previous military experience, George Washington was given the rank of major in the militia of the colony.

In 1754, Governor Dinwiddie famously sent Major Washington on a mission into the Ohio Country. He was to tell the French, who were building a series of forts there, that the land in question belonged to the King of England and that they, the French, should therefore withdraw from the region. The next few years – from Great Meadows/Fort Necessity to Braddock's defeat and on to Forbes seizure of Fort Duquesne (thereafter Fort Pitt) plus the defense of the Virginia frontier in the early stages of the French and Indian War – formed an important part of Washington's military education. It took him from valorous exercise to humiliating defeat, to heroic leadership under abysmal circumstances, and from purely selfish and parochial views to an ability to see, if not always understand, a bigger picture. It also made him, by 1758 when he resigned his position, the best known soldier in the 13 colonies.

In that year, he married Martha Dandridge Custis, a very well-to-do widow. In this fashion, he attained the wealth that enabled him to enter into the ranks of the great families of Virginia.

In 1758, he also entered the House of Burgesses. While normally remaining in the background, he was never without influence. As relations between the colonies and the mother country grew strained after 1763, he was normally to be found on the side of the colonial legislatures and their definition of what constituted the "rights of Englishmen," as applied to the colonies. The restraints imposed by Parliament were rejected as unworthy of Englishmen.

He was one of Virginia's representatives to the First Continental Congress in 1774. He also returned with the delegation to Philadelphia in 1775. With hostilities imminent, it was notable that Washington, alone among the delegates, was dressed in military uniform. After Lexington and Concord in June of 1775, and with a British Army besieged in Boston by New England militia, Congress adopted the army and selected George Washington as its commander in chief.

Since the form of the American Government from 1775-1783 had no formal executive, but functioned by committee for the most part, Washington became the most visible symbol of the Revolution and remained so throughout the era. His embodiment of the revolutionary ethos was perhaps best symbolized in two moments.

The first, in the spring of 1783, occurred at Newburgh, N. Y. when a proposal was floated (the Newburgh Conspiracy) that the officers lead the army against the Congress, demanding long overdue back pay and benefits. Washington quelled the abortive effort by sheer force of personality. In a speech to his officers, he dramatized his own sacrifices during the war by pausing to put on a pair of spectacles and saying to his men, "Gentlemen, you must pardon me. I have grown gray in your service, and now find myself growing blind." In the speech, he appealed to their better natures – to the nobility of the sacrifices they had made for their county and to their honor. As the officers left the meeting, the Newburgh Conspiracy ended. That ought to have put to rest any notion that he intended to seek power on his own, like Oliver Cromwell or Napoleon Bonaparte. In that context, we might also note that Bonaparte himself once noted, referring to his early military success before his thrust to power, "They wanted me to be another Washington." Clearly, like Cromwell, he was not.

The second moment came at the end of the war when, the peace treaty having been agreed to, he at once took horse, went to the Congress and returned to them his commission as commander in chief. Having held power, he gracefully relinquished it and returned to Mount Vernon, proving that he was a man who could be trusted with power, without fear of abuse. In a few years, his countrymen would remember the man who could be trusted with their liberties.

We can conclude our rapid survey of his pre-presidential experience with another sentence or two. Having reluctantly returned to public life in 1787, he assumed the chair as presiding officer of the Constitutional Convention in Philadelphia and threw the weight of his influence behind the new Constitution and its ratification. It was also a foregone conclusion that, assuming ratification, he would be the first President.

When the 69 electors cast the ballots to elect the first President, all – without exception – cast their ballots for George Washington.

Current American scholars have ranked Washington fourth among the Presidents, after FDR, Lincoln and Theodore Roosevelt, in this category.

2. Party Leadership (political)

Here, Washington is ranked at 20th, just barely within the upper half of Presidents. The category poses peculiar difficulties for Washington. No other President within the top 10 ranks lower than he. The basic problem is that in Washington's time there were no political parties. By his second term their outlines could dimly be glimpsed, but they had not yet formally coalesced. Furthermore, Washington and many other influential figures of the day opposed their influence as pernicious. Washington devoted much of his Farewell Address to warning against the formation of political parties.

In a broader sense, Washington was a political being, but an 18th Century political being. He was the product of a deferential society, one in which each man knew his place. That society was being democratized almost daily, but Washington, trying hard to dignify both his new office and his new government, was not unduly sensitive to that fact. For example, he abhorred the notion that anyone would think that he harbored any monarchical sentiments, which his detractors somehow suspected. Nevertheless, as president, he never shook hands, but rather bowed to those introduced to him. He did this at least in part because he felt the office needed to be bolstered by outward signs of respect.

In this context his politicking was quite unlike that of a modern President. So, he might think, if, hypothetically, we appoint a South Carolinian to post X what impact will that have on the South Carolina congressional delegation, or on the way Carolinians view the new government? He also relied heavily on private conversation and persuasion, preferring words over dinner or a glass of wine, as well as previous ties of affection or service, to exhortation or bargaining as a means of swaying minds or votes.

It would then be impossible to fault our respondents for the verdict returned. The problem is that the question, while quite important for the survey as a whole, does not fit this particular President very well at all.

3. Communication Ability (speak, write)

Washington is 12th in this category, just inside the top 30 per cent. He was, like most active leaders of his generation, a prodigious correspondent. Again, like many such leaders, much of his correspondence of the war years was actually written by staff officers like Alexander Hamilton. Once they caught his mode of thinking, they could be relied upon to deal with most day to day matters.

He did not fancy himself a literary stylist or orator. Speculation that he was somewhat reticent due to the weakness of his formal education might not be entirely incorrect. By 18th Century standards, his writing was relatively plain. His presidential speeches, if he regarded them as really important, were often farmed out for initial drafts. Sometimes he sent out a draft for editing and/or amendment. It would seem that like many modern Presidents he resorted to speech writers while keeping the tone and tint of a speech his own.

In the case of his most famous speech, the Farewell Address, there were two efforts. In preparation for his first effort at retiring in 1792, he turned to James Madison, then still one of his closest confidants. Washington was persuaded to accept a second term by Madison, among others, but as 1796 approached – and with it Washington's absolute decision to retire to Mount Vernon – he by then felt himself abandoned by Jefferson and Madison. As a result, he turned to Alexander Hamilton for the new effort. Drafts flowed back and forth between the two men. Despite Hamilton's brilliance and capacity, few if any would suggest that the final draft of the Farewell Address is Hamilton's. It clearly is Washington's.

As an orator, few of Washington's efforts are notable. Off the battlefield, he never needed to raise his voice to be noticed or heard. His presence commanded attention others needed to seek, and conversation rather than eloquence was his great gift as a communicator. On the other hand, as we have seen, his speech to his assembled officers on the occasion of the Newburgh Conspiracy is a study in the drama and impact of carefully crafted oratory.

He would never write with the stylistic panache of Thomas Jefferson; few ever would. The depth of thought and lucidity of argument of John Adams in, e.g., The Novanglus Papers , was not an effort that Washington was prepared to attempt. Rather, Washington's way is represented best in a perhaps apocryphal story. As the story goes, at the meeting of the First Continental Congress Washington rose and announced that he was prepared to raise, equip and lead into battle a thousand men (a regiment) at his own expense. Example rather than eloquence was his strength.

4. Relationship With Congress

In this realm, only FDR and Lyndon B. Johnson are accorded higher overall rankings than Washington. His influence remained high throughout his presidency, though higher during his first term. In part that was certainly due not only to the presence of "His Excellency" but also due to his intensely close relationship with James Madison. As leader of the House of Representatives and known to have been one of the principal figures at the Constitutional Convention, Madison functioned as what would now be seen as the majority leader of the House. He also, however, was a member of Washington's unofficial cabinet of advisors. Thus, when Washington arrived in New York for his inauguration Madison was delegated by the House to prepare an address of welcome to the President-elect. Then, at Washington's request, he drafted the President's response to the address of the House. By the second term, that relationship had been weakened, as Madison moved increasingly under Jefferson's influence.

The President was always conscious that every step he took, every action he performed, established precedents. He was, to all intents and purposes, defining the role of the President day by day. In that context, he was scrupulously careful to avoid trespassing on the constitutionally defined duties and territory of the legislative branch. For example, he was unwilling to veto legislation of which he merely disapproved. He believed he should veto only those measures he felt to be unconstitutional. That precedent would hold through five additional presidencies, until that of Andrew Jackson.

Washington also believed it necessary to avoid even the appearance of seeking to influence congressional elections. Therefore, he refused to discuss the qualifications of candidates for the House of Representatives. Senate membership was at the time determined by the state legislatures and would be for more than another century. This precedent would endure only until Jefferson's presidency.

In the earliest stages of the new administration, significant responsibilities loomed. First came the new government itself. General Washington had to convert the new government of the United States from a parchment document to a working institution. Even in that day, the creation of departments, their staffing and the systematic creation of a logical, working bureaucracy all required time and energy. In what would now be called "upper management," the President insisted upon verifiable credentials and references. Someone, known to the President or perhaps the cabinet secretary involved, would have to vouch for the individual's character. Of course, at the very top, the cabinet, that someone was the President. Later, subordinate officials would recommend their assistants and subordinates. It should be noted that Washington was rarely satisfied with official advice; he ranged widely for guidance and information. Then, too, we must remember that all appointees were subject to senatorial confirmation until an essentially clerical, non-policy level was reached.

With considerable support from the President, Madison ably took responsibility for shaping the Bill of Rights and shepherding it through the Congress. Ratification by the states was completed in 1791. Once again, we need to keep in mind Madison's unique role in this period. Probably the single most important member of the House, he was also functioning as a member of the inner circle of the executive branch. That blending of roles would be impossible today without cries of violating the separation of powers. In the more intimate world of an infant nation around 1790, Madison's dual role certainly brought the executive and legislative branches into useful and amiable cooperation.

The prime necessity of the new government was an adequate financial system. It was the inability of the government under the Articles of Confederation to meet the fiscal needs of the nation that had doomed that government. In the House, Madison moved quickly to establish an adequate tariff on imports to provide the government with a revenue source, the first in American history.

As the Congress recessed in 1789, the House of Representatives charged the new secretary of the treasury with recommending a method to resolve the financial problems of a new nation with deep debt and without credit resources. In 1790, Hamilton presented the House with the first great American state paper, The Report on Public Credit. It was a brilliant work providing an overarching structure for the financial stability of the new government. It created a wholly satisfactory way of dealing with the public indebtedness of the United States. Together with a proposal to establish a Bank of the United States, it constituted a viable means of stimulating economic growth. Accepted by generations of historians and economists as a salutary method for providing stability and growth, it also resolved the problems of indebtedness and credit virtually overnight.

For clarity's sake, let us take a moment to outline Hamilton's proposal and define some of the terms that characterized Hamilton's scheme. It was symbolized by the terms "Funding and Assumption." Funding involved the existing debt, foreign and domestic. In round numbers that was about $50 million. Of that amount, about 20 per cent was owed to foreign creditors, the remainder to American citizens. Virtually no one opposed payment in full of the foreign debt. The American debt, which traded at about 25 cents on the dollar was another matter. Many wished simply to write it off. Others among Hamilton's critics thought that since much of it was no longer held by the original owners (who had loaned it to the government, or had been soldiers given paper instead of money) but by speculators whom it would be appropriate to pay it off at perhaps 30 cents on the dollar.

Hamilton's plan called for full payment. If the country wished to borrow again, he said, it was these men, this "interest" (in the 18th Century sense) who would be the available source of credit.

In the Report on Public Credit he further recommended that the federal government add an additional $25 million to the debt. That represented debts incurred by the states as a result of supporting the war. These monies constituted "Assumption" – that is the assumption by the federal government of debts owed by the states in support of the establishment of independence.

Effectively he proposed to call in all the old, worthless paper certificates representing the national debt and issuing new paper at about a one-third lower rate of interest.

The debt would be addressed by the use of a "sinking fund" – a specific portion of the annual revenue that was unalterably pledged to the purpose of paying off the debt.

The report also hinted at the later creation of a Bank of the United States, as an agent of the federal government and an engine of economic development. It was to be dominated but not controlled by the United States government.

Hamilton's plan also, unintentionally, introduced political havoc into both Congress and the cabinet and provided the first specific impetus to the formation of American political parties. Before the beginning of the administration, Hamilton had been one of Madison's closest political collaborators during the struggle over ratification of the Constitution. Madison, in turn, had been one of Hamilton's strongest supporters for secretary of the treasury. This issue would begin their separation, as Madison stood with Jefferson against so-called "Funding and Assumption." In so doing, Madison adopted a less nationalist and more parochial view than he had earlier espoused.

Hamilton, with Washington's support in the cabinet, fought a titanic political battle, opposed by his erstwhile colleague, Madison, in Congress. Ultimately, however, the administration's plan for the public management of the debt was accepted. Jefferson and Madison were persuaded to withdraw public objection and even throw minimal support to Hamilton for Funding and Assumption. Hamilton agreed to provide votes in Congress for the permanent location of the national capital in the south, on the Potomac River. It was probably the new government's first "log roll," or exchange of support for political favors. For his part, Washington largely remained above the battle on the proposal to establish The Bank of the United States."

In foreign policy, too, though the debate would be more ideological, contentious and bitter, the administration would ultimately prove successful in its dealings with the Senate. As the French Revolution produced war clouds over Europe, so it produced travail for the United States. From the European wars, which would endure, with short intervals, from 1793 to 1815, there arose whole areas of problems for American shippers and markets, seamen and merchants. Among the problems would be interference with free trade on the high seas, seizures of American vessels, and the impressment of seamen. Washington was convinced that the new nation, grappling with economic problems dating from the Revolution, in need of international trade for internal prosperity and hard-pressed to handle the endemic problems of a nation in process of creation, simply could not afford a war against either Britain or France.

In an effort to resolve some of the problems, Washington asked Chief Justice John Jay to go to England and attempt to negotiate a commercial treaty dealing with neutral rights on the high seas, the impressment of American seamen into foreign service, trade relations and the continued occupation by the British of trading posts in the northwestern territory of the United States. The resultant negotiation led to a deeply flawed treaty but one that avoided war. The Jeffersonian faction, increasingly called Republicans or Republican Democrats – which ultimately evolved into the modern day Democratic Party – saw the treaty as a sellout to Britain, as opposed to the ideologically "purer" France of the French Revolution. They saw it as confirmation of their suspicions that Washington had monarchical leanings. The Federalists, the party which encompassed Washington and his policies, though he was never a member of it, saw the Republicans as radicals who would unhesitatingly bring an American "Reign of Terror" into being.

The Senate ratified the Jay Treaty with a notable lack of enthusiasm. The House of Representatives thereupon demanded to be shown all documents relative to the Treaty under threat of denying funds to implement the ratified treaty. Washington, who had been so tender of the prerogatives of the Congress, now proved tender of those of the executive branch as well. He rather pointedly informed the House that the Constitution gave them no power in the area of foreign affairs, and went on to issue the first claim of executive privilege in denying access to the documents. He prevailed, though it added to what was, for him, the trauma of his last years in office.

5. Court Appointments

This forms another area in which Washington is ranked highly. Here our respondents assign him a rank of second, behind only Franklin D. Roosevelt.

One of the principles Washington considered in appointing men to office, in addition to character, was geography. If the new nation was to function as one, then all areas would need to be represented in that nation. It is not surprising, then, that among the 11 men he nominated between 1789 and 1797 and who accepted and were confirmed by the Senate, nine states were represented.

No President has ever appointed so many members of the U. S. Supreme Court. Of course, under the Judiciary Act of 1789, he had an initial six appointments – the chief justice and five associate justices. His first appointment was that of John Jay of New York as chief justice. Jay, the former secretary of foreign affairs under the Articles of Confederation, had been his first choice for secretary of state, but Jay had asked for the court instead. The five nominees for associate justice were William Cushing of Massachusetts, James Wilson of Pennsylvania, Robert H. Harrison of Maryland, John Blair of Virginia and John Rutledge of South Carolina. Harrison declined the nomination, and James Iredell of North Carolina was named in his place in 1790. Rutledge resigned before he ever heard a case to become the chief justice of North Carolina. Thomas Johnson of Maryland was nominated to replace him. In 1793, William Paterson of New Jersey was placed on the court and, in 1796, Samuel Chase of Maryland.

It is almost impossible to think that any group of justices on the Supreme Court was ever better pedigreed. John Jay, as well as Cushing, Rutledge, Blair, Johnson and Chase, had all served as chief judge of the Supreme Courts of their respective states. Jay, Wilson, Johnson and Chase had all served in the Continental Congress. Rutledge, Ellsworth, Wilson, Blair and Paterson had all been members of the 1787 Constitutional Convention. Johnson had been governor of Maryland three times. Iredell had been attorney general of North Carolina and had been deeply involved in recreating the laws of North Carolina under its Revolutionary Constitution. He also had served on the North Carolina Supreme Court. Iredell, as well as Blair, Wilson and Cushing had served at the Constitutional Ratifying Conventions of their respective states.

A list of other offices held and duties discharged would be little more than gilding the lily. Let us simply provide a few more lines for Ellsworth and Jay as a completion of the bona fides of the group.

Ellsworth, who was educated at Yale and Princeton, was one of the authors of the so-called "Great Compromise" at the Constitutional Convention. In addition, as a U. S. senator, he was the primary author of the Judiciary Act of 1789, which established the broad outline of the role, structure and function of the judicial branch.

Jay was a product of King's College (later, Columbia University). Before the Revolution he had been a member of the Committees of Correspondence. As a member of the New York Provincial Congress, he had been the principal author of New York's Revolutionary Constitution. He had served as president of the Continental Congress. He resigned that office to serve as minister to Spain. Though the Spanish crown never recognized the government of the United States before the Peace of Paris of 1783, Jay did, somehow, manage to wheedle a loan from Spain. He joined Adams and Franklin in Paris to negotiate a peace with England. There, he was insistent that no negotiation begin until Britain had, in effect, recognized the independence of the United States.

Thereafter he served as secretary of foreign affairs for government under the Articles. In the wake of the Philadelphia Convention, he joined Hamilton and Madison in writing The Federalist Papers to persuade New Yorkers to ratify the new Constitution.

This group indeed possessed a pedigree. It is our assumption that the relative paucity of cases and issues to come before this court is the primary reason Washington's selections are rated second rather than first.

6. Handling of the U.S. Economy

Once again, we find President Washington among the top 10 per cent, in third place. While the ranking is enviable, it seems a trifle low. When Washington stood in New York to take his inaugural oath, the economy of the United States and the fiscal status of the new government were each virtually nonexistent. There was no revenue stream immediately available to the government and no machinery in place to engender, collect or distribute such revenue. Less than two and one-half years had passed since economic distress and class conflict in Massachusetts had led to the uprising known as Shays' Rebellion, August-December 1786. Taxes were being levied by one state against another. There was a large unpaid, and seemingly unpayable, public debt owed to both foreign creditors and to citizens of the United States. Loans were being sought merely to meet the interest payments on that debt. State paper money issues were of varying and frequently dubious value.

The government of the United States maintained ministries in foreign countries, but their efforts to negotiate commercial or other treaties could safely be ignored by their host governments. They knew that the variant commercial policies of the constituent states of the United States made it impossible for Americans to successfully discriminate against any foreign nation in its own favor or that of any "most favored nation."

Spain refused to allow Americans living in the Trans-Appalachian West (Kentucky and Tennessee) to transit the lower Mississippi River or to use the port of New Orleans to market their produce. The bitter truth was that the United States could do nothing about it. Similarly, the British continued to occupy posts in the northwestern territory even though they had agreed to vacate that region under the terms of the Treaty of Paris of 1783.

As Abraham Lincoln was to say in other circumstances, so Washington might have complained, "the bottom's out of the tub."

Eight years later, when Washington at last left Philadelphia for Mount Vernon, he left behind a prosperous nation. Government debts were well secured and a system of investment and payment provided for. Loans had been and could be negotiated on very favorable terms. Spain had made the Mississippi River and the port of New Orleans available to American commodities under the Pinckney Treaty. The defeat of the northwestern Indians at the Battle of Fallen Timbers by General Anthony Wayne, and the Jay Treaty with England, had opened the Northwest Territory to settlement. This was bad news for the American Indian tribes but good news for the small frontier farmer, for speculators and for the economy.

Much of the credit for the startling alteration in the fortunes of the United States was owed to the intellect, energy, imagination and dynamism of Washington's young secretary of the treasury, Alexander Hamilton. Only 32 years old, Hamilton had begun his studies of the financing of governments, with particular emphasis on the English model, before the end of the war. In between two wartime combat assignments – one early in the war through the Battles of Trenton and Princeton, the other late in the war, at Yorktown

– Hamilton served Washington as a member of his personal staff for four years.

The politics of funding and assumption were explosive, involving as they did sectionalism, agrarian against commercial interests and the marginally leveling ideas of Thomas Jefferson versus the Federalist concept of the natural rule of "the better sort."

Some of the quarrel was at least partially cosmetic. Jefferson and Madison and their Virginia constituents rabidly opposed Assumption. Virginia had labored to deal with her debt; other states had not. If the concerns of Virginians were provincial, they were not necessarily unjust. Once they were allowed a place at the federal trough, with promises of monies made available to Virginia, the objections became less vociferous and were more subject to compromise, particularly after the Virginians also were guaranteed the permanent location of the national capital on the banks of the Potomac.

In any event, funding, assumption and the national bank did garner the necessary congressional votes, did pass and were put in place. If Jefferson felt uncomfortable then, he must have been more so when, as President, he consulted his own secretary of the treasury and was told that it was best to leave Hamilton's arrangements in place.

What seemed to some to be nearly miraculous had taken place during one presidency, much of it virtually during a single term. Hamilton himself has told us that it was the general presumption of Washington's support for the program that enabled him to carry the day.

Third place is a high ranking, but we do doubt that equally significant problems existed between 1993 and 2001 when President Clinton, whom our respondents have ranked in second place above President Washington, was "handling" the American economy.

7. Luck

In this area, George Washington is ranked second, just after Theodore Roosevelt.

No one can deny that, during his lifetime, George Washington was blessed with good fortune. He survived, with multiple bullet holes in his clothing, Braddock's defeat in 1755 and faced equivalent dangers on a significant number of other occasions when he appeared in the forefront of battle. His politico-military survival in the face of numerous defeats in battle during the Revolution similarly attests to his luck, as well as his talent.

His presidency began with the country in dire economic straits, though it ended in triumphant prosperity for both the nation and its citizens. Was the selection of Hamilton as secretary of the treasury and the President's staunch support of him and his economic plans – contrary to the advice of some of the president's advisors, such as Jefferson and Madison – luck or purely good judgment? When we consider that Robert Morris was Washington's first choice for treasury secretary, we may be excused for suggesting that – initially, at least – luck may indeed have played some role.

Similarly, in foreign affairs, Washington's presidency is coterminous with the French Revolution, the Reign of Terror and the start of the Wars of the French Revolution. Events spawned by the French Revolution would threaten the United States with the specter of war with one or more European powers. Washington knew that at that time the nation possessed neither the financial nor military resources to wage such a war. His first secretary of state, Jefferson, was a Francophile who felt that France represented the future and that America, France's ally since 1778, should support its position. He, at best, only weakly supported Washington's policy.

The President's efforts to negotiate with Britain led to the unsatisfactory Jay Treaty, but did provide the nation with another 15 years of peace. It also paved the way for attacks, veiled and otherwise, upon him and his reputation and character by such former confidantes as Jefferson and Madison, as well as others, which were a source of great personal anxiety to Washington.

Persistent quarrels with the Indian tribes of the Northwest Territory led to two of the worst defeats ever suffered by an American Army, Generals Josiah Harmar, in 1790, and Arthur St. Clair, in 1791. It was not until 1794, that General Anthony Wayne, through the Battle of Fallen Timbers and the subsequent Treaty of Greenville, managed to quell disturbances in what was then known as the Ohio country.

The interior settlements of the trans-Appalachian West were, in 1789 and after, facing huge problems concerning the sale of their crops. Issues of sheer bulk made it virtually impossible to ship grain east over the mountains. Roads, if they existed, were execrable. Spain, which controlled both banks of the lower Mississippi River and the port of New Orleans, refused to grant the settlers of Kentucky and Tennessee transit rights on the river or access to the port of New Orleans. Here, Washington would, indeed, enjoy the blessings of fortune. European diplomatic problems came to America's aid. Spain, wary of possible war with England, was puzzled by the news of the Jay Treaty. It seemed such a poor bargain from the view of the United States that it was assumed there must be secret protocols. Perhaps they provided for an Anglo-American assault on New Orleans and Spanish Florida. In that state of mind, Spain summoned the American minister to Madrid and moved to appease the Americans. The Treaty of San Lorenzo, also called The Pinckney Treaty of 1795, saw Spain accept the United States' definition of the northern boundary of Florida, granted the right of transit on the Mississippi to western Americans and granted them the right of deposit for their goods in the port of New Orleans.

8. Ability to Compromise

In this category we find another third place ranking. We think that this, too, was a difficult category for the respondents because Washington's time in office was qualitatively different than that of other presidents.

In 1789, everyone was starting from scratch. Everyone, or nearly everyone, was then a Federalist. That is to say, virtually all members of the House and Senate had supported the Constitution and its ratification. The two most active members of the government, Hamilton and Madison, had been close collaborators during ratification. With Chief Justice John Jay, they were the authors of the celebrated Federalist Papers, urging New Yorkers to ratify the Constitution. Both were also intimate members of Washington's inner circle. Jefferson, a reluctant secretary of state, did not join the cabinet until 1790. He did not leave his post in Paris until September, 1789, and had not yet joined in any debates, other than via correspondence.

It would be well here to note that a portion of Jefferson's seeming pique may have stemmed from his late arrival on the scene. When Jefferson left Paris to come home, Hamilton was already hard at work at treasury. When Jefferson took his oath of office, Hamilton's Report on Public Credit already had been published.

Parochialism was present but, initially and primarily, as a background note. Little that was terribly controversial had yet been proposed. The Report on Public Credit and the issues surrounding the French Revolution were symbols that would unleash partisan ideology and the formation of parties. They would also complete the dissolution of the bond between Madison and Hamilton and begin Madison's estrangement from Washington and solidify his intense political bond with Jefferson.

One result of all of this, from its chronology to its geography to its ideology, was that on many key issues, Washington was rarely given an opportunity to compromise. He was rather presented with a choice, from one side or another, with a clear indication that no compromise was sought or desired. On the contrary, he was asked to throw his support behind one side or the other.

As a general rule, he appears to have given Hamilton primary support on economic and fiscal issues and Jefferson on diplomatic issues other than neutrality. Thus, when he found it necessary to issue what history calls the Neutrality Proclamation, sensitive to both the Congress and to Jefferson's

Francophile position, he scrupulously avoided even the use of the word, neutrality. Similarly, he tolerated the presence of Edmond-Charles Genet, known widely as "Citizen Genet," as France's minister to the United States until Genet directly challenged the President. By then, even Jefferson agreed that Genet had become more trouble than he was worth.

Perhaps the clearest indicator of President Washington's willingness to compromise may be seen in the Jay Treaty. The President was convinced that the nation could not afford a war against either France or Britain. The Jay Treaty was a pact that clearly indicated that Britain regarded the United States as a second-class state. It failed even to address issues of neutral rights on the high seas, which was the Jay Treaty's reason for being. Washington was prepared to accept it, and to sacrifice political capital to do so (though most of the public ignominy went to Jay) because it cleared the British from the Northwest Territory posts and because it achieved his overarching goal, peace – or, at least, the absence of war.

9. Willing to Take Risks

The very fact that Washington agreed to become President is a strong indicator of his willingness to take risks.

It is unlikely that any scholar who has written anything about George Washington in the last half-century or more has failed to indicate how deeply he valued his reputation and character. He was fully aware of his achievements and jealous of his reputation. An old anecdote tells us that in 1783 King George III, being told by the painter Benjamin West that Washington would return power to Congress and go home, replied, "If he does that he will be the greatest man in the world." The king's statement, of course, represented the level of integrity and rectitude to which General Washington aspired. In fact, that was exactly what he did. Particularly as he entered his second term, feeling the hostility of Jefferson, he lamented the damage to his reputation that the presidency had cost him. The sly aspersions cast upon him by Madison and Jefferson concerning his aging and his declining faculties wounded him deeply. But of course, he had put himself in harm's way when he agreed to run in 1788 and, again, in 1792. He had, knowingly, taken the risk

Here, our experts have ranked Washington ninth. Again, the unique character of this presidency, particularly his deference to the Congress and even, when feasible, to his direct subordinates, makes it difficult to quarrel with a ranking that places him just outside the top 20 per cent. And yet we note that he never gave specific public support to Hamilton's Report on Public Credit, and, it appeared to many that Hamilton fought a titanic battle alone. It is Hamilton who tells us that the aegis of Washington was essential to his success. Are we perhaps seeing another example of a hidden hand?

We have already spoken of Washington's willingness to support the ratification of the Jay Treaty and to spend the political capital of his reputation for preservation of peace with Great Britain in 1794-1795.

In that same period, the events of the so-called Whiskey Rebellion took place. In 1791, Congress had placed an excise tax on whiskey to help defray the costs of funding and assumption. In western Pennsylvania, the tax was considered particularly onerous. Transportation of grain to market was difficult due to distance, bad roads, bulk and cost. Grain converted to whiskey was more portable and more useful. Whiskey was so important in the economy of the region that it served as a medium of exchange. Distillers began to refuse to pay the excise and to physically resist the excise men. Associate Justice James Wilson issued a writ saying the area was in a state of rebellion. President Washington called out 13,000 militiamen from Pennsylvania, New Jersey, Maryland, and Virginia. They formed at Harrisburg, PA in September of 1794. Washington personally reviewed them and then traveled with them for a few days. It was a much larger force than he usually had commanded during the Revolution. Confronted with overwhelming force, the rebellion collapsed. Two men were convicted of treason, but the President soon pardoned them on grounds of diminished capacity.

For the first time, the federal government had demonstrated its ability to enforce obedience to civil authority. By calling out such a large force, Washington greatly diminished any risk of armed resistance. His later magnanimity also undoubtedly did much to minimize resentment. A risk was considered, analyzed and minimized. Action was taken. Action succeeded.

10. Executive Appointments

This category garners a ranking of first for President Washington. In General Washington's day there were only four cabinet officers – the secretaries of state, treasury, war and the attorney general. There was a postmaster general, but he was not included in policy discussions or deliberations.

The first secretary of state was Jefferson – although, since he was returning from a diplomatic assignment in France and reluctant to serve, he did not join the cabinet until January of 1790, nine months after Washington's inauguration. Treasury fell to Hamilton. The department of war went to Henry Knox of Massachusetts, who had been one of Washington's key generals during the Revolution, and Edmund Randolph of Virginia assumed the duties of attorney general. Washington's penchant for geographical diversity in appointments is well illustrated here. It would have been more thorough had his first choices, John Jay of New York at state and Robert Morris of Pennsylvania at treasury, agreed to serve.

It is, in any event, an enviable list, perhaps more so if we remember that in the early days of the administration James Madison, who was the leader of the House of Representatives, was also a close presidential advisor.

In this context, we might note that the professors responding to this survey ranked Jefferson and Madison first and second in intelligence among all American Presidents. Where, in terms of SAT scores, Hamilton would rank in that company is an unanswerable but intriguing question. Certainly, that cabinet had a quality of brilliance difficult to match.

Henry Knox, who had become chief of artillery of the Continental Army before Boston in 1775-1776, fought in that capacity to the end of the war. He then became the commanding general of the army after the peace and had been secretary of war for Congress under the Articles of Confederation, from 1785 until, at Washington's request; he became the first secretary of war under the Constitution.

Edmund Randolph had been part of the Virginia delegation to the Constitutional Convention. It was he who proposed the so-called Virginia Plan at the convention. He did not sign the final document, but did campaign for its ratification.

Few cabinets have been as well qualified and, with Jefferson and Hamilton, perhaps none since has displayed as much evidence of brilliance.

The quarrel between Jefferson and Hamilton foreshadowed the emergence of the political party system. It was rooted in a North-South dichotomy and a commercial-agricultural — as well as a slave-free — divide. The political reality was that Hamilton, to Jefferson's chagrin, was the more dominant figure. Perhaps it was because the economic and financial problems that had brought down the Confederation government so desperately needed solution, and Hamilton's plans clearly seemed to offer the best hope. Indeed, they did provide the solution. Perhaps the fact that Hamilton was on the scene and on the job months before Jefferson arrived resulted in Hamilton's dominance. Perhaps Hamilton's prominence stemmed from Hamilton having served for so long during the Revolution as Washington's aide and secretary. In any event, Jefferson seems to have gone from reluctance to serve, through pique and annoyance until he resigned in 1793.

11. Overall Ability

Trailing Abraham Lincoln and FDR, Washington is ranked third in this category.

Once again we feel constrained to note that this was not a modern presidency. Washington's personality was an integral part of his presidency. As is well known, he searched for a proper tone for the presidency – one that would not be overly elevated and perceived of as aristocratic or monarchical nor one that seemed overly familiar. The President's view was that this new, republican entity would need to be presented with some dignity. When he received the public, usually once a week at a formal session, he did not shake hands; he bowed. Most Americans seemed to find that acceptable. The custom was retained until Jefferson became President.

Washington's long military experience, culminating in his eight years as commander in chief of the Continental Army, stood him in good stead as president. No one else in North America had any similar experience in organizing, motivating and managing any equivalently large and complex organization.

In that experience he also had faced the need to juggle political complexities in appointing subordinates. After the appointments, it became necessary to reconcile differences while still juggling political complications and somehow remaining focused on the primary goal.

The first test of his abilities was the necessity of converting a piece of paper, the Constitution, from an abstract concept into a workable system, the government of the United States. In what might appear to be slight of hand, he seems to have accomplished that almost without exerting visible energy.

Deference is certainly owed to his collaborators and subordinates, particularly to Hamilton and Madison, but his presence and the confidence and trust he generated played a major role in the smooth path from abstraction to reality. Between 1789 and 1791, Congress passed legislation to provide the government with a revenue stream from import duties and a mechanism to collect and distribute that money. It also drafted, in 1789, a Bill of Rights for transmission to the states for ratification. In 1790, Congress drew upon Hamilton's ideas for a master plan for the American economy. After passage, virtually overnight, that plan converted the United States from a disreputable and impecunious status to financial respectability. In matters of foreign policy, as Europe erupted into the world-wide phenomenon of the Wars of the French Revolution, President Washington, through the Neutrality Proclamation and the Jay Treaty kept the nation at peace throughout both his terms.

Similarly, the use of overwhelming force in the Whiskey Rebellion, followed by judicious magnanimity in its aftermath, proved that this

American government, unlike that under the Articles of Confederation, could do more than merely preside over a fractious nation. It could govern.

12. Imagination

Respondents in this category have assigned Washington a rank of ninth, just outside the top 20 per cent. Interestingly enough, he thus joins three other of our earliest Presidents who are ranked in the top 10 in this category – Jefferson, Madison and John Quincy Adams. The 20th Century also has four – Theodore Roosevelt, Wilson, FDR and Kennedy. The remaining two are assigned to the mid-nineteenth century James K. Polk and Lincoln.

Certainly, from early in his young manhood through his presidency, the American West engaged Washington's imagination, fervidly and constantly. As he matured, the interest shifted from a personal, frequently financial one into a grander vision of an American West, perhaps one of the few he shared with Jefferson. In this area, his vision was quite wide ranging, involving schemes for canals, for example, to help make the burgeoning American frontier physically reachable and to tie it economically to the East.

We also believe that his desire to emulate Roman leader Cincinnatus – to perform heroic deeds and then lay down power and return to his farm – represents an imaginative construction. It is, if you will, a towering ideal – a man summoned to service by and for his people and granted power precisely because they are convinced that he can be trusted to wield power without abuse. Thus in 1783, fulfilling that trust, the task assigned him by Congress in 1775 having been discharged, he went to Congress, resigned his commission and went home.

Only reluctantly in 1787, persuaded by Shays' Rebellion and other problems and by James Madison among others, did he return to public life at the Constitutional Convention and later agreed to accept the presidency. This would seem to be the only genuine presidential draft in American history. Hoping to retire at the end of his first term, he was again persuaded of his indispensability by Madison and others, and accepted a second term. Four years later, when 1796 loomed, he was no longer amenable to persuasion. He would not accept another term, to which he certainly would have been elected. He went home.

The two-term precedent Washington established would endure for another 144 years, until 1940, when Franklin Roosevelt would seek and win a third and then a fourth term. In the wake of that experience, the nation would amend its constitution to forbid any one again from seeking a third term by adding the 22nd Amendment to the Constitution.

When we speak of imagination, we must not forget to think of his presidential national tour. The President, hoping to bind the union more closely together, toured all the states, seeing and being seen. The laborious nature of such a tour, given the roads and accommodations of the 18th Century, made it an almost Herculean venture. But it was imaginative, right down to the exclusion of Rhode Island in the first instance because the state had not ratified the Constitution, and then visiting the state after it had entered the union.

In historical terms, it is instructive to contrast Washington's imaginative construct with the concepts that seem to have driven his historic near contemporaries, Cromwell and Bonaparte.

13. Domestic Accomplishments

Here, George Washington is ranked third among the presidents, following Franklin Roosevelt and Abraham Lincoln.

A logical question might be, since his administration created the country and saved it from the ash heap of history, should he be ranked higher? That point may certainly be argued, but in this ongoing exercise of nearly 30 years, we do not have a ballot.

Our assumption is that Lincoln, who saved the republic from destruction during the Civil War, is accorded second place for that achievement, and that FDR is granted pride of place because he wrestled with the Depression and led the country through the travail of World War II.

As to Washington, as we have seen in 1789 he came to lead a government which owed massxive debts it could not pay. That had no source of revenue. Which had a constitution but no government. Under his leadership the new government created a plan to service the debt which worked exceptionally well. That government created a revenue stream and the necessary bureaucracy to manage it. In an astonishingly short period of time, not only had his administration solved those problems but drafted and sent to the states a draft Bill of Rights as well.

At least in passing we should mention that Washington is responsible for the development of the institutional functioning of the cabinet system in the national government, and for the free use of the veto, which the Constitution granted to the President.

In the same vein of constitutional development, we would also point out that in the wake of the Jay Treaty, the House of Representatives, which did not share the Senate's willingness to accept that treaty, demanded to be shown all papers and documents relevant to the negotiation and conclusion of the treaty. Washington, who was almost preternaturally sensitive to the prerogatives of the legislative branch, now reacted strongly to protect those of the executive and, as we have seen, rejected the demands of the House, enunciating the doctrine of executive privilege.

In Washington's era, there was an area nestled between domestic and foreign policy – dealings with the various Indian tribes. Washington offers to the observer an assortment of activities, including diplomacy with the tribes, warfare, and the independent actions of the frontier people, warlike and otherwise, that the government often could not control. Included in the array of tasks was more conventional diplomacy with the European nations, which hoped to gain advantage by utilizing their influence with the Indians. The Treaty of New York with the Cherokee, General Wayne's defeat of the Northwestern tribes at the Battle of Fallen Timbers and the resultant Treaty of Greenville – as well as the Jay and Pinckney treaties – had the effect of opening both the Northwest and Southwest Territories to settlement and the ultimate creation of new states, which began before Washington left office. This made possible an average of the admission of one new state every three years, from the end of Washington's second term through the admission of Missouri in 1821.

Quickly summarized, a nation on the verge of bankruptcy in 1789, which had suffered civil unrest in the preceding few years, and which had feared possible disunion, by 1797 was prosperous, united, growing and at peace both at home and abroad.

14. Integrity

This constitutes one of the five categories in which our respondents have ranked George Washington first. He is followed by Lincoln and John Adams.

His contemporaries offer welcome insight. When he heard of Washington's death, his fellow Virginian and Revolutionary War veteran, General "Light Horse Harry" Lee said that he was "First in war, first in peace and first in the hearts of his countrymen." Nearly 10 years earlier, in a codicil to his will, Benjamin Franklin had left to George Washington a cane made from a crabapple tree. With the cane, he left a sentiment; "My fine crab-tree walking stick, with a gold head curiously wrought in the form of a cap of liberty, I give to my friend, and the friend of mankind, General Washington. If it were a scepter, he has merited it and would become it." (June 23, 1789.) These words of praise, which rather bookend his presidency, would seem to demonstrate the respect and esteem in which he was held by his peers.

We would suggest the following as a rationale for this ranking. First and foremost, we believe that the experts saw, as did his contemporaries, the clear reality that Washington, unlike most men, could be trusted with power. He would use it wisely and for the public good but, more importantly, he would not seek it for its own sake. Nor would he abandon principle to retain it. He would assume it as necessary and, when the necessity had ended, he would equally readily resign it.

When called upon to staff the new government, he was importuned by friends and acquaintances, who sought to remind him of long-standing associations and friendships. He responded that all appointments were to be based strictly on merit. This introduced a theme of his presidency, which was rectitude. Despite the fears of Jefferson and a few others, he lacked interest in monarchical style or power. So, he would not try to introduce legislation into either house of Congress. To do that, he felt, was a legislative prerogative. He also refused to veto acts of Congress he did not like. He would use the veto freely, but only when he believed there to be constitutional grounds for such an action.

Though perhaps not directly related to the conduct of his presidency, for Washington as for most of his generation, class and geographical region, the issue of slavery loomed large. His views on slavery altered over the years. By the 1760s he had already decided that the slave economy of the Virginia tobacco planter was unwise. Twenty years later he was prepared, at least partly, to acknowledge that slavery was a moral blight.

Nevertheless, as President he allowed Madison to quash anti-slavery petitions which would effectively deny debate on the issue for 20 years. The only justification for Washington's behavior in this area would seem to be two factors:

First, that the creation and stabilization of the new government seemed more immediately important. And second – and this was Lincoln's later explanation – the Founders believed slavery to be already anachronistic and doomed to wither away. None of them was likely to have foreseen the synergy created at the end of the 18th Century by the industrial revolution in textiles, the opening of an American South, the rich soil and frost-free weather of Georgia, Alabama and Mississippi, so well adapted to cotton culture and Eli Whitney's invention of the cotton gin.

We do know that personally in later life, Washington stopped buying and selling slaves, purchasing only an occasional slave in order to unite families. In his will, he quite imperatively provided for the freeing of his own slaves, expressly forbidding any delay in the process. As Joseph Ellis has written, "There it was, a clear statement of his personal rejection of slavery… He was, in fact, the only politically prominent member of the Virginia dynasty to act on Jefferson's famous words in the Declaration of Independence by freeing his own slaves."

It may be well to conclude this section by again citing the words of his successor as president, John Adams, who was not always the most generous of men in assessing his contemporaries. An elderly and annoyed Adams mused about mankind, so often duped by its leaders but still willing to trust in mere assertions of probity and integrity. He "quoted ... a Renaissance pope; 'If the good people wish to be deceived, let them be deceived'... Then he added, 'Washington, however, did not deceive them.'"

15. Executive Ability

In this category President Washington is tied with Abraham Lincoln for first place, a ranking with which it is difficult to argue.

As we saw with Eisenhower, General Washington's military experience was an effective preparation for the presidency. In fact, in the early stages of his presidency it would be true to say that between 1775 and 1783 he had overseen larger, if not more complex, operations than he did in 1789 or 1790.

Once again it would seem that his physical and psychological presence formed an important positive factor in his executive style. Familiarity, as well as reputation, was also significant. Two members of the cabinet had served as members of his military family during the revolution. Hamilton served as his key aide and Knox as Washington's chief artillery commander. Each knew him well and was intrinsically compatible with him. Attorney General Randolph had acted as his attorney on a number of occasions. Washington had served in the House of Burgesses and the Continental Congress with Jefferson, and his letters attempting to persuade Jefferson to enter the cabinet were very flattering.

Certainly, within the group as both a public figure and a personality, he must have been thoroughly dominant. From his military experiences and perhaps from his management of Mount Vernon, particularly during the Revolution when he managed the estate by correspondence, he had learned the art of delegation and used it effectively.

Early in the first administration, he seems to have sought to present an impression of almost presiding over rather than directing the administration. Thus, when Congress was debating the issues of funding and assumption he maintained a discreet silence. Hamilton battled furiously, but – publicly, at least – the President did not.

In foreign policy, much more clearly the bailiwick of the executive branch, he was more direct and more overt. There were those who questioned whether the President had the right to announce neutrality by proclamation. If Congress had to declare war, did it not have a role in determining peace policy? He was, however, determined not to allow the country to be drawn into the European War. Similarly with the Citizen Genet affair, while solicitous of Jefferson's admiration for French egalitarianism, Washington could only be pushed so far. Fortunately, Jefferson arrived at the notion that Genet was not worth the trouble he caused, and his recall was demanded.

Hamilton certainly became the most influential member of the cabinet. It is clear, however, that it was an earned influence, not merely affection. Hamilton's energy and genius at economic planning and his ability at improvisation spoke to the most urgent needs of the nation and of the administration. It is highly unlikely that Washington ever lost sight of the fact that it was economic and fiscal failure that had brought down the government under the Articles of Confederation. That fact alone, without the brilliance and careful creation and analytical defense of his economic plans, would probably have been enough to guarantee Hamilton's primacy in any cabinet. It also remains true, however, that Washington's thoughts were more often compatible with those of Hamilton than those of Jefferson.

Finally, in this truncated summary, we should mention his energy and drive as well as his imagination. During his first administration he toured all of the states of the Union. First he went to the northern states and then, in a second tour to the southern states. Thus, President Washington, who surely symbolized the nation more at that time than the flag did, went out and showed himself to the people almost as a modern candidate would do. He was not, of course, selling himself, but the new government. As the nation debated laws and policies, the people could also see the man who represented the national struggle and attainment. As they celebrated the hero, perhaps those on the losing ends of policy debates were somewhat mollified.

Where the location of his stops on the tour warranted, he was careful to provide anecdotes from his revolutionary military travels that linked him to the locale. Given the state of the roads, accommodations and infrastructure, as they then existed, these tours demanded not only energy but stamina and determination as well.

His skills as planner and director were displayed almost serially as the new government began to function. The first item on the agenda was the provision of income for the government. Next came the drafting and transmission to the states of the Bill of Rights, which fulfilled an implicit promise made to the anti-Federalists during the debates over ratification. Ultimately, well before the end of Washington's first term, Hamilton's economic plan established a sound foundation for the national economy, and the abstraction the Constitution had been in April of 1789 had been shaped into a functioning, responsive government.

16. Foreign Policy Accomplishments

The foreign policy problems of the United States faced peculiar complications raised by the American settlements west of the Alleghany Mountains. north of the Ohio River, the development of settlement was being impeded by recalcitrant Indian tribes who were encouraged by British traders working out of the old British posts, which should have been abandoned under the terms of the Treaty of Paris of 1783.

The southwest frontier found Spain, rather than Britain, as the principal impediment to settlement and development. Thriving settlements existed already in Kentucky and Tennessee. They would enter the union in 1792 and 1796 respectively. Spanish colonial authorities controlled much of the lower Mississippi River and the port of New Orleans. The agricultural commodities of the southwestern American settlers were too bulky to be transported back over the mountains to the east. They needed the use of the river and of New Orleans to market their crops. Spain, fearful of a possible American invasion of Florida/Louisiana, hoped to keep the Americans weak by denying them access to markets. Spain also sought to persuade the frontier people of the trans-Appalachian West to agree to submit to Spanish colonial control by allowing them to retain the Protestant religion and offering attractive terms for land ownership. Bribes also were offered to American officials.

These problems formed a constant background to the diplomatic activity of the United States as Europe began to explode. As we have seen, at the time of Washington's inauguration the United States faced a contemptuous world. If the United States appointed a minister to London or Paris or Madrid, the government of the nation involved could afford to completely ignore that official. In commercial affairs, there was never a need to make a treaty with the United States. The government under the Articles lacked the authority to create or collect customs or to grant favored status to one nation over another. All such real power had been retained by the states. If Boston hoped to gain favorable terms with English goods by threatening a discriminatory tariff the goods would simply be shipped to Rhode Island or Connecticut and later smuggled into Massachusetts.

Once the new government was in place with uniform tariff laws, and particularly once the Hamiltonian program was created, officials of the United States could speak with authority. Under the circumstances, European capitals now found it advisable to attend to voices representing the United States.

Even as Washington was inaugurated, France was embarking on that series of events which, lasting for a quarter of a century, would encompass the French Revolution and the Napoleonic Era. By 1793 these events led to a general European war, which would include an Anglo-French War, which, in its turn, would, with the exception of two brief periods, encompass the years from 1793-1815. One result would be to catch the United States, as a principal neutral carrier, in a vise between the plans and designs of two great powers.

This would involve the nation in difficulties with France and Britain regarding "neutral rights on the high seas." In addition to questions of what goods neutrals might carry, from where to where and under threat of what penalties, Great Britain also added the question of the "impressment of seamen" to the mix.

For George Washington it was a settled principle that the United States in its circumstances at the time could not afford a war with a great power, and that a war with Great Britain would be suicidal. Britain was not only a great power. She also was, as a result of the import duties paid on British goods entering the American ports, the major source of revenue for the new government.

By 1794, he had sent Chief Justice John Jay to England to attempt to settle the issues between the two nations. Unfortunately for Jay, Hamilton's indiscreet comments to the British minister badly undermined his position. Jay was to deal with Britain's continued occupation of the northwest posts, to end the impressment of seamen, to get Britain to accede to the United States' definition of neutral rights on the high seas and to open British trade, particularly with the British West Indies, to American shipping.

The result was the Jay Treaty. It was a bad treaty from the American perspective, except that it prevented war. Trade with the West Indies, the prize for American commercial interests, was made possible, but only on unacceptable terms. Trade with the British East Indies, of only marginal interest, was made available on favorable terms, as was trade with the British Isles. Neutral rights and impressments, which initially were to be the justification for the treaty, were ignored. Influenced, at least in part by General Wayne's victory at Fallen Timbers, the British did agree to withdraw from the northwest posts. Washington reluctantly submitted the treaty to the Senate for ratification only because it avoided war. The Senate ratified the treaty with Washington's influence exercising a significant role.

Wildly unpopular in commercial ports, the treaty was popular in the Northwest. There, coupled with the Battle of Fallen Timbers and the Treaty of Greenville, its impact was to open the territory north of the Ohio River to settlement. The area thereafter boomed.

The Jay Treaty also provided the U.S. with a dividend via the law of unintended consequences. The Spanish thought the treaty must be a sign of a Anglo-American bargain, for which Spain's North American possessions might be the target and the western Americans the weapon. The Spanish foreign minister approached the American minister, Thomas Pinckney, and proposed what became the Treaty of San Lorenzo. Spain agreed to the American definition of the boundary between the United States and Florida, the right of American citizens to ship their goods down the Mississippi River to New Orleans and granted the right of deposit in New Orleans for those goods. Spain had decided it was wise to appease the Americans.

Almost simultaneously the major problems of the Northwest and Southwest Territories of the United States were resolved. Both would enjoy more than a decade of untrammeled development.

17. Leadership Ability

Washington is ranked first in this category, in a tie with Franklin D. Roosevelt. The ABC's of leadership are not obscure, but neither are they spelled out in a manual. Once again, as a man of the 18th Century, General Washington and the Americans of his day marched to a different drummer than did most of his successors.

George Washington is the only American who has ever received the unanimous vote of the Electoral College. He did so in 1788, and he did so again, after his first term, in 1792. No scholar, to our knowledge, has ever suggested that had he sought a third term in 1796 he would have been denied. Usually, in fact, he is praised for what is seen as an act of self-denial by his voluntary surrender of power.

It also seems clear that by his ability to transcend region, a task Jefferson and Madison found difficult or impossible, he helped bring unity to the nation, just as he helped establish its national economic foundation. The quest for unity was not a mere result. It was an outcome actively sought, as witnessed by his tour of all the states during his first administration.

He also, as he left office, urged what might be called an isolationist tradition in foreign policy on the nation. That is, the recommendation in the Farewell Address to avoid entangling alliances. It can be suggested that such a policy proved generally wise, at least until after the first third of the 20th Century.

His careful use of geographic patronage enabled him to bring into positions of power men of talent, surely, but men of talent carefully selected to assure each part of the nation that its interests would not be overlooked. For most of his time in office, as we have tried to illustrate, he was forced to wrestle with the issues of war and peace, and their impact on American prosperity forced upon him by the French Revolution and the events subsequent to it. The response to each issue was always measured, though not necessarily always elegant. The stated policy aim, however – peace to permit the nation to grow and prosper, strengthen and develop – was invariably achieved in a climate of some dignity. Washington's dignified, even aloof, demeanor seemed often to hide the degree of drive and energy he brought to his administration and to his style of leadership.

Finally, we note that it seems unlikely that any other President coped so successfully with such a beleaguered economy in such a brief period of time.

18. Intelligence

The professors have ranked Washington as 13th among his peers, below William McKinley and Jimmy Carter.

It seems strange that a man who could take command of and organize an army in the field from scratch, lead it on active service for eight years, provide for technical and logistical support, virtually singlehandedly run his own intelligence service and deftly maneuver between his enemies in arms and his enemies in politics, would not appear brighter to the respondents. Particularly so, when the same man six years later would take the paper charter of the Constitution of the United States and create from it a working government – a government that would quickly solve the financial crisis that had ruined its predecessor.

If Hamilton and Jefferson were, at least for a few years, prepared to sublimate their own ambitions in service to such a figure, one might assume that, whatever else might be said, he was not without substantial acumen.

We suggest that this ranking may perhaps be based primarily on credentialing – on Washington's lack of formal education. Perhaps his lack of any higher degree of education may have weighed against him. It is an issue that certainly plays a legitimate role in the question, but perhaps not quite as large a role as we think it may have here.

19. Avoid Crucial Mistakes

Given the difficulties that Washington confronted – the economy, the foreign policy issues growing out of the French Revolution and the subsequent wars and the hostility of the northwestern tribes – it seems obvious that had crucial mistakes been made the history of the United States would have been dramatically different. Indeed, there might not have been such a history.

Our respondents seem to have recognized that reality, since once again this is one of the five categories in which he is ranked above all other

Presidents.

20. Present Overall View

While Washington may, indeed, have been "first in the hearts of his countrymen" in 1799, as Light Horse Harry Lee described him, in the SRI poll the respondents' current overall view in 2002 placed him third.

Chapter 5 - John Adams – March 4, 1797-March 4, 1801

"I pray heaven to bestow the best of blessings on this house and all that shall hereafter inhabit. May none but honest and wise men ever rule under this roof."
– Prayer of John Adams, written on the first morning he occupied the White House. (David McCullogh, John Adams, p. 551)

"Facts are stubborn things, and whatever may be our wishes, our inclinations or the dictates of our passions, they cannot alter the state of facts and evidence."
– John Adams to the jury in the so-called Boston Massacre trial. (David McCullogh, John Adams, p. 68)

John Adams is the second President in this triad. Of the six Presidents we are examining, he is the only one who has not been ranked in the top 10. His overall rank was twelfth. He is also the only one of this group to serve only one term. He is one of the three who served as vice president before assuming the presidency. He was the first President to serve in Washington, D.C. and to occupy the White House – or the President's House, as it was then called.

When he boarded the stagecoach to leave Washington on a March morning in 1801, the day of Jefferson's inauguration, he was writing an end to a virtually unbroken string of service that went back to his tenure in the First Continental Congress – or even a decade earlier to his prominent role in Massachusetts' opposition to the Stamp Act of 1765. It would seem that few had served as long and as continuously. None served longer. Nor had anyone served as long at such distances. He had been on one sort of diplomatic mission for the new nation in Europe for most of the decade between 1778 and 1788.

With the arrival of a new century, John Adams departed from center stage and leading roles in American history.

1. Background (family, education, experience)

In this category, Adams is ranked third overall, within the top 10 per cent. We believe this owed much to his strengths in education and experience, rather than to family. John Adams' father was a farmer, a shoemaker and a church deacon. He had married above his station. Mrs. Adams was a Boylston. For his time and social station, John Adams was very well educated. Born in Braintree, MA in 1735, when he graduated from Harvard College in 1755 he was ranked 15th in a class of 24. At that time, however, class rank was not based on academic achievement but on social standing. In that context, Adams ranked in the bottom half of his class. In academic standing he was one of the top three. He taught school for a few years while he pondered his future. Deciding not to become a minister, he turned to the law and was admitted to the bar in 1758.

He quickly proved to be a successful attorney. In the fall of 1764 he married Abigail Smith. Their marriage would prove to be one of the great American love stories.

As his practice and reputation grew, more and more of his time was spent in Boston. Finally he found it necessary to move the practice from Braintree to Boston. Whether this relocation was also connected to his gravitation toward that political group, which included his cousin Samuel Adams, that would come to be known as the Whig or Patriot party seems unclear. In 1765, he wrote and published A Dissertation on the Canon and Feudal Law, an essay that stipulated that the rights of the colonists – that liberty itself – was not a gift of statute or government but a right derived from God. It was an entitlement, not a privilege.

Later that year, he drafted the so-called "Braintree Instructions" requiring that the Braintree delegate to the colonial assembly uphold the principle of "no taxation without representation" in the face of the Stamp Act.

In 1770, though a rising star among the Whigs in Boston, he risked his popularity in the wake of the Boston Massacre by agreeing to defend those British soldiers and their commander who had fired on a protesting mob, killing five. Seven months later, the captain was acquitted. Of the eight enlisted soldiers tried, six were acquitted and two found guilty of manslaughter. As punishment they were branded on their thumbs.

The case seems almost typical of Adams. A rising leader, he had gained substantial popularity a year earlier as he defended four seamen being tried for the murder of a British officer who had tried to impress them into the Royal Navy. They, too, were acquitted. However, in 1770, almost instinctively, he risked his popularity by taking the Boston Massacre case because he thought it proper to see that the accused had competent counsel.

By then, Adams was clearly recognized as a Whig leader. That summer (1770) the Boston Town Meeting elected him to the colonial assembly. In the calm between political storms, his law practice flourished.

After the Boston Tea Party, December, 1773, and Parliament's passage of the punitive "Intolerable Acts" in the spring of 1774, he was chosen as one of the Massachusetts delegates to the First Continental Congress, which met in Philadelphia. For all practical purposes, he would be in the business of the American Revolution and/or the nation for the next 26 years. Perhaps no one but Washington would be so continuously in service, and even Washington got to stand down from 1783-1787.

Adams returned to Philadelphia in 1775 for the Second Continental Congress and subsequent sessions until his departure for France and diplomatic duties. In that period, he played a leading, perhaps the leading, role in Congress. It was he who would nominate George Washington as commander-in-chief of the Continental Army. It was Adams who was perceived to be, if not the dominant figure of the radical faction in the Congress, its first among equals. He served on no fewer than two dozen committees of the Congress, including the Board of War and Ordnance – which, in essence, functioned as an 18th Century legislative department of defense. Here, he came closest to executive service before his presidency. In 1776, bolstered by Tom Paine's Common Sense and by events, he was one of the most prominent proponents of American independence. At the end, the motion for independence was moved by Richard Henry Lee of Virginia and seconded by John Adams.

He also served on the Committee to draft a declaration of independence and, it is said, was the member most insistent that Thomas Jefferson draft the document. When, later in 1776, a delegation was sent to New York to meet with the Howe brothers, (Admiral Richard and General William, representing Great Britain), to discuss reconciliation, Adams was again chosen as a member of that committee with Benjamin Franklin and Edmund Rutledge of South Carolina. There were few significant committees of the Continental Congress between 1774 and 1777 that could not count John Adams among their number. It should, however, also be remembered that virtually all committees had at least one Massachusetts delegate assigned. Since the Howe brothers lacked authority to do anything other than accept colonial submission and grant pardons to some, but not others, the meeting came to nothing. Notably, John Adams was not among those whom the Howes' were authorized to pardon.

In the fall of 1776 the Congress sent Silas Deane of Connecticut as an envoy to France to seek an alliance. Later, they appointed Benjamin Franklin and

Thomas Jefferson as commissioners to join Deane. When Jefferson proved reluctant to serve, Arthur Lee of Virginia was appointed in his stead.

After a brief return to Braintree and Abigail, Adams returned to the 1777 session of Congress. It was poorly attended in the wake of the defeats suffered in New York in 1776, and despite Washington's victories at Trenton and Princeton. Even Thomas Jefferson failed to appear, to Adams' great chagrin.

In November of 1777, Adams left Philadelphia for home, intending to refuse re-election and remain there. Later that month he learned that Congress would appoint him as a commissioner to France in the place of Silas Deane, who had been recalled. Adams decided to accept the appointment and to take his son, John Quincy Adams, then 10 years old, with him. They sailed in February of 1778 from Massachusetts. It is probably impossible today to understand how hazardous a winter crossing of the Atlantic was in the 18th Century, never mind such a crossing in the face of a hostile British navy. With one brief exception, Adams would remain in Europe for the next decade.

By the time Adams arrived in Paris, the alliance, spurred on by the American victory over English General John Burgoyne at Saratoga, had already been concluded, and he found little opportunity for significant activity. He did, it would seem, bring a modicum of administrative order to the affairs of the commissioners. He worked on financial accounts, extracting fiscal details from French suppliers, preparing reports for the Continental Congress and addressing himself to such issues as the disposition of prize ships taken by American privateers and issues regarding American prisoners of war.

In early 1779, the commissioners found themselves unemployed since Congress had appointed Franklin as minister plenipotentiary to France. Arthur Lee was sent to Madrid to seek Spanish assistance. No instructions were sent for Adams. He and John Quincy took ship for home and reached Massachusetts in early August.

In less than a month, he had been elected Braintree's representative to the Massachusetts Constitutional Convention and took his seat, at Cambridge, on September 1st. He was completely in his element there and appears to have largely drafted the Massachusetts constitution in under a month. The delegates had printed copies by the end of October. Often amended in the ensuing 230 years, it is the oldest functioning constitution in the world.

The ink on the constitution of the commonwealth was barely dry when Adams was informed that the Congress had chosen him as minister plenipotentiary to negotiate a treaty of peace with Great Britain as well as a commercial treaty. Adams again accepted, and – once again with John

Quincy and John Quincy's younger brother, Charles, in tow – sailed for Europe. They arrived on the Continent in December of 1779 and reached Paris in February of 1780.

In Paris, Adams proved to be an annoyance to the French foreign minister, Charles Gravier, the Comte de Vergennes, who liked his American diplomats more pliable than Adams. By August of 1780, Franklin wrote to Congress that Adams had given offense to the French. Vergennes certainly would have welcomed his recall. Under the circumstances, Adams left France for Holland to try to secure aid from the Netherlands for the United States.

This was a bold and purely independent act on Adams' part. He had no credentials in Holland and no diplomatic standing until the following year, when he was authorized to seek loans from the Dutch for the support of the Revolution. Adams threw himself into the study of Dutch culture, history and language and into the cultivation of friendship with influential Dutch citizens. In addition, he went to work and produced a virtual cornucopia of pro-American propaganda.

In the spring of 1781, in violation of all contemporary diplomatic standards, Adams addressed himself directly to the Dutch government, suggesting the wisdom of an alliance between the two republics. He carefully ensured that his formal letter was widely published and circulated in the Dutch and other European press. Then, he awaited events.

While he waited, Vergennes made every effort to secure Adams' recall. French influence and, in all likelihood, bribery, moved Congress, but not enough. Adams' plenipotentiary powers were revoked and a new commission of five members was appointed. They were Franklin and Adams, already in Europe, and John Jay of New York, also in Europe, in Spain. The other two were Henry Laurens of North Carolina, who had been captured en route to Europe and was confined to a British cell, and Thomas Jefferson, who, once again, declined to serve, leaving only three. Congress also had decreed, as Vergennes wished, that the commissioners were to agree to nothing that France had not approved.

In October of 1781 General Charles Cornwallis had surrendered the British Army at Yorktown to General Washington. When news of the capitulation reached Europe, Adams seized the moment and called upon the Dutch government for a response to his spring letter proposing recognition of the independence of the United States. He publicly called upon citizens of the Netherlands to make known their opinions on the matter. On April 19, 1782 (the seventh anniversary of the Battles of Lexington and Concord), Holland recognized the United States and John Adams as its representative. In June, he negotiated a loan of five million guilders, then about $2 million, and in October, he signed a treaty of commerce between the two nations. The preceding month, he had received a letter from John Jay, by then in Paris, telling him that the British were prepared to negotiate and urging him to get to Paris as quickly as possible.

Now the commissioners began to disobey their instructions. Jay and Adams both insisted, without regard to French views, that the recognition of the independence of the United States was not negotiable. It was, rather, to be a necessary precondition for negotiations. Franklin, while he was more willing to accommodate the French, ultimately agreed. All three men decided to negotiate with Britain while ignoring the wishes of the French government and in complete defiance of congressional instruction. The Americans persuaded the British to cede to the United States all lands lying between the Allegheny Mountains and the Mississippi River and to cede navigation rights on the river. British demands for compensation for loyalist losses during the war simply were to be passed on to the individual states for their consideration. Adams was successful in his strenuous arguments for the protection of the rights of American fishermen off the Grand Banks.

The reality was that the commissioners had made a separate peace treaty with the British, disregarding not only their instructions from Congress but the terms of the treaty of alliance as well. Vergennes would have to grin and bear it as best he could. The final draft of the treaty was signed at Paris in September of 1783. The three men had acquitted themselves well and acted in the best interests of their country. Few diplomatic acts in American history so clearly have been successful.

At war's end Adams was appointed as commissioner to negotiate a commercial treaty with Britain. Jefferson, who had now agreed to come to Paris to replace Franklin, was reunited with his friend Adams. Their friendship would be rendered even more enjoyable when Abigail joined John in London. From 1785 to 1788 he was the United States minister to the Court of St. James. Upon his return to the United States he was elected as vice president under George Washington (1789-1797) and then served as President from 1797-1801.

If we arbitrarily date his revolutionary service as beginning with the Stamp Act in 1765, we can stipulate that he served his country from the time he was 29 for 36 years, until he left the presidency at age 65 in 1801. He served as a revolutionary agitator and propagandist, as a legislator and a proponent of independence. He had been in fact, in Jefferson's phrase, "the colossus of independence." He was a quasi-administrator and executive on the Board of War and of Ordnance, a political philosopher, a diplomat and vice president. Few men would ever approach the executive chair with as broad and as varied a background and as much experience as did John Adams.

2. Party Leadership (political)

Like Washington, Adams' relation to elective politics was unique. When he became President the outlines of a party system were in the process of emerging but were not yet clear. The fact that Jefferson, his presidential opponent, was now his vice president would seem to aptly symbolize the political confusion of the time. So, too, would the almost visceral dislike of Alexander Hamilton for Adams; and vice versa. Both are probably correctly described as Federalists, but even before Adams' election Hamilton had tried to undercut him by trying to manage the Electoral College vote to elect not Adams but the Federalist vice presidential candidate, Charles Cotesworth Pinckney, leaving Adams (presumptively) to another vice presidential term. It is, indeed, an interesting question as to whether Adams could have been elected at all without ill-advised French depredations on American shipping in protest of the Jay Treaty and the Neutrality Proclamation and the equally poor decision to allow the outgoing French minister to the United States to work directly for Jefferson's election.

As President, Adams would confront Jefferson and Madison and the emerging Republican Party on the one hand and Hamilton and his Federalist faction, often called "High Federalists," on the other. Given the complexities created, it is hardly surprising that our phalanx of experts has given him a rank of 30th in this area.

The difficulties of Washington's second term, stemming from the Wars of the French Revolution, left sensitive issues for Adams. The French government believed that the United States had not lived up to its obligations to France stemming from the 1778 Treaty of Alliance between the two nations. The official American position was that obligations existed between governments, not between geographic entities, and that due to the French Revolution the treaties no longer existed. The French rejected this position and felt it necessary to retaliate against the United States. The Americans, of course, were angered by the French seizure of American flagged vessels. Initially, Adams had general Federalist support because he and Hamilton were in agreement that a war with France was not in the best interests of the United States.

By way of illustrating its disapproval of American policy, France ostentatiously heaped honors on the head of James Monroe, the outgoing American minister to France, who, like his leader, Jefferson, was a Francophile. Furthermore, France refused to recognize the minister appointed by Adams, C. C. Pinckney, and ordered him out of the country. This contemptuous treatment led a number of Federalists to propose breaking diplomatic relations with France.

Thus began the confrontation with France that would dominate policy and political activity during Adams' term as President. Diplomacy, issues of war and peace and domestic issues – dominated perhaps by the Alien and Sedition Acts, which were themselves responses to the foreign policy issues of the Franco-American problem – would bedevil Adams to the end of his term.

Since these problems loom so large that they virtually define Adams presidency, they figure prominently in the rankings awarded Adams by our academic experts in a number of categories. It seems appropriate then, for clarity's sake to outline them here. The foreign policy issue might be defined in this fashion.

A. Adams assumes the presidency with France angry as a result of American policy under Washington. The Directory (the term applied to the French form of government from1795-99) regarded American ratification of the Jay Treaty as a violation of the 1778 Treaty of Alliance between France and the United States. France also believed that American policy after 1794 favored Britain against France, despite Washington's Neutrality Proclamation. Under the circumstances, The Directory authorized the seizure of American ships suspected of trading with the English. To stress its position, the outgoing minister to France, James Monroe, who was a pro-French Jeffersonian, was lavishly entertained and heaped with honors, while the new American minister was ordered out of the country. This was a violation of protocol and a direct diplomatic insult.

B. When President Adams became aware that his appointee, C.C.Pinckney, had been ousted and was in exile in Holland, he almost simultaneously was made aware that the French Navy was seizing American vessels in the Caribbean and that The Directory had made a public announcement that American shipping was subject to seizure. A crisis seemed to confront the country. There was considerable speculation about the possibility of war, though the Jeffersonian faction (the Republicans) would surely oppose such a measure. Adams called for a special session of Congress in mid-May of 1797.

C. When Adams addressed the Congress on May 16th he and Hamilton still were in agreement that war should be avoided. He spoke of the offense given to the United States by French conduct but also of favoring efforts at conciliation. To that end he recommended that Congress take measures to strengthen the defense establishment while diplomatic efforts sought a negotiated settlement. Federalists applauded while Republicans decried his suggestions as overly belligerent and hostile to France. Adams at that point, appointed John Marshall of Virginia and Elbridge Gerry of Massachusetts to join C.C. Pinckney to form a commission to seek negotiations with France. By the time they sailed, more than 300 American vessels had been seized by the French.

D. At this time in world history, "seas rolled and months passed" before events taking place in Europe could possibly be known in the United States. Thus, nearly a year had passed before Adams reported to Congress, in March of 1798, that the commission had failed and that the country would need to look further to its defenses. One result of this was to be the creation of a new, separate, department of the navy, with Benjamin Stoddert of Maryland as its first Secretary.

Possibly to avoid inflaming public opinion, the President sent no details to the Congress, merely a relatively bald statement of results. Republicans, defenders of the French, now became convinced that Adams was withholding information which would put The Directory in a better light or, alternatively disclose some error or scandal in the Adams administration's conduct of diplomacy. The Republicans therefore demanded that all papers that had any bearing on the mission be made available to Congress. The commission, the documents disclosed, after being received in a half-hearted manner was then approached by three officials of the French foreign office (redacted to X, Y and Z) who were demanding bribes as a precondition for negotiations.

National reaction to the disclosures proved to be an anti-French rage and a rallying cry, "millions for defense but not one cent for tribute" was born. Congress also repealed the French treaties of 1778, and the United States Navy was ordered to patrol south into the Caribbean in defense of American shipping. This led to an undeclared naval war (the Quasi War) that would last until 1800. The small American Navy acquitted itself well and proved formidable in ship-to-ship combat.

E. Congress also authorized the expansion of the American army to 10,000 men. Washington was called out of retirement to take command. Washington's preference and politics necessitated the appointment of Alexander Hamilton as second-in-command. Adams who believed that Hamilton had Napoleonic ambitions, was unhappy with this arrangement but worked to insure that the army (which he felt would never be necessary) would never reach the level authorized.

When negotiations in France collapsed, Marshall and Pinckney had returned to the United States, but Gerry had remained in France. Since he was the only Republican on the commission, the "High Federalists" saw this action as treason, or nearly so. Even Adams, who had been the one to insist on the appointment of his old colleague from the Continental Congress to the commission, was momentarily taken aback. Then word reached him that Gerry had remained only to avoid a complete rupture and that France understood that war with the United States was not in her best interest.

In early 1799, on the strength of assurances he had received from Europe that France was prepared to receive an American envoy with appropriate civility, Adams acted. Suddenly, and without prior notification, the President sent to the Senate the nomination of William Vans Murray of Maryland as minister to France. He was then the minister to Holland and had been in frequent contact with Talleyrand, the French foreign minister. There was objection to Murray, mostly from Federalists, but he had done much to lay the groundwork for the new reality. Adams finessed the matter by keeping Murray but also by creating a new commission. Murray would be joined by the chief justice, Oliver Ellsworth, and by Governor W. R. Davie of North Carolina.

F. The final result, In September of 1800, was the Treaty of Montefontaine. The Quasi-War would end, France agreed to the abrogation of the treaties of 1798 and commerce between the two nations was restored. The United States agreed not to seek damages for French seizures. It signified a diplomatic triumph for the United States, and a dozen more years of peace and prosperity for the United States.

After Adams reported the failure of the Marshall, Gerry and Pinckney commission effort to Congress the Republicans had hints that something had gone wrong. Hoping to embarrass Adams and the Federalists, they demanded a full report on all communications from the commission. The "High Federalists," laughing up their sleeves in all probability, supported the Republican position. Adams decided to acquiesce. The Republicans had overplayed their hand. Full disclosure led to public anger and demands for war with France. Adams, who had no desire for war, took advantage of the mood and asked Congress to provide funds to improve the nation's defenses. He rejected or temporized on demands for war but readily accepted appropriations, particularly for the navy. It was at this time that a separate department of the navy was established. This initiative would stand the nation in good stead during the next two decades and fit well with Adams' long-held beliefs about the importance of naval power. Congress also appropriated funds to establish a 10,000-man army.

Talleyrand, who also did not want a war, quickly signaled that France had no desire for armed conflict. If the Americans would send another envoy, Talleyrand said, he would be appropriately welcomed. Adams was happy to respond positively. That also enabled him to outmaneuver Hamilton, who very much wished to lead that new army. Adams was determined that the army would not be needed.

By 1800, France agreed to the abrogation of the treaties of 1778 and to accept the American definition that "neutral ships make neutral goods," at least for the moment. In turn, the United States waived the right to seek indemnities for illegally seized vessels and cargo.

In this area, the most significant of his presidency, Adams succeeded in controlling the Federalist majorities in Congress, which had been increased in the 1779 elections. At least until that time, Adams had enjoyed Hamilton's cooperation.

Also associated with this period, these events and with partisan politics were the Alien and Sedition Acts, which were seen by many as war measures. The war reference is to the undeclared naval war with France (the Quasi War). Though Adams did not seek the legislation, nor urge its passage, he did not oppose it and he did sign it into law.

The acts consisted of the following:

1) The Naturalization Act of 1798, which increased from five to 14 years the period of residence necessary before one could seek naturalization;

2) The Alien Acts and the Sedition Act. There were two Alien Acts. One, often called the Alien Friends Act, empowered the President, in dealing with an alien with whose native country the United States was not at war, to expel any such alien he deemed dangerous. The Alien Enemies Act dealt with aliens with whose native state the United States was at war. It gave the President the right to order them out of the country or to imprison them.

3) Finally, the Sedition Act defined criticism of high government officials as a crime punishable by fine and imprisonment.

Clearly, the Naturalization Act, while perhaps onerous, was constitutional. The Alien Friends Act would not pass constitutional muster today. It was in any event self-limiting, as was the Sedition Act. Both had sunset clauses and were to expire before the end of the Adams administration.

Adams never enforced the Alien Acts, though the Sedition Act – clearly unconstitutional to modern eyes – did result in trials and convictions that, politically, seemed to have backfired. There was not sufficiently draconian action to quiet critics but there was enough to create political martyrs. Republicans repealed the Naturalization Act in 1802. The Sedition Act and the Alien Friends Act expired before the Republicans took power, and the Alien Enemies Act still is in effect.

Overall, while Adams is ranked quite low in this category, he seems to have been able to hold his own with Congress. This would seem to be particularly so when we contemplate the fact that his opponents for influence with

Congress included not only Hamilton, but also House leader Albert Gallatin for the Republicans and, in the deep background, Jefferson.

3. Communication Ability (speak, write)

In the upper quarter of American presidents, Adams places 10th in this category. Like most of his contemporaries, including Jefferson, the bulk of his work was political and devoted to the defense of the "rights of Englishmen," or colonial rights, during the pre-revolutionary and revolutionary period. The briefest of bibliographies would include the following:

Dissertation on the Canon and Feudal Law 1765
The Novanglus Papers 1775
Defense of the Constitutions of the United States of America 1787
Discourses on Davila 1790

All were focused on political rights and governmental forms.

He also was a formidable speaker in legislative bodies. As a result, he became one of the foremost leaders of the radical faction in the Continental Congress. His advanced position on such issues as independence brought him both friends and enemies, but made his leadership indisputable.

While he was a towering intellect, he lacked Jefferson's felicity of style and, quite properly, deferred to him as principal draftsman of the Declaration of Independence. He was an accomplished essayist and pamphleteer who fared less well when he pursued longer forms. As a communicator, Adams was certainly effective. His work was well organized and cogent. He usually was persuasive, and few disparaged the clarity of his efforts, whether written or spoken. Jefferson spoke almost reverently of Adams' oratorical skills during the culminating debates on independence in the Continental Congress.

4. Relationship With Congress

President Adams is ranked 20th in this area, just within the top 50 per cent.

He was the first President to succeed to the office, so he, like Washington, had no precedents to guide him. His relative weakness in this area undoubtedly owes something to that fact. His administration coincided with the Fifth and Sixth Congresses. In the Fifth Congress there were 106 members of the House of Representatives, with 57 Federalists and 49 Jeffersonian Republicans. The Sixth also had 106 House members, with 60 Federalists and 46 Republicans. As we have seen, Adams' political problems in dealing with Congress were complicated by the division of the Federalists into the "High Federalists" and the remainder of the party. The former were more loyal to Hamilton than to Adams.

The major political issue during the years of the Adams presidency, as we have noted, was the quarrel with France, which had grown out of the wars of the French Revolution. The origin of those problems was discussed in the second category: Party Leadership (political).

It was in this context that the commission of Marshall, Pinckney and Gerry was sent to Paris. From their treatment emerged the infamous XYZ Affair and the resultant political furor and legislation.

The significance of naval power for the United States had been near and dear to John Adams' heart since the Revolution. It was, therefore, quite logical that he took advantage of the mood and the moment to request the establishment of a separate navy department for the American defense establishment. A permanent U. S. Marine Corps also dates from this period. So, too, Congress voted to raise and fund a 10,000-man army. Adams was less enthusiastic about this, since he felt there was absolutely no danger of a French invasion. Without that, there would be no one for the new army to fight.

All were agreed that Washington would be summoned from retirement to command the army. It was however, clear that, at his age (then 66) it was unrealistic to assume he would, or could, keep the field. Hamilton very much wanted to be the second in command – which would be, actually, tantamount to command. Due to Washington's insistence, he would receive the honor, but Adams and events would keep him on a short leash. No real recruiting took place before 1799. By then much of the fervor of 1798 had died down. In the meantime, the undeclared naval war with France, the so-called "Quasi-War," proved very successful for the United States Navy. Over a two-year period American naval vessels were victorious in every action but one.

In early1799, Adams moved to re-establish good relations with France and another commission was appointed. The commission was dispatched and gently received. Negotiations proceeded, aided by the fact that Napoleon had now ousted The Directory and wanted to avoid any American complications to European problems. In September of 1800 a treaty was concluded.

Just as they had been unhappy with Adams' nomination of Murray in 1799, so too did the Federalists dislike the treaty. But, under the political circumstances, it was not possible to reject it. The Senate split the difference and gave the treaty "conditional" ratification – an interesting if dubious constitutional construction. The Republicans, who dominated the Senate of 1801, would complete the process, at least in a formal sense, by the unconditional ratification of the treaty after they came to power.

It seems logical to conclude that Adams did quite well in managing a Congress over which he held relatively little sway. For the first two years he, with Hamilton's compliance, damped down the pro-war volatility in Congress. For the next two, despite Hamilton's resistance, he utilized a combination of astute manipulation of political circumstances as well as the manipulation of men to achieve his goals.

To appropriate a sports cliché, "It may not have been pretty, but it was a win." Whether that would justify a higher ranking in this category is a matter over which we have no control.

5. Court Appointments

Among 41 American presidents, John Adams is ranked third in the quality of his judicial appointments. Coincidentally, his ranking is numerically the same as the number of the appointments he made to the Supreme Court.

Adams' first Supreme Court appointment came in December of 1798, when he sent to the Senate the name of Bushrod Washington to be associate justice. He was a Virginian and the nephew of George Washington. Adams had first offered the post to John Marshall, who had declined and suggested the younger Washington in his place. Bushrod Washington had studied law under James Wilson and, again coincidentally, it was to Wilson's seat that he was appointed. He would serve just one month short of 31 years. The second appointment came in December of 1799. That was Alfred Moore of North Carolina. Moore served just over four years before resigning and wrote only one opinion. The third, of course, was that of John Marshall of Virginia as chief justice, a position he found more agreeable than the associate justice post that he'd rejected earlier. Marshall served from the end of January of 1801, until July of 1835, longer than any other chief justice to date.

Bushrod Washington graduated from William and Mary in 1778 and was admitted to the practice of law in 1784. After military service in the latter stages of the Revolution, he was a supporter of the Constitution at the Virginia ratification convention. By 1798, his extensive political and legal background, together with the fact that no Virginian had served on the Supreme Court since 1795, led to his appointment as associate justice. He seems to have been a quite competent jurist though his virtually constant agreement with Chief Justice Marshall probably has dimmed his own luster. In the more than a quarter of a century they served together, he dissented on only three occasions. He has been commended for his judicious demeanor and behavior when functioning, as they all then did, as a circuit court judge.

A year after Bushrod Washington's appointment, Adams sent to the Senate the name of Alfred Moore of North Carolina as an associate justice. He would serve from December 10, 1799, to January 26, 1804, at which point he resigned. Moore was admitted to the bar in 1775. During the Revolutionary War he had served as an officer in both the North Carolina militia and the Continental Line. In 1782, the North Carolina legislature elected him attorney general. He later served as a Superior Court judge in 1798 and 1799, until Adams elevated him to the Supreme Court. Poor health seems to have been a problem for him throughout his tenure. That may have been the reason that he was absent while the Marbury V. Madison case was argued before the court.

There can be no doubt that the reason for Adams' excellent ranking for judicial appointments lies primarily in his nomination of John Marshall as chief justice of the Supreme Court of the United States. Marshall would lead the Court, not simply preside, from the end of January, 1801, until his death. No other chief justice has been as influential overall.

Born in 1755, he was the eldest of 15 children. Well taught at home, he was also a student at the Reverend Archibald Campbell's school, which James Monroe also attended. He served during the Revolutionary War in the Virginia militia and, from 1776-1780 was a lieutenant in the Continental Line. After his military service, he attended William and Mary. Like Jefferson (his distant cousin), Marshall read law with George Wythe. He was, like Bushrod Washington, an early member of Phi Beta Kappa. As a member of the Virginia ratifying convention in 1788, he vociferously supported the proposed constitution.

As chief justice, Marshall did much to make the Supreme Court a truly co-equal branch of government, particularly in the decision he wrote in Marbury v. Madison in 1803. There he propounded the doctrine of judicial review, stipulating the authority of the judiciary as the ultimate arbiter of constitutional law. That decision established the power of the Supreme Court (not uncontested by Presidents) to declare laws and acts and executive orders constitutional or unconstitutional. Interestingly enough, the Marshall court never again declared a federal law unconstitutional.

In McCulloch v. Maryland in 1819, the Supreme Court forbade states to enact laws it held to be in violation of the federal Constitution. This was carried further two years later in Cohens v. Virginia, which established the supremacy of federal versus state law by overruling the Virginia Supreme Court. In Gibbons v. Ogden in 1824, Marshall ruled against a New York State law granting a monopoly of commerce on the Hudson River. His ruling stipulated that the interstate commerce clause of the United States

Constitution deprived any state of authority in such areas. If the Federalist Party rapidly passed out of existence after the election of 1800, John Marshall saw to it that the Federalist concepts, particularly that of the supremacy of the national government as opposed to states' rights, did not.

6. Handling of the U. S. Economy

The result of our polling in this category places Adams 11th among the Presidents, just outside the top 25 per cent. In truth, of course, the concept of a presidential administration trying to manage the economy was more than a century away.

Adams did assume office with advantages that Washington had not possessed. The Hamiltonian financial program was well entrenched and under full sail. The government had adequate revenues, and its credit was good. The Land Ordinance of 1785 and the Northwest Ordinance of 1787 had pointed the way west for farmers and frontiersmen, though the new century would be well underway before an adequate system of federal land distribution would be in place. The Jay Treaty, the defeat of the northwest Indian tribes and the Treaty of Greenville did open the Northwest Territory, at least to squatters and irregular settlement. The Pinckney Treaty fulfilled an equivalent role for the Southwest Territory. The wars of the French Revolution created foreign policy problems for the new nation and for the new administration, but they also offered economic opportunities for its citizens.

Wartime disruptions of normal European patterns of distribution and consumption tended to increase the value of American commodities. Belligerent blockades appeared to offer bonanzas to neutral carriers. The practices were dangerous, but if blockaders and decrees could be eluded the practices also were highly lucrative. Many of America's foreign policy difficulties of the next two decades grew out of those perceived opportunities. Taken all in all, the four years of the Adams administration offered considerable stimulus for economic development and little in the way of economic hardship.

7. Luck

Our respondents gave Adams a rank of 29th in this category.

Entering into this assessment, we believe, was the fact that he succeeded George Washington. If, as we have said, Washington was blessed with a rather majestic personal presence – size, demeanor, athleticism and so forth – he also was bolstered by his image as a hero. Adams, too, had played a major role in the creation of the United States and the founding of its governments, but no one was likely to refer to him as the Father of His Country. Washington was elected President twice by the unanimous vote of the Electoral College. Adams won an electoral majority of three votes. The Jeffersonian faction would, not infrequently, mock him by referring to that vote. Whether such mockery had any influence on the electorate, it surely bothered John Adams.

During his first administration at least, Washington often was deferred to, even by those like Jefferson, who disagreed with the President. Adams not only had the enmity of his overt political rivals, the Jeffersonian Republicans, but also the highly dubious and unreliable loyalty of Hamilton and the High Federalists.

The hostility of the French government centered on Adams, whose presidential ambitions in 1796 France had opposed. Adams, of course, had little to do with the formation of Washington's policies. The hostility, however, would prove a complicating factor in the conduct of foreign policy during his presidency.

The vice presidency of Jefferson, soon to be rendered anachronistic by the ratification of the 22nd Amendment to the Constitution, deprived Adams of the type of loyalty that he, himself, had shown George Washington during the eight years of his vice presidency.

Adams also was hindered by his own personality. While a man of great honor and integrity, he was capable of anger and could prove petty and petulant. When he allowed that aspect of his personality to take control, he was quite capable of injuring his own interests and weakening his own causes by presenting a virtual caricature of himself, which his enemies often found politically useful.

His luck also was poor in that the dominant events of his presidency, American relations with France, were abysmal as a result of the French Revolution and its resultant wars. Whether one speaks of the XYZ Affair or the Alien and Sedition Acts, almost every salient action of his presidency was, in some fashion, a child of the French Revolution. In that context he had limited political leverage.

8. Ability to Compromise

Here, at 34th, we find John Adams' lowest ranking.

It seems to us that this placement owes a great deal to his sometimes aggressive ego and his not infrequent willingness to disparage former colleagues and associates. If, on the other hand, we look at his handling of the major issue of his presidency, relations with France, we find a different Adams. He was sensitive to the honor and position of the United States. He was, nevertheless, willing to speak softly, to hold anger in abeyance and to offer and even reoffer the olive branch.

When, shortly after his inauguration, the French government refused to receive the American minister to France, a clear insult to the United States, the President, far from erupting into anger and acrimony, sought, and won from the Congress a three-man commission to go to France and negotiate. The immediate result was a further insult – the demand for a bribe as a precondition of negotiations; the XYZ affair.

Adams took advantage of the public outcry and hostility toward France to beef up America's defense posture spending. Otherwise, he temporized. An undeclared naval war (the Quasi War with France) satisfied the most belligerent elements of public opinion.

By early 1799, Adams having received reassurances that France was prepared to receive in good faith a new American representative, sent the necessary nomination to the Senate for confirmation. There was some congressional unhappiness. To quiet that unease, he agreed to a new commission rather than a single minister, and the movement to normalize relations went forward.

Agreement was reached in Paris in September of 1800, to general public satisfaction. Since the prospect of peace was generally well received, a reluctant Federalist Senate agreed to the treaty. It might not fulfill a textbook blueprint for compromise, but it surely seems to be one, and one essentially engineered by John Adams.

Historians, almost without exception since that day, and aware of the strong public support Adams had in the off-year elections of 1798-1799, have believed that his dogged pursuit of peace not only achieved his goal, but also probably ensured his defeat and Jefferson's victory in the election of 1800.

While not successful with his domestic internal enemies, Adams seems to have done well with conciliation and compromise in the major foreign policy problems that confronted the nation. This ranking might be perceived as rather low.

9. Willingness to Take Risks

Appearing in the top third, Adams is ranked 13th in this category. Any examination of Adams' career clearly indicates a willingness to take risks. As a young man he was a significant leader in the pre-Revolutionary movement against British authority. When the movement became truly continental, he was one of the most prominent and vociferous leaders of the independence faction in the Continental Congress. His role was so prominent that when the Howe brothers were authorized to pardon Americans willing to return to loyalty in the summer of 1776 Adams' name was conspicuously absent from the list.

During the near decade of his diplomatic efforts in Europe, 1777-1787, he also proved willing to take risks to carry out his duties. These ranged from the willingness to risk a wintertime trans-Atlantic passage to Europe in which he placed himself in the physical danger of the crossing as well as the inherent danger of circumstances. Any British naval Captain would have rejoiced at capturing him. That very fate befell Henry Laurens of South Carolina after he was appointed as an American peace commissioner. Laurens ended up in the Tower of London, the only American ever imprisoned there

In pursuit of what he conceived to be the best interests of the United States, Adams was willing to oppose the wishes of the French foreign minister, Vergennes, who sought to have him recalled. On a different level lay his virtually independent diplomacy in Holland. So, too, in the course of his presidency, he was constantly running risks, though most of these were political rather than physical. From the initial French rejection of his envoy through the XYZ affair and the Quasi War with France, he risked his popularity, such as it was, and his political capital in order to buy time for the French to perceive where their own self-interest lay. It was only near the end of his own administration that he would find vindication.

He later would say that he wished no epitaph other than, "Here lies John Adams, who took upon himself the responsibility of peace with France...."

10. Executive Appointments

Once again, we find ourselves confronted with a unique situation due to a lack of precedent. Adams was the first President ever to succeed to the office.

Confronted with a cabinet of George Washington's choosing, he elected to keep them in place. They were Timothy Pickering of Massachusetts as secretary of state; Oliver Wolcott Jr. of Connecticut as secretary of the treasury; James McHenry of Maryland as secretary of war and Charles Lee of Virginia as attorney general. Later, due to the threat of war with France, and the emphasis on naval affairs, the Department of the Navy was created, and Adams appointed Benjamin Stoddert of Maryland as the first secretary of the navy.

The decision to retain Washington's cabinet members proved to be a cardinal error. Except for Lee, they were individually and collectively adherents of Hamilton, who disdained Adams and frequently opposed his policies. Pickering, in particular, who was fiercely anti-French, would be a problem. All would serve at least until 1800. When Adams finally demanded Pickering's resignation, he refused to quit, and Adams was forced to formally dismiss him. John Marshall succeeded Pickering at the state department, and Samuel Dexter of Massachusetts first replaced McHenry as secretary of war in May of 1800, and then Wolcott at treasury from January to May of 1801. Dexter even briefly conducted some of the duties of secretary of state after Marshall became chief justice in the waning days of the Adams administration.

In any event, Adams' error was evident relatively early, and historians since have speculated as to why he endured the situation for most of his presidency. Endure it he did, however.

His ranking here, 14th, moves him just outside the top one third of presidents and we do not find that difficult to accept.

11. Overall Ability

President Adams is accorded a ranking of eighth in this area.

John Adams displayed many talents and abilities in his life and political career, from the practice of law and the defense of revolutionary ideals through the organization of illegal legislatures, to the American Revolution, and to independence. He was then sent to Europe to carry out diplomatic missions for the new nation, which he had helped to create. He also found time to act as the principal author of the Constitution of the Commonwealth of Massachusetts. After the ratification of the United States Constitution, he served as the first vice president and the second President of the United States. At that point, after just about a full generation of service to his colony, state and nation, at an age at which one could now claim Social Security benefits, he retired to his home to lead a life of study, reading, learning and correspondence until his death, 25 years later in 1826.

To all the tasks of his lifetime Adams brought a native intelligence that verged upon and probably reached brilliance. To this intelligence he added a lifelong habit of reading and study. He was not only smart but erudite. It should be noted that his reading was active. It was his habit, biographers have noted, to annotate the books he read, often agreeing or disagreeing with the author in marginal notes.

He was not, physically, a large man, but seems to have possessed a great deal of stamina and a willingness to work through minor illnesses, pain and discomfort. As President such problems would plague him.

He could be disparaging about the achievements of others, particularly if they seemed to threaten to obscure or eclipse his own. On the other hand, he seems never to have allowed his vanity to interfere with his duty. If it was politically astute to have a delegate from Virginia move the motion for independence, then John Adams of Massachusetts would cheerfully second the motion. Certainly we know that in the Continental Congress, through 1776, he was a determined, vigorous and effective champion of independence.

His disposition to friends was exemplary. Even if they espoused a different side of a major issue, he would strive to retain the personal friendship in the face of the political or ideological break. It is particularly notable that he was quick to forgive an injury – though not, perhaps, with Hamilton. When Benjamin Rush sought in later years to restore communication between the estranged friends, Adams and Jefferson, it is worth noting that it was Adams who took the first step, though a reasonable case can be made that he was "more sinned against than sinning." The ability to forgive is a useful virtue in politics and in life.

Adams was honest and frank. He did not find it necessary to share every thought or every recollection of a slight, but it was not difficult to know where he stood on issues he regarded significant. He was usually wise, though he was also, on occasion, erratic. It does, though, seem correct to say that wisdom was usually dominant unless he was convinced that further argument was futile. It seems that only in those circumstances was he erratic or guilty of obviously overly emotional behavior.

In short, he brought a highly developed intelligence to the service of his country, driven by duty and honesty. He would sacrifice his comfort and even his affection for his beloved Abigail to the moral obligations imposed by position or responsibility.

12. Imagination

The responses here have given Adams a ranking of 12th place. Certainly, Adams has never been considered a particularly imaginative man. The type of soaring imagination that scholars discern in his younger contemporaries, Hamilton and Jefferson, has not been seen in Adams by historians.

Perhaps in his great love for Abigail he most closely approached imaginative heights. In their correspondence, she was always Diana and he, Lysander. Perhaps too, in his reading he gave rein to his imagination. While certainly learned in the classics and political philosophy, particularly Cicero and the law, he was also an aficionado of Shakespeare and Cervantes, and very fond of poetry.

In another sense, we might suggest that Adams – and, indeed, all the Founders – was quite imaginative. After all, in a period of 20 years, in a world of monarchies, they created a republic. In a world of colonial powers and obedient colonies, they would stage and win the first modern, colonial revolution.

Adams seems to have understood that waging that struggle, the fury of redefining the world, imposed burdens that at least temporarily imposed crucial limitations.

He would write, "I must study politics and war that my sons may have liberty to study mathematics and philosophy. My sons ought to study mathematics and philosophy, geography, natural history, naval architecture, navigation, commerce and agriculture in order to give their children a right to study paintings, poetry, music, architecture, statuary, tapestry and porcelain."

The statement itself betrays substantial imagination coupled with Adams' strong sense of duty and responsibility, which were among his most conspicuous character traits.

13. Domestic Accomplishments

Adams is ranked 19th in this category.

Assuredly, a major reason for his relatively low score in this category rests in the events of 1797 to late 1800, which forced Adams to maintain a laser-like intensity on foreign policy, in particular on relations with the French. In effect, little time or energy was left for new initiatives in domestic affairs. Since the nation, at the time, was prosperous and at peace, there were no outcries for greater activity by the federal government, which was not then perceived as the government.

However, it is equally true that those actions and events, captured in the phrase "The Alien and Sedition Acts," weigh more heavily against Adams in our time than in his own. Those events were primarily a response to foreign policy issues. There is a certain irony in our perception of them in a domestic context.

During the summer of the second year of the Adams' presidency, amidst the furor of the XYZ Affair and the vociferous incantation of warlike slogans – and the start of the undeclared naval war with France – the Federalist-controlled Congress passed a series of measures historically known as the Alien and Sedition Acts. Clearly, the acts had a dual function. One was to deal with possible espionage or sabotage or at least the threat of incidents arising from French enmity. The second purpose was to diminish the electoral threat of the Jeffersonian Republicans.

To Adams' credit, we would again note that none were proposed by him, nor did he lend support to their passage. On the other hand, neither did he oppose their passage nor hesitate to sign them into law. Adams clearly saw them as war measures, and their passage occurred along with bills for naval expenditures and the creation of the department of the Navy.

They were, in part, a Federalist response to their fears of French and Irish immigrants entering the United States. They were also a response to radical pamphleteers, many of whom were radical immigrants whose writings tended to glorify Jeffersonian Republicans and to attack the dominant Federalists. Since the immigrants seemed to be pro-Republican and Jefferson supporters, the question was how might such activity be curbed? How might Federalist fears be allayed?

Ultimately there were four acts. Three would focus on aliens, the fourth on sedition. Each act fell short of what had been proposed by the more extreme Federalist sponsors.

It is customary to begin by first addressing the Naturalization Act of mid-June, 1798. Original efforts to prevent the foreign-born from ever voting or holding office were voted down, despite Federalist majorities in Congress. The version ultimately enacted merely increased the period of residence necessary for citizenship from five to 14 years. Even then it passed in the separate houses by only a single vote in each. While seen as churlish, it clearly was constitutional. With the arrival of the Jefferson administration and Republican majorities, the five-year residency requirement would be reestablished.

On June 25th Congress passed the first of the Alien Acts, which is sometimes called the Alien Friends Act. This act dealt with resident aliens with whose nation of origin the United States was not at war. It stipulated that the president might expel any such alien he determined to be a danger to the United States. No reason was required and no hearing was necessary. Though this was less extreme than the original proposal, it was, in modern terms, clearly unconstitutional. A "sunset" clause was included in the legislation. It was to expire in 1800, and it did so. Five more years would pass before, in the case of Marbury v. Madison, the Supreme Court would assert the right of judicial review. In the interim, both Madison and Jefferson would assert, respectively and in varying degrees in the Virginia and Kentucky resolutions, the right of a state to nullify an act of Congress. Jefferson's Kentucky Resolution, the more radical of the two, called for states to declare abhorrent federal legislation null and void within the boundaries of the state. Such arguments would be turned to good use by southern radicals in decades yet to come.

The Alien Enemies Act dealt with resident aliens who had emigrated from a nation with which the United States was at war. Passed in early July of 1798, it was satisfactory to all concerned, Republicans as well as Federalists. The act empowered the President, in time of war, to designate such aliens as hostile and have them arrested or deported as he deemed appropriate. Here, however, unlike the Alien Friends Act, both law enforcement and the courts were involved. In short, there was due process. Since Adams avoided war, the act was never used.

In an interesting irony, due to the French role in the hysteria that produced the acts, the Sedition Act dates from July 14, 1798, the ninth anniversary of Bastille Day and the start of the French Revolution. Succinctly put, the Sedition Act made it a high misdemeanor to engage in any conspiracy to oppose the legal measures of government or to prevent their execution. Penalties might range up to $5,000 and five years imprisonment. A lesser offense, a misdemeanor, would result from publishing any false or malicious story directed against the President or Congress. That offense carried a penalty of $2,000 and two years in prison. Like the Alien Friends Act, it too contained a sunset clause, expiring on March 3, 1801, the last full day of the Adams' administration.

In the case of the Sedition Act, unlike the Alien Acts, indictments were sought, charges were filed, and trials took place. Citizens, mostly newspaper editors, were convicted. As has been said, the Sedition Act did not muzzle the radical press. However, its enforcement did provide Republicans with bona fide martyrs for the election of 1800.

Making appropriate allowance for modern interpretations of the Alien and Sedition Acts, it is certainly not surprising to find that in this category Adams barely manages to stay within the upper half of American presidents.

14. Integrity

Integrity, like the categories of Court Appointments and Background, provides a strong area for President Adams. As in those categories, expert opinion ranks him third. Only Washington and Lincoln are ranked higher and, interestingly enough, he is immediately followed in that department by his son, John Quincy Adams.

Throughout his adult life John Adams would, again and again, give evidence of his character and integrity. His marriage was an example of love and fidelity. Few men have given evidence of being more devoted than Adams and yet, when duty called, he would, in response to the business of the Revolution or the nation, absent himself from home for months at a time, even for years if necessary.

As a successful young legal practitioner in the 1760s, he threw himself into the defense of the "rights of Englishmen," even rejecting an offer to be the advocate general of the Massachusetts Bay Colony Court of Admiralty, which would certainly have rewarded him handsomely.

He was self-critical, aware of and concerned with his own weaknesses. In his letters and in his diary and elsewhere, we find him taking himself to task for his vanity and irascibility.

When in France after 1777 he found himself seemingly abandoned and even ignored, if not insulted, by the Continental Congress. Nonetheless, he remained doggedly at his post, carrying out whatever tasks he could, pursuing his duty, until he was able to negotiate both a treaty and a loan with Holland. He went on then with John Jay and Benjamin Franklin to conclude a successful peace treaty with Great Britain.

From 1789 to 1797 he served as the first vice president of the United States. Though often ignored, he invariably supported President Washington when called upon to cast his vote in the Senate.

As President, surrounded by men who were members of his administration but minions of his political enemies, he persistently and courageously pursued a policy designed to prevent a war with France and to present a peace with honor to his country. In a time of confusion and political flux, his devotion, commitment and intelligence enabled him to achieve his objectives, even though such success probably cost him whatever chance of reelection he might have had.

There certainly can be no questions about his integrity.

15. Executive Ability

In 14th place, Adams, once again, lies just outside the upper third.

Without doubt, Adams brought intelligence, even brilliance to the presidency. He also brought to the office a great deal of experience in foreign policy and diplomacy. He did not bring with him any direct executive experience. Some claims might be made for his early experiences on the Board of War and Ordnance of the Continental Congress, and, perhaps even some vicarious experience based on his eight years as Washington's vice president. The latter claim would certainly be open to question, since he was not really a member of the inner circle of the Washington administration.

On the other hand, he also brought to the presidency a high degree of vanity, a tendency to be dismissive of the talents of his contemporaries and a cantankerousness that often made it difficult for colleagues and collaborators to cooperate with him. His disposition, erratic and often irascible, was not aided by a series of physical and emotional problems that ranged from the loss of teeth and frequent oral pain to illness and the ailments and fatigues of age. In these years, too, President Adams was forced to confront the fact that his daughter, Abigail, had married a weak man whose failures were virtually irremediable. Emotionally, this was heartbreaking and chronologically linked to the descent of Adams' second son, Charles, into alcoholism.

Perhaps these factors played a role in Adams' seeming determination to conduct more and more of the affairs of state from home in Braintree, which had by then been renamed Quincy. Each year, he seemed to linger longer before returning to the capital. In 1799, he spent more than half the year at home. In that era, if Congress was not in session, there were few compelling reasons for the chief executive to be physically present in Washington.

With a cabinet of dubious loyalty, a vice president (Jefferson) who opposed his policies and sought to undermine him politically and in the face of machinations by Hamilton and the "High Federalists," Adams' determination to linger in Massachusetts becomes understandable. Nevertheless, it would seem likely to have strengthened the position of his enemies and to have lent greater credibility to tales of the President's eccentricities.

Despite all this, Adams remained strong enough and smart enough, aided by circumstances, to outmaneuver Hamilton, McHenry, Wolcott and Pickering, and to maintain his policy of quiet diplomacy with France and temporizing at home, which would culminate in a diplomatic triumph in 1800.

In short, we believe that our experts seem to have recognized Adams' ability, albeit at the same time weighing his deficiencies, and to have assigned to him a rating that seems to have taken into account the singular reality of his time and place, as well as his single-mindedness and talents.

16. Foreign Policy Accomplishments

Accorded a rank of 12th in this area.

In effect, just one foreign policy issue arose during Adams' term of office – relations with France.

The issues surrounding the problems between France and the United States appear to be entirely or nearly entirely the product of French policy. Indeed, the hostile outlines of French policy seem to be fully developed before Adams was in office long enough to take any foreign policy initiative. At the end of four years we find a thematic unity. That unity is the consistency of the policy of the Adams' administration. He would, at least prevent the two nations from formally going to war. He would display admirable patience in avoiding war with one of the "Great Powers" of the period and allowing the small power to have more than a decade of economic and political development before its strength would be tried. Relations between the two nations would be restored on terms honorable to the United States and, as a bonus, Adams would solidly establish the foundation of the United States Navy, a project near and dear to his heart.

Given the realities of the day, this may be another category in which an increase in his ranking might be seen as appropriate.

17. Leadership Ability

The experts who responded to our survey provide Adams with ranking of 18th in this category.

Clearly, John Adams was a leader of exceptional skills. Equally clearly, he does not rank at or very near the apex of American Presidents. Historically, however, he cannot be denied a legitimate claim to being one of the most prominent participants of the American Revolutionary Era as well as one of, if not the, most significant leaders of the Continental Congress.

It may be that Adams' skills at persuading delegates, organizing blocs of votes, maneuvering committees, and the like, indicate that his leadership skills might have been better suited to a parliamentary form of government, rather than one led by an energetic executive. Certainly, in this context, we cannot ignore the view of Jefferson about Adams' very real role in the success of the movement for independence. His acknowledged leadership of the Board of War and Ordinance in the Continental Congress testifies not only to the confidence of his colleagues but to his capabilities and talents as well. It does not, however, speak directly to executive ability or skills.

Leadership weaknesses may be perceived in his presidency, perhaps particularly in his lengthy absences from the capital, ranging up to half a year away at a time. On the other hand, Congress in that age was rarely in session.

His continuance of Washington's cabinet and his retention of them for most of his presidency clearly indicate a major error. In his defense, it may be said that Adams was treading virgin ground. No one had ever been in this circumstance before, or ever would be again. It is an interesting point that historians have rarely dwelt at length upon the question as to whether or not Pickering, Wolcott and McHenry might have owed Adams an ethical duty to either support him or resign. Still, retaining them was not a sign of leadership particularly since he allowed the situation to go uncorrected for so long.

His foreign policy manipulations, however, did show leadership. And there, take it as we will, he does seem to have outmaneuvered Jefferson, Hamilton, most of his own cabinet and the largest portion of the Congress, not to mention the French.

18. Intelligence

Ranked sixth in intelligence, Adams falls within the top 15 per cent of

American Presidents. We might note, parenthetically, that his son, John Quincy Adams is ranked third.

By all standard measures, John Adams was possessed of an acute intellect. We have noted elsewhere his academic class rank at Harvard among the top three. His reading ranged widely from the Greek and Roman classics to the most contemporary works of his time. He may have been contemptuous of Rousseau, but he had read him and knew the work of which he was so dismissive. He read both Latin and Greek and, when he was sent to France, he immediately turned his attention to the study of the language, as he would do again in Holland.

His historical circumstances tended to confirm the dominance of law and government and the underlying philosophical texts in his reading, but he also ranged widely over religion and other, more worldly, topics. He knew the works of the Enlightenment authors. David McCullough's excellent biography of Adams notes that among the moderns – which is to say, his general contemporaries – his tastes were eclectic and included Adam Smith, Condorcet, Rousseau, Mary Wollstonecraft Shelley and Joseph Priestly. The need to know would seem to be a driving force. He was not impressed by Rousseau, but was aware he needed to be familiar with his work.

His correspondence with Jefferson, Benjamin Rush and others, in the waning years of their lives, still shows us a lively intellect and a questing, and questioning mind. Adams was prepared to plumb every topic. In their correspondence, for example, it is clear that there were topics Jefferson preferred to eschew. There seem to have been no barriers for Adams. All topics were open.

He was, at least in a parliamentary setting, a brilliant organizer and a man who, by force of thought and argument, could sway men to accept his conclusions. A study of Adams during the first three meetings of the Continental Congresses would seem to illustrate a master at work.

By virtually all of the standard measures we use to evaluate or assess the quality of an intellect at the remove of two centuries or so, it seems necessary to accept John Adams as brilliant. It would seem impossible to rank him any lower than our respondents have done.

19. Avoid Critical Mistakes

Here we find President Adams in 15th place. He is ranked just ahead of Madison and just behind presidents Cleveland and McKinley, who are tied at 13th.

Clearly in terms of foreign policy Adams did avoid critical mistakes. If then, the ranking is based on mistakes in domestic policy, we will, we think

140

necessarily, need to assume that it stems from the Alien and Sedition Acts.

We think it proper to assume that if Adams had initiated, sponsored or vigorously espoused the acts, their net negative effect would have been greater. We would also assume that his reluctance to enforce the alien acts probably produced a mitigating factor which, while it took him out of the upper third of the Presidents in this category, did not take him very far out.

We also would suggest that some respondents may have seen some signs of political weakness in maintaining Washington's cabinet members. That decision, they may have concluded, constituted a critical mistake in the area of politics rather than policy, but which, nevertheless, severely weakened his administration.

20. Present Overall View
John Adams is tied with Dwight Eisenhower, in ninth place, in the rankings for present overall view.

Chapter 6 - Thomas Jefferson – March 4, 1801 – March 4, 1809

"We hold these truths to be self-evident, that all men are created equal, that they are endowed by their Creator with certain unalienable Rights, that among these are Life, Liberty and the Pursuit of Happiness ...."
– Thomas Jefferson, The Declaration of Independence

As Thomas Jefferson was to be the third President of the United States, so, also, he is the third member of this group and also the third of the six men we have examined to have served as vice president of the United States.

The fact that he was the principal author of the Declaration of Independence provides him with a considerable claim to the initial expression of the ideological basis of the American nation.

An interesting footnote to his role among American Presidents may lie in the fact that he is the first opposition leader to win the office – that is, he was not just the first non-Federalist president, but he represents the peaceful succession of the opposition to power. He is the first president of the 19th Century, and he is the first President to begin his term in the new national capital, Washington, D. C.

He is, then, at least externally, as he liked to think of himself, a President of new beginnings. Having stipulated that, let us turn to our examination of Thomas Jefferson.

1. Background (family, education, experience)

The experts who responded to our 2002 survey ranked Jefferson second in background. Only John Quincy Adams surpassed him. Certainly, among this group of Presidents, his family background in terms of wealth and social position is ranked superior to those of Washington and Adams. It is also substantially superior to those of Truman and Eisenhower. Of the six men we examine in these two groups, only Franklin Roosevelt, whom our experts rank fifth, can even begin to contend with the position our respondents have accorded Jefferson.

Like Adams, Jefferson's father had married above his station. His mother, Jane Randolph Jefferson, was a member of the planter elite. Her status entitled him to a place, albeit not a prominent one, among the mythical First Families of Virginia. His father, Peter Jefferson, had done well as a surveyor and mapmaker, and Jefferson was born to a family well-endowed with land and slaves. As was customary, the family owned a number of farms, or plantations, each with enough slaves to till it. He would always have 75 to 100 slaves at his home plantation, Monticello.

He was born at Shadwell, in Virginia, in April of 1743. As is well known, he died at Monticello, July 4th, 1826, the 50th anniversary of the Declaration of Independence, the same day that John Adams died.

Peter Jefferson prized education. In the absence of any system of public education in Virginia, Mr. Jefferson, like many other planters, provided a tutor for young Jefferson's education at home. At 9, Thomas was placed in a local private school. The future President was 14 when his father died, and his guardians entrusted his education to the Reverend James Maury for two years. Disliking Maury, Jefferson, at 17 in 1760, persuaded his guardians to allow him to matriculate at William and Mary College. There he happily and diligently pursued his studies. He seems to have been an exceptional student. After that, he read law with George Wythe, one of Virginia's best lawyers and a lifelong role model for Jefferson. He was admitted to the bar in 1767 and proved to be an adept and effective attorney. In 1769, he was elected to the Virginia House of Burgesses. The next decade would see him occupied almost constantly with service in one or more legislatures, either with the Continental Congress in Philadelphia or, primarily, in the Virginia House of Burgesses.

It is clear that in pre-Revolutionary Virginia, Jefferson was a persistent, if quiet, member of the radical wing of the Burgesses. When, for example, the royal governor had adjourned or dismissed that body and it met privately as a rump session Jefferson usually was included. He was certainly involved in the establishment of a permanent Virginia Committee of Correspondence to keep in touch with similar committees in other colonies, and thus enabled to maintain continuous contact with other revolutionary thinkers.

It was during this period, in 1774, that he drafted the document known as A Summary View of the Rights of British North America. Intended as a possible set of instructions for the Virginia delegation to the First Continental Congress, to which he had not been selected, it was not adopted. However, it did come to be published. It is usually celebrated as one of the earliest examples of the complete denial of any power of the British Parliament over the American colonies. Colonial rights, Jefferson averred, were natural rights derived from nature or from the Creator but not from men – a view he and John Adams shared. The widespread dissemination that followed its publication made an early contribution to Jefferson's reputation outside Virginia as both a patriot and an effective literary stylist.

As the meeting of the Second Continental Congress approached, Virginia chose seven delegates. Jefferson came in eighth, probably because of his youth. He had just entered his 30s and had served as a Burgess for only six years. When Peyton Randolph returned to Virginia to serve in the House of Burgesses Jefferson was sent to Philadelphia as his replacement.

War broke out at Lexington and Concord in April. When the Congress decided that a public defense of the colonists and their actions was needed, Jefferson was chosen to serve on the committee. It should be noted that political reality virtually demanded that a Virginian as well as a Massachusetts representative serve on all major committees. His contribution to the resultant product, The Declaration of the Causes and Necessities of Taking Up Arms, 1775, was really that of principal draftsman. The result, amended in deference to John Dickinson and other more moderate members, was somewhat more restrained than the Summary View. But, as was true of the Summary View, the Declaration of Causes can also be seen as prefiguring in philosophy, organization and rhetoric the Declaration of Independence, which would be his next composition and, indeed, his magnum opus.

The publication in January of 1776 of Tom Paine's Common Sense, plus the reality of the war and the actions of King George III and Parliament, provided a political tipping point. Thus, as spring came, so came a spate of political actions, all tending toward the independence of the colonies. The formal motion for independence was introduced in June of 1776 by the Virginia delegation. On July 2nd Congress voted to declare independence. A committee to draft a justification for the action already had been appointed. It included John Adams, Benjamin Franklin and Thomas Jefferson. Debated for two days and nights, the draft was adopted on July 4th. Although Adams and Franklin certainly had offered advice and proposed changes, the declaration clearly was Jefferson's creation. It was he who writhed under the criticisms and additions, corrections and deletions from the floor, which, most historians believe, actually strengthened the document. In any event, Thomas Jefferson had produced the first and arguably the most important of the great state papers of the United States.

He has been subject to criticism because, some would say, there is little or no originality in the document. Such criticisms ignore or misunderstand the purpose of the document, the object of the exercise. It was designed to persuade. So it begins with an introduction, couched in language that assumes a "right of revolution" and suggests that when the right was exercised it was necessary to prove that it was justly undertaken. It then expatiates on the philosophical rationale for the right of revolution. George III's right to wear his crown was based on the events of the "Glorious Revolution," (1688-1689), which paved the way for a significant growth of parliamentary power in England. Jefferson's philosophical justification has its deepest roots in John Locke's defense of precisely that revolution. It therefore was difficult, even for the king and his ministers, to argue against Jefferson's point. In short, it was standard Whig doctrine of the period to which most Englishmen and colonists adhered. It was accepted political doctrine.

For most of Jefferson's contemporary readers and auditors, the crux of the argument then lay not in the so-called philosophical portions of the piece that so engage the modern reader, but in the statement of charges forming the larger portion of the work. The crux of the contemporary argument then lies in the acts of commission and omission of which the king is accused. Justification is to be found in that long list of assertions, most of which begin with the words, "he has ... ." The purpose was to prove, and to Jefferson and his colleagues they did prove, that an objective review did, in fact, justify the idea that "... a long list of abuses and usurpations ... evinces a design to reduce [the colonies] under absolute Despotism [then] it is their right, it is their duty to throw off such a government ... ."

Oddly enough, the declaration was virtually Jefferson's last service to the Revolution at the national level until nearly the end of the war. By September of 1776 he had returned to Virginia, where he functioned as a legislator and reformer from 1776 to 1779 and then as governor until 1781.

In Virginia he labored as a political reformer. He worked hard to bring an end to primogeniture and entail, forms of property holding that tended to the benefit of the established families by maintaining and strengthening their hold on their property. That, in turn, acted to preserve the political power of the aristocracy, of which he was, of course, a member. He also worked to end the establishment of religion in Virginia and sought to broaden the electoral franchise by proposing that men who were unable to satisfy the property qualification for voting be given 50 acres by the state, which would enable them to qualify as voters.

Jefferson's terms as governor took place under difficult circumstances. He faced two invasions of the state, one under Benedict Arnold and the second under Lord Cornwallis. He was hampered in his responses to Virginia's problems because the executive, as was common under revolutionary constitutions, had little power. In an ironic twist, Jefferson's own proposals for executive authority in post-colonial Virginia would have resulted in even greater weakness. His own idealism insisted that without coercion the citizens would step forward to defend the state. He therefore had no preparations in hand when crises arose and he found that his expectations were not matched by reality. All in all, his executive experience proved to be the nadir of his political life, with the possible exception of the last year or so of his presidency.

It would be disingenuous if we failed to address the question of slavery. Thomas Jefferson, on occasion, could wax lyrical about liberty as the natural condition of mankind. He was known to suggest that slavery was wrong and was bad for the master as well as the slave. Despite that, he never proposed an end to the institution. He was a Virginia aristocrat whose property and lavish lifestyle depended on slavery.

He maintained that he could not afford to free his slaves because of his indebtedness. He freed only five slaves throughout his long life. It appears, however, that much of that indebtedness was due to a lifestyle in which he denied himself absolutely nothing. Virtually every author who has written significantly about Jefferson in the last 20 or 30 years has at least mentioned the 40 crates of furnishings, wines, and so on that he brought back from France with him in 1789. Thereafter, when, as secretary of state he set up housekeeping first in New York and then in Philadelphia, he not only provided expensive furnishings for the homes he rented but also undertook extensive renovations upon them. Nor should we forget to mention that Monticello was under virtually constant renovation at no little expense, even though slave labor allowed for considerable economies.

If Jefferson's attitudes and actions as a slave owner had to be encapsulated briefly, the words ambivalence and insensitivity would spring to mind. Certainly, his mature actions on the subject do not compare well, for example, with those of George Washington.

By June of 1783, he was back in Philadelphia as one of the Virginia delegation to the Confederation Congress. His last term of legislative service was not, however, to be without distinction. Indeed, in some ways, his leadership in this period was to be more distinguished than his earlier service. By the time he returned, the Confederation Congress was far from its zenith. It frequently was unable to even muster a quorum. There were, for example, extensive delays in pulling together the nine state delegations necessary to conduct business, even to ratify the peace treaty with Great Britain. The quality of individual members had also deteriorated. Under these adverse circumstances, Jefferson labored diligently and effectively.

In this period, he is best remembered for his work on the Ordinance of 1784 which, though never effectuated, was the precursor to the Land

Ordinance of 1785 and the Northwest Ordinance of 1787. The Ordinance of 1784 was an ordinance of governance that proposed that all new states created by the United States be admitted to the Union on an equal footing with the original 13. In 1784, this was not an unusual position, but it was one Jefferson had proposed in Virginia almost a decade earlier. It also proposed, as would the Northwest Ordinance, territorial government developing through evolutionary stages, with greater degrees of self-government at each stage. It also proposed that slavery be prohibited in the territories after 1800. All of these, at least perhaps because of Jefferson's interest or initiatives, would appear in the Northwest Ordinance of 1787, though the prohibition of slavery then would apply only to the territories north of the Ohio River.

In 1784 he was appointed to diplomatic service in Europe. This time, he accepted. For a period of about nine months, he, John Adams and Benjamin Franklin were all in Paris together. After that, John Adams went to London as the first American minister to the Court of St. James, while Jefferson replaced Franklin in Paris.

Given the lack of authority held by the Confederation Congress, European governments could ignore American diplomatic representatives with impunity. As a result, American diplomats in the period (1784-1789) showed little return on investment. Jefferson found France charming and became a lover of the nation and its people. He returned to the United States just as the French Revolution was beginning. He saw its potential as both beneficial and dangerous, but, on the whole, leaned markedly to the optimistic side.

As he left France, he seems to have anticipated returning to resume his diplomatic duties. However, after he arrived home, he was persuaded to join the Washington administration as the first secretary of state.

His experience during Washington's first term, particularly the antipathy he developed in regard to Secretary of the Treasury Alexander Hamilton, led him into opposition to administration policies and to all things Federalist. Quite quickly, opposition seemed to rally around him, leading to the emergence of what was to become the Republican Party, the predecessor of the modern Democratic Party.

When Washington refused to seek a third term, Jefferson was John Adams' opponent in the race for President in 1796. Due to a then constitutional anomaly – the original constitution required that the second place vote-getter in the electoral college become vice president – he emerged as Adams' vice president. It was directly from that office in 1800 that he was to be elected President. We should probably mention here that he was the first American to be elected President as a result of the "Three Fifths Compromise." That is, under that Constitutional formula, slaves were counted as three-fifths of a person for purposes of representation and taxation. While not allowed to vote, 60 per cent of their number in the census was counted. That number boosted the number of members of the House of Representatives and presidential electors allowed each slave state. The electors thus provided proved to be a factor in Jefferson's electoral margin in the election of 1800.

Like his immediate predecessor, John Adams, President Jefferson brought to the presidency considerable legislative experience, more at the state level than Adams, less at the national level. He also brought diplomatic experience. Unlike Adams, he had executive experience as both governor of Virginia and secretary of state. Some controversy might surround each of the latter, but undoubtedly they constituted experience.

2. Party Leadership (political)

Jefferson, who is ranked third among our presidents in party leadership, professed to abhor the very idea of political parties, as did most of the Founders. He once fervently said that if he could not go to heaven without a political party he would not go. Yet, in one of the paradoxes so characteristic of his life, he is not only highly regarded as a political leader by our experts but is also seen by many as the founder of what became the modern Democratic party.

We saw in our overview of the Washington administration that two discrete phenomena launched the first American party system. In chronological order they were the French Revolution of 1789 and the Hamiltonian economic system – funding, assumption and the Bank of the United States. Within the cabinet, Jefferson found himself on the wrong side on both issues. He distinctly favored France in its quarrels with Britain, while Hamilton and Washington thought Britain was too essential to American security and prosperity to be alienated. Despite Washington's best efforts this fundamental difference would never be solved.

On Hamilton's financial recommendations, particularly "Assumption," Jefferson and Madison had particular, even parochial, problems as Virginians, and those problems tended to be conflated with broader, more ideological issues. They saw them as conflicts between republican virtues (Jefferson) on one hand versus aristocratic, even monarchical corruption (Hamilton), on the other. Jefferson and Madison agreed to a log roll in which they bargained Republican votes in the House of Representatives in favor of both funding and assumption. In exchange, they received Hamilton's promise to provide Federalist votes in the House of Representatives for permanently locating the national capital on the Potomac River – plus a substantial monetary payment to Virginia. Suspicion remained, however. Indeed, it was not long before Jefferson persuaded himself that, somehow, Hamilton had run a confidence scheme on him and Madison. Few, other than Jefferson, have found the suspicion convincing.

By the time Jefferson resigned as secretary of state in December of 1793, he was already identified with the emergence of an opposition party, then called the Republican Party. Posterity, however, might suggest an earlier date, May, 1791, not much more than a year after he had entered the cabinet. That year, with Congress in recess, Jefferson and Madison went north into New York, the home state of Alexander Hamilton. Both men would maintain that it was just a simple "botanizing" expedition – and, indeed, they traveled up the Hudson Valley as far north as Lake George. Some cynical historians, however, have noted that their paths also took them into conversations with Robert R. Livingston and Aaron Burr and other well-known political opponents of Hamilton. Indeed, some have suggested this trip was the distant origin of the long-time alliance between northern urban political bosses and the Southern Barons, which would be the mainstay of the Democratic Party's electoral strength into the 1960s.

Jefferson's 1794 return to Monticello and his plantation brought refuge in the bosom of his family and his plans for the ongoing rebuilding of Monticello, scientific and agricultural activities and, undoubtedly, for a man who hated confrontation, surcease of stress. But it did not preclude or even seriously impede his return to public life in time for the presidential election of 1796. That was the first contested election in American history, and the first party-oriented election as well. John Adams would represent the Federalists, who were far from unanimous in their support for him. Jefferson would be the champion of the Republicans. Jefferson did, indeed, protest his lack of interest, and Madison did provide him with a rationale as to why he must run. A cursory view, however, does not suggest that vehement arguments were necessary.

Adams' election elevated Jefferson, who ran a close second, to the vice presidency. While he congratulated Adams, their old friendship had begun to deteriorate, and Jefferson began to absent himself from Philadelphia, then the second temporary capital. Through that period, he cemented his political alliances by extensive correspondence as well as by the use of surrogates. Jefferson, probably due to his dislike of direct disagreement, was prone to the use of trusted deputies to forward his ideas and arguments. So too, as had been customary in the early days of revolutionary argumentation, many polemics on all sides of an issue were published anonymously under assumed names or classical allusions, Indeed, from 1791 to 1793, Jefferson had hired Philip Freneau, a Princeton classmate of Madison's, as a state department clerk in a not very subtle effort to subsidize a newspaper, The National Gazette, which often had savaged the policies of the Washington administration, of which Jefferson was at least a titular member.

But even as Republicans blackguarded Federalists as aristocrats and would-be monarchists, and Federalists belabored Republicans as radicals who lusted to set up "Madame La Guillotine" in the squares of Boston, Baltimore, and other cities and towns, neither side recognized that the western world was undergoing a sea change. The world into which John Adams and Thomas Jefferson were born was, in essence, a deferential society. Men had their designated place in it, with women in subordinate roles, and each man occupied a specific place in a hierarchical society, from bottom to top. The lower orders would, for example, knuckle their forelocks or remove their hats when in the presence of a social superior. That world was dying even as they were being born into it. Jefferson was an aristocrat and a leader. Adams, by dint of talent, education, initiative and hard work, had become a leader. Ironically, Adams would, as he aged, become something of a defender of the old order, while Jefferson became the champion of the new.

In this context, Jefferson, as a political leader, had something of a head start. The Republicans represented the newly forming society. The Jefferson who had written that "all men were created equal," (assuming they were male and Caucasian), was virtually defined as the leader of a new polity.

There seems to be a profound irony in a situation in which the men who represented the best of the old order – Washington, Adams and the like, exemplars who had created a new government, provided a stable, republican polity and a well-founded economic system – then found themselves virtually dismissed as the new order found no place for them.

The Jefferson who became President even physically illustrated the new order. In France as a diplomat, Jefferson, as seen in contemporary portraits, is quite the dandy, coiffed and groomed to perfection, more than fit to grace a Parisian salon. Portraiture showing Secretary of State Thomas Jefferson shows us a gentleman again. On the other hand, this is an American gentleman, much toned down from Jefferson in Paris. President Jefferson, receiving accredited diplomats in varying stages of dress, may have given offense to one minister or another, but he was something of a familiar and comfortable presence to the majority of his fellow countrymen. Certainly, that was his intent. Even physically, he seems to have had command of the new politics.

Perhaps the strangest element of the period lies in the fact that both sides, Federalists and Republicans, sought to prove to the world that free men were capable of governing themselves. Both seem ultimately to have believed that a society needs both liberty and order. Not even the Hamiltonian caricature that so bedeviled Jefferson would have thought to propose any form of government lacking representative forms. Rather, Federalists tended to emphasize order; Republicans, liberty.

Jefferson, aided and abetted by Madison and others, created and dominated a political party that, perhaps unconsciously, understood the newly emergent social and political reality and stood prepared literally and symbolically to lead it into the 19th Century and beyond.

3. Communication Ability (speak, write)

Once it has been stipulated that President Jefferson was the principal author of the Declaration of Independence, little remains to be said about his literary skills and talents. He was an exceptional author and propagandist who, in the Declaration, encapsulated the Whig political philosophy in a brief, cogent and eloquent two paragraphs, just about one page. In the Anglo-American world, as we have demonstrated, it was almost impossible to disagree with. George III's family had been enthroned by the English based precisely on the basis of the same philosophical points. Except for the nearly poetic quality of the prose, it was a simple, bald statement of largely agreed upon political principles. The next three pages of the text form the gist of the argument, justifying the colonies in resorting to the agreed-upon right of revolution (whether in 1688-89 or in 1775-1776) on the basis of specific grievances. They constituted proof, Jefferson was arguing, that the Americans had an obvious case for independence.

To that credential we should certainly add A Summary View of the Rights of British North America Asserted and Proved, and his large contribution to the Declaration of the Causes and Necessities of Taking Up Arms, both of which provided reasons for his prominence in 1776. Both of them also fortify the case for his reputation as a writer of strength, beauty and grace.

It is principally because of his skillful prose that our experts have ranked him fourth in this category, in the top 10 per cent, trailing only FDR, Lincoln and Theodore Roosevelt. As a speaker Jefferson seems to have been uncomfortable and disappointing.

He was always unhappy as a public speaker. It was not that he was an inept speaker, but rather that he did not like the function. Perhaps this was connected to his dread of confrontation. Thus, in avoiding or evading public speaking, he was able to avoid personal discomfort. It is notable that, as President, he abandoned the public delivery of what is now called the State of the Union address. He had a written document prepared and sent to Congress where it was read by the clerk of the House. That precedent continued until the presidency of Woodrow Wilson.

In any event, we are left with the view espoused by so many, perhaps most, scholars since 1776: the declaration constitutes the central ideas upon which the existence of the United States is based. Its author deserves the laurels for the power of the document.

4. Relationship With Congress

Once again, we find President Jefferson in fourth place, among the top 10 per cent of American Presidents. In relation to this question, perhaps the easiest and most obviously relevant fact is that he never found it necessary to exercise the veto. He is the only President ever to serve two full terms who never vetoed or pocket-vetoed any act of Congress.

An examination of the party affiliations of the House of Representatives, publicly provided by the office of the clerk of the House, helps to explain the lack of any vetoes. Jefferson's first Congress, the Seventh, shows the House with 107 members. Of those, 68, or 63 per cent, were Republicans. His last, the 10th Congress, bolstered in numbers by the Census of 1800, had 142 members in the House, with a Republican majority of more than 80 per cent, with 116 Republicans and only 26 Federalists. Margins in the Senate were not dissimilar.

Despite his ever growing majorities, the President left little to chance. When the legislature was in session it was virtually impossible for a member to avoid the President. Invitations to intimate dinners at the President's House showered down upon the members. He seems to have kept score, maintaining a sort of check list of those who had graced his table. When partisanship became too rancorous, he simply separated the parties, entertaining Republicans one night and Federalists another. Certainly good food and good wine, for both of which he was renowned, as well as good conversation, for which he was also famed, must have, to some degree, disarmed his foes and gratified his friends. Modern Presidents can only think how useful it must have been to be able to dine with all of the members of the House and Senate during one or two sessions of a Congress.

While the exercise was pragmatically useful, it also spoke to the Jeffersonian style. Joyce Appleby (in her Thomas Jefferson, 2003, p. 42) tells us that in one period of less than four months he held 47 dinners. His guests ranged from senators to diplomats and included individuals of current interest and acclaim. In any event, joined to his voluminous correspondence and the work of longtime associates and surrogates, such as James Madison and Albert Gallatin, it all illustrates the distinctive style of an early party leader who also wore the mantle of a paragon of the American Revolution.

5. Court Appointments

The Siena Research Institute's academic experts have placed Jefferson ninth in court appointments. We see no reason to disagree with at such a determination.

With regard to the Supreme Court, President Jefferson had the opportunity to nominate only three associate justices, even though the court expanded from six to seven members during his term of office. His appointees in chronological order were William Johnson, Jr. of South Carolina, who served from March of 1804 until August of 1834 and was the first Republican on the court; Henry Brockholst Livingston of New York, who served from November of 1806 till March of 1823, and then Thomas Todd, born in Virginia, appointed from Kentucky, the first member from the new Seventh Circuit, who served from March of 1807 till February of 1826.

For Jefferson, the federal judiciary in general, and the Supreme Court headed by his distant cousin, John Marshall, in particular, served as a profound annoyance. It represented Federalism entrenched in a political system which he otherwise completely dominated.

In 1803, in the wake of the Republican victory in the repeal of the Judiciary Act of 1801, Chief Justice Marshall handed Jefferson and his partisans a paltry victory and a major defeat in the case of Marbury v. Madison. Marshall denied Marbury redress but took the occasion to sternly lecture the administration as to how it ought to have behaved and, adding insult to injury, boldly used the occasion to claim and to illustrate the far greater implied power of judicial review.

When Jefferson turned to the impeachment of federal judges as an instrument to control the judiciary, the impeachment, conviction and removal of Judge John Pickering opened a specific area of controversy. Pickering was clearly incompetent, whether as a result of dementia or alcoholism. Where the vagueness of the law on impeachment would seem to some to have required thoughtful deliberation, the Republican House of Representatives shouted the measure through. Then, with barely a pause, they turned their attention to Associate Justice of the Supreme Court Samuel Chase. There were persistent rumors that after Chase was impeached and removed Chief Justice Marshall was next. The House quickly impeached Chase but, despite its Republican majority, the Senate failed to convict.

It is in light of that brief circumstance that Jefferson would have been likely to assess his own appointees. William Johnson would certainly have gratified the President. He proved to be nearly immune to Marshall's intellect, rhetoric or charm. In his three decades on the Marshall Court he was the principal dissenter, writing something approaching half of all the dissenting opinions – though even Johnson, in 1808, would criticize the President for exceeding his authority. Henry Livingston, on the other hand, proved to be more malleable and seems to have succumbed to Marshall's persuasion/ He came to accept a more aggressive, nationalist view of the Constitution. In general, scholars see him as usually in agreement with the chief justice.

Thomas Todd, after relocating to Kentucky at the end of the American Revolution, was by 1806 serving as chief judge of the state's appeals court. When, in 1807, the federal courts added a new, seventh, judicial district, and an equivalent post for an associate justice on the Supreme Court, the western states – Kentucky, Tennessee and Ohio – urged Jefferson to appoint Todd to the Supreme Court. This new seventh justice would "ride circuit" in those states, and Todd was recognized as an expert in western land law. Todd's expert knowledge would, obviously, be germane to such pleadings.

In general it seems fair to say that, while Todd wrote few opinions, he was drawn toward Marshall's views. Jefferson, then, would not have been pleased with the opinions of either Livingston or Todd.

Overall, there seem to be no significant questions of competency, but only Johnson would appear to have maintained an attitude toward the law and the Constitution that Jefferson might have found acceptable.

6. Handling of the U. S. Economy

At 14th, this is Jefferson's second lowest rating.

Unknown to most Americans, including the President, great economic changes were in the offing. Samuel Slater had opened the first cotton textile mill in the United States in 1793. Coincidentally, Eli Whitney applied for a patent on his cotton gin the same year. These unrelated events, combined with the opening of the so-called "black belt" (rich, dark alluvial soil, lots of frost-free days each year) South to the cultivation of cotton, set the stage for a combination of agricultural, commercial and industrial development, as well as for a revived life for slavery in the American South.

Within 25 years of Jefferson's inauguration, New York State would complete the Erie Canal and, shortly thereafter, railroads would begin to exert a substantial economic impact on the nation. It was, however, not much earlier that Americans, other than Alexander Hamilton, began to seriously consider the federal government as an engine of economic development, a notion that Jefferson would surely have found abhorrent.

Jefferson's election campaign had promised a simpler, more frugal federal government as well as the rapid reduction of the national debt. He moved rapidly to forward the former goal, but events, both positive and negative, conspired to prevent the latter.

His hopes to dismantle the Hamiltonian system were aborted when his secretary of the treasury, Albert Gallatin, who as a Republican spokesman in the Congress had opposed much of Hamilton's plan for the Bank of the United States, told Jefferson that the bank was necessary to the efficient functioning of the government.

The Hamiltonian excise taxes were eliminated, which made the federal government even more dependent upon revenue from customs duties. Since commerce with England generated the largest portion of that revenue, this condition would prove to significantly complicate foreign policy problems. Meantime, the nation was growing from a population of less than four million in 1790 to over five million in 1800, above seven million in 1810 and just under 10 million in 1820.

In anticipation of general westward expansion, government under the Articles of Confederation had carefully crafted land ordinances for the survey, sale and governance of the western territories of the United States. Government under the Constitution followed suit, but found itself responding to political pressure and was, fairly steadily, lowering prices and selling smaller plots of land in response to public demands.

Nevertheless, settlers frequently ignored the government. That is, they moved in, settled on the land as squatters, cleared, planted, harvested and moved on again. The net effect was another diminution of the income for which the government had hoped.

Overall, then, as Jefferson tried to move toward frugality, even the small income on which the government had planned proved to be fleeting. This created stress and, when acted upon by unplanned turbulence, would adversely affect both the administration and the economy.

Ultimately, it would be foreign policy issues that would stamp Jefferson's imprint on the economy, and that stamp would – barring the Louisiana Purchase – be a predominantly negative one. As Jefferson and Madison, like the Washington and Adams administrations before them, wrestled with the European conflict unleashed by the wars of the French Revolution and Napoleon, they initially were blessed with peace and tranquility. The Peace of Amiens, March, 1802, brought a temporary halt to the hostilities between England and France. Coupled with the Treaty of Luneville of 1801, this meant a general European peace. Unfortunately for Jefferson's plans and predilections, it would endure only until May of 1803, after which war would break out again, lasting until 1814. We might also note that it was at the end of the period of the Peace of Amiens that France found itself prepared to sell Louisiana to the United States.

With war again a reality, the Jefferson Administration found itself fending off violations of American neutral rights on the high seas by both France and England. Frustrated and believing England the greater culprit, in 1806 Jefferson had Congress pass the Non-Importation Act which called upon Britain either to end the impressment of American seamen and to accept American definitions of neutral rights or to face trade restrictions, including the complete prohibition of the importation of some British goods into the United States. The President's goal was a commercial treaty to achieve those ends. When Britain proved stubborn on the impressment issue, Jefferson refused even to submit the draft treaty, which was not wholly without merit, to the Senate.

Britain, meanwhile, tightened the noose on American trade with a series of "Orders in Council." Napoleon, in turn, kept the pressure on American trade on his side with the so-called "Berlin" and "Milan Decrees," which threatened American shipping. It seemed, indeed, that all American merchant vessels stood in peril.

For those who doubted the danger, 1807 made it evident. A ship of the United States Navy, the frigate U.S.S. Chesapeake was outbound for the Mediterranean. Within American territorial waters, she was intercepted by the more powerful British 50-gun ship-of-the-line, H.M.S. Leopard, which demanded that she heave to and allow the British to search her for British deserters. When Chesapeake's captain refused, the Leopard opened fire. Chesapeake, which was not prepared for combat, fired off a gun or two for honor's sake but was forced to submit to the indignity. Whatever might be said about impressments or "free trade and sailors' rights," this clearly was an act of war.

Jefferson was obviously unsure of what to do. The nation was not prepared for war, and such preparation would clearly mean an end to the frugal federal government to which he was pledged.

Probably harking back to the prewar era of the American Revolution, he now proposed that Congress enact an embargo. American ships were to be forbidden to sail in any European trade. Indeed, they were forbidden to sail at all, without special license. If no American ships were on the high seas, then no insult could be offered to the American flag. There could be no cause for war. The Embargo Act, passed in December of 1807, would be in effect well into the spring of 1809.

The American economy reeled. The great northern seaports saw literally tens of thousands thrown out of work – sailors, longshoremen, clerks, sail makers and many more in ancillary occupations that depended on seafarers for their living. "All told, some 30,000 American Sailors lost their jobs, as did another 100,000 workers in [related] maritime trades." The nation's commercial economy was severely disrupted. During much of the period, the President devoted his efforts, with some single mindedness, to the enforcement of the embargo.

The agrarian heartland, the largest part of the Republican Party's political base, was only marginally affected at first. The 1807 crop had gone to market before the embargo was enacted. It may be significant that it was only after the 1808 agricultural crop languished and commodity prices fell that the Republicans began to modify the nation's position.

The President would ultimately, in the waning days of his term, be forced to sign a repeal of the embargo. Significantly, it does not appear to be a choice he made of his own volition. In any event, it seems fair to suggest that the Embargo Act was probably the fastest-acting, as well as one of the most economically harmful acts, of any American administration. It appears to us that the Embargo Act has to be the primary cause of Jefferson's ranking in this category.

7. Luck

As a general proposition, it seems fair to suggest that Jefferson, who has been ranked sixth in luck, was blessed with good luck in his first term and found fortune more adverse in his second.

During the first term a brief but real cessation of European hostilities occurred. Allowing for the time it then took for word to travel, Jefferson enjoyed more than a year, perhaps a year and a half or two, of that peace. In that period, which began during his first year in office, there were no issues to confront in regard to British or French violations of neutral rights on the high seas. Coupled with the after-effects of the Jay Treaty and the Quasi-War with France, the President was able to concentrate on domestic policy to a large degree. In addition, his policy of frugality was more easily maintained when there were no foreign policy clashes.

The Louisiana Purchase also was connected to this phenomenon. Succinctly put, historians suggest that Napoleon, then first consul of France, sought to reestablish a French colonial empire in the Western Hemisphere centered on what are now Haiti and then the Louisiana Territory. To that end, under the terms of the secret Treaty of San Ildefonso in 1800, Napoleon forced Spain to cede Louisiana, including New Orleans, to France.

When Jefferson became aware of this, he was alarmed. The right to market goods out of the port of New Orleans, granted by the Pinckney Treaty, 1795, was an economic necessity for the trans-Appalachian states and territories of the United States. Controlled by a weak European power such as Spain, the Americans could afford to tolerate foreign ownership, regarding it as essentially titular. In the hands of a strong, aggressive power like France danger seemed apparent. The President ordered the American minister to France, Robert Livingston, to begin to negotiate for the purchase of the port of New Orleans. He would soon send James Monroe, as minister plenipotentiary, to assist in the process. He even drafted a letter to Livingston, probably meant to be read by the French, saying that if France continued to hold New Orleans the United States might be forced to seek out an alliance with England.

Good fortune for the Americans resolved the potential dilemma. There had been a successful slave revolt in Haiti in the 1790's. Haiti, the former French colony of Saint Domingue, was the key to Bonaparte's scheme. That colony was the major producer of sugar cane of that day, and sugar was a particularly lucrative commodity. French troops, sent to the island, failed to put down the rebellion. That failure was linked to stubborn Haitian resistance, to courageous and competent rebel leadership – particularly that of Toussaint L'Ouverture – and to the devastating effects of malaria and yellow fever on French troops. In effect, tropical diseases acted as a force multiplier for the rebels by seriously reducing both the absolute number and the combat effectiveness of the troops sent.

Napoleon also knew that the Peace of Amiens was about to come to an end and that the British Royal Navy would make an overseas empire difficult and expensive to manage or defend. Money from the Americans for the purchase of the territory would prove useful in financing any new war.

Thus it was that Livingston and Monroe were able, on April 30, 1803, to virtually double the size of the United States and make it a trans-Mississippi power, for only $15 million. The purchase encompassed some 828,000 square miles and all, or part of, what would become 15 states. When the Americans asked the French what the boundaries of the Louisiana Territory were, the reply was said to be that they had made a bargain and should "make the most of it." Jefferson was startled at the size of the acquisition and had some constitutional qualms about the legality of the action. He was, after all, a "strict constructionist." However, strict construction or loose, he was not about to allow the opportunity to pass. It was probably the single most popular act of his administration.

Jefferson's presidency represented the ascendance of the common man. As we have already illustrated, the era of deference was passing and social change, as well as the principles embodied by both the American and French Revolutions, gave the Jeffersonian political faction a genuine claim to being the first legitimate popular government.

George Washington, of course, had enjoyed great personal popularity, almost reverence, but he did not function as a popular political chief. In a society increasingly intolerant of bars to progress or disadvantages to the "lesser sort," Jefferson seemed to represent the emergent or emerging popular will. His accession to power had also marked the first peaceful transfer of power from one political faction to another in a society in which the political party process was not yet broadly established.

The end of the Peace of Amiens and the resultant international tensions – as well as specific acts such as the Chesapeake Affair, the Orders in Council and the Berlin and Milan Decrees – all brought increasing pressure on the Jefferson Administration in the second term. Jefferson faced unpleasant choices.

The administration seems to have found itself unable to conceive of alternatives to economic warfare and/or actual war. Shunning war, it turned to trade restrictions. It relied on the poorly thought out and economically disastrous Embargo of December, 1807. It basically forbade Americans to trade abroad, which crippled portions of the economy. Furthermore, it proved futile in that it failed to solve the problem it was meant to address.

The Republicans would survive, politically, with Madison elected as Jefferson's successor in 1808, though with reduced, if still significant, majorities. New England, however, hard hit by the embargo, returned to the Federalist political camp.

8. Ability to Compromise

He is ranked in ninth place here.

Clearly, with his ample and carefully nurtured congressional majorities, President Jefferson rarely faced a need to consider compromise. His behavior in the closing days of his administration, as well as his irritation when members of the Continental Congress amended his original draft of the Declaration of Independence, suggest that it was probably not his strong suit. Indeed, this ranking may be slightly on the high side.

He certainly was capable of dealing with cold, hard facts, as when Secretary Gallatin informed him that the Bank of the United States would have to be retained. He also was realistic when, in the final settlement with the Barbary Pirates, the United States, having denied ransoming captives, still paid Tripoli a $60,000 ransom for the release of the last Americans still held prisoner. In each case, a face-saving formula was devised. In the case of the Bank, the President contented himself with selling the federal government's shares in the Bank to the English financial house, Baring Brothers. In the light of Republican apprehension over foreign ownership of shares in the Bank of the United States and Andrew Jackson's later demonization of the Bank due to foreign influence, there is an interesting degree of irony in this Jeffersonian formulation. In regard to the payment to the Barbary powers in the Treaty of 1805, the administration simply "spun" the issue. The administration issued a resounding statement that in the United States, to a government "... bottomed on the will of all, the life and liberty of every individual citizen became interesting to all." Payments to the other Barbary States continued until 1816.

The best argument for his ability to compromise probably lies in the style in which he managed the meetings and deliberations of his cabinet. In those meetings, he appears to have presided rather than dictated. The meetings seem to have been a sort of open forum in which the secretaries felt free to disagree and offer additions, corrections and deletions to ideas or proposals brought before them. If to such a concept we add, as we did in the case of Franklin Roosevelt, the tendency of members of the cabinet to serve for extensive periods of time, it seems difficult not to envision amicability and compromise. It would also correlate well with the President's well known aversion to confrontation. However, the very presence of the President in those meetings cannot have been without influence.

On the other hand, if we examine the Embargo Act and its aftermath, then we might draw a less gentle picture of the President. Enacted at the President's behest in late 1807, the embargo had devastating effects upon the commercial cities of the Northeast and their hinterland. The President's popularity fell dramatically, particularly in that region. The South and West did not begin to really feel the pinch until after the 1808 agricultural crop headed to what proved to be a marginal market. It would seem that the President saw no alternative to the embargo. For whatever reasons, he refused to abandon or even to modify his position.

As tension and anger mounted, it appears that President Jefferson simply abandoned the reins of government to his successor, Secretary of State James Madison, and to Secretary of the Treasury Albert Gallatin, though he continued to urge the rigorous enforcement of the embargo. Certainly, no memories of the Kentucky Resolutions seemed to linger. (It is amusing to speculate how Jefferson would have responded if Massachusetts, for example, had sought to nullify the Embargo.) Finally, in February of 1809, the Congress, with no presidential leadership and unhappy with the 1808 election results, repealed the Embargo Act. A reluctant President signed the repeal.

Few alternatives were available, but it seems that Thomas Jefferson either could not or would not conceive of either an alternative or an amelioration of the embargo. He appears not to have even considered compromise on a matter of great importance to the nation. Rather, he seems to have acted, perhaps stubbornly, as a prisoner of circumstance or as an angry martyr.

9. Willing to Take Risks

Here, Jefferson is found in seventh place. We find the ranking somewhat on the high side, since we see the administration as essentially cautious.

On the political front, Jefferson certainly acted expansively when the preliminary negotiations to acquire New Orleans moved to include the entire Louisiana Purchase. Because of the state of communications of that era, great credit must be given to Monroe and Livingston for the initiative they displayed. On the other hand, it does not appear to have posed any risk at all. It was, politically and historically, a wonderfully popular action. Even many Federalists were loath to oppose it.

Otherwise, his political activity was primarily the effort to root out the federalism that had been the principal promise of his campaign. Even there, in areas such as patronage, he acted cautiously and deliberately. Certainly, the new broom would sweep clean, but it was neither as precipitate nor as obvious as the Jacksonians would be in the next generation. Few Americans, and probably none in the administration, were concerned that the interests of the Bank of the United States were being superseded by state banks.

In foreign affairs, too Jefferson did not seem overly aggressive except, perhaps, with the Barbary States. He did, as he had wished to do since the late 18th Century, halt all payments of "tribute" – of what we might call "protection money" – to Algiers, Morocco, Tripoli and Tunis. Washington and Adams, like the leaders of European powers, had paid to protect American trade in the Mediterranean. Angered by the new policy, the Pasha of Tripoli declared war on the United States in May of 1801. While Congress never reciprocated with a formal declaration of war, it did pass an act authorizing the use of the United States Navy to protect American commerce in the region. Naval units dispatched by the President effectively would wage a war in the region until 1805. The seizure of Derna in Tripoli, in addition to adding a line to the Marine Corps hymn, ended the war on a satisfactory, if not triumphant, note and on terms to which we have already alluded. It strikes us as a genuine stretch to suggest that the Tripolitanian War represented any sort of a real risk to the United States.

In dealing with France and Great Britain in the period after the Peace of Amiens, Jefferson, if anything, appears genuinely risk averse. Even the impressment of seamen from a United States Navy frigate in the so-called

Chesapeake Affair brought no threat, or even intimation of force against Great Britain.

To describe the Jefferson Administration as forward looking and, perhaps, ground breaking in a number of ways would seem appropriate, but we find it difficult to celebrate or censure it as a risk-taking administration.

10. Executive Appointments

In fourth place for the third time, Jefferson again appears in the top 10 per cent.

Seeing Adams' example directly in front of him, and representing an opposition party, there was little risk that he might repeat Adams' error in retaining his predecessor's cabinet. Two members did, however, in the course of the transition, serve beyond Adams' term. Samuel Dexter of Massachusetts who served Adams as both secretary of war and of the treasury served, at least technically, until May of 1801. Similarly, Benjamin Stoddert of Maryland, who had served as the first secretary of the navy, also served briefly into the Jefferson administration. No particular significance attaches to either of these anomalies.

The cabinet Jefferson seated was a distinguished one. For secretary of state he chose his long-time friend and political associate, and almost alter ego, James Madison. To the treasury department, he sent Albert Gallatin. Gallatin was a Swiss immigrant who had served in both the House and Senate, acting as a sort of Republican spokesman against Hamilton and his plans. He was one of the few Republicans at the time with reasonable credentials in the world of finance. The secretary of war designate was Henry Dearborn of Massachusetts. His revolutionary war military record was extensive. Originally a New Hampshire man, he had fought at Bunker Hill and marched with and served under Benedict Arnold on the ill-fated Quebec campaign, where he was captured at the end of 1775. Exchanged in 1777, he fought at Ticonderoga and at Saratoga. He also served at Valley Forge and fought at the Battle of Monmouth and in the Clinton-Sullivan campaign against the Iroquois. As a member of Washington's military staff, he was also present at Cornwallis' surrender at Yorktown. After the war he relocated to Maine, then a province of Massachusetts, and served two terms in the House of Representatives before being selected for the cabinet. All three men served from 1801 to 1809. Gallatin indeed served well beyond and into Madison's Administration.

Levi Lincoln, also of Massachusetts, was Jefferson's first attorney general and served from 1801-1804. John Breckinridge was the second. A Virginian by birth, he had relocated to Kentucky where he had served as attorney general and as speaker of the house. Kentucky sent him to the Senate in 1801. In 1805 Jefferson nominated him as Lincoln's replacement. He died at the end of 1806. He was, quite briefly, succeeded by Robert Smith, who was, in turn, replaced by Caesar A. Rodney of Delaware. Rodney served from 1806 until the end of the administration. Like Gallatin, Rodney remained in Madison's Cabinet until 1811.

The fifth cabinet member was Robert Smith, the secretary of the navy. Born in Pennsylvania and a graduate of Princeton, Smith had moved to Maryland to practice law. His brother, Samuel Smith, was a United States Senator from Maryland. Robert served in both the upper and lower houses of the Maryland legislature and served as a presidential elector. He was nominated and confirmed in 1801.

The President had initially thought to appoint Smith to replace Levi Lincoln as attorney general, in 1805. The plan called for the nomination of Jacob Crowninshield to replace Smith at the navy department. Crowninshield, however, ultimately declined to serve. Thereafter, after a brief period in which Smith served as both head of the navy department and attorney general, he reverted to his role as secretary of the navy until 1809, with Rodney becoming attorney general.

Secretary of State, Madison brought exemplary credentials to the office. He was a distinguished figure, both as a result of his role in the formation of the Constitutional Convention of 1787 and the pivotal role he played there. He, perhaps more than any other man, had persuaded Washington to attend and participate in the Constitutional Convention. That, of course, meant that Washington would be chosen to chair the meeting and, as a result, that his prestige would attach itself to that document. Madison also played a major role in persuading Washington both to accept the presidency and to accept a second term in office.

With the formation of the new federal government in 1789, Madison was initially Washington's closest advisor and also, in effect, what we would now call the majority leader of the House of Representatives. In that capacity, it was Madison who compiled the draft of the Bill of Rights, which the Congress sent to the states for ratification. That process was completed in 1791. By that time, he was already moving away from Washington and the Federalist camp and toward his friend, then Secretary of State Jefferson. Madison's entry into that camp and its opposition to the ideas of Secretary of the Treasury Hamilton increasingly distanced Madison from Washington.

With Jefferson, Madison also participated in the process of creating the Republican Party. In part political philosopher, he was also part political mechanic. In 1791, he and Jefferson took their famous "botanizing" expedition to New York while Congress was in recess. The botanical results seem little known, but many historians date the long-term alliance of northern, urban political leaders with the agrarian interests of the South, the long enduring strength of the Democratic party, from this expedition.

As secretary of state, Madison's purview extended to three major issues – the conflict with the Barbary States, the Louisiana Purchase and the matter of neutral rights on the high seas. The last two rose out of the tensions and wars created by the French Revolution and Napoleon Bonaparte. Madison also played a significant role in the establishment of the Embargo.

To a large degree, though they remained close collaborators, the President preferred to function as his own secretary of state. When he was the American minister to France in the 1780's, Jefferson had opposed paying tribute to the Barbary States. As President, he stopped payments to Tripoli and a four-year war ensued.

When France forced Spain to retrocede the Louisiana Territory, the port of New Orleans became a key pressure point for the United States. As things developed, events in Europe and in Haiti made the Louisiana Purchase possible. The President and the secretary of state followed up quickly, and the Louisiana Purchase was consummated.

The renewal of the European conflict after 1803, coupled with the military weakness of the United States, led to a weak response to the Chesapeake Affair, the Embargo Act and, what seemed to be predictable American economic dislocation.

In the face of strong presidential leadership, one may speak of cordial cabinet consultation, or even of the close bond between the President and the Secretary, but it is difficult to point with any surety to any strong cabinet initiatives, other than Madison's highly positive input on the idea of the embargo. The embargo seems to have originated with the department of state.

Gallatin also brought strong credentials to the treasury department. In addition to the specifics mentioned above, he had seen some limited military service with the militia in Maine during the latter stages of the Revolution. It was, however, primarily after he had left Massachusetts for Pennsylvania that he began to make his mark. In the mid-1780s he began to acquire land in western Pennsylvania, where he pursued various entrepreneurial activities. These included the early manufacture of glass near Pittsburgh. By 1800, glass would form a significant part of his fortune.

In 1795, he was elected to the House of Representatives, where he quickly became probably the most influential of all the Republican members in the area of finance. When Madison left to return to Virginia, Gallatin became the Republican leader in the House. His combination of financial knowledge and political leadership made his selection as secretary of the treasury in 1801 virtually automatic. Arguably, during Jefferson's administration he was the most significant and successful member of the cabinet.

In his new role Gallatin worked tirelessly to fulfill Jefferson's campaign goal to reduce the size and cost of the federal government and to eliminate the national debt. Unfortunately for those plans and promises, the administration also had to deal with the cost of the Tripolitanian war and the financial implications of the Louisiana Purchase. President Jefferson also complicated Gallatin's plans when he fulfilled various campaign promises by eliminating excise taxes, stamp taxes and other impositions of Hamilton's programs that he considered to be onerous. Gallatin did well, but with costs up and revenues down he faced a distinctly uphill battle.

Gallatin planned to pledge 75 per cent of the annual revenue of the United States to debt reduction. He did, seemingly miraculously, reduce the national debt from $80 million to $45 million, despite the cost of the Tripolitanian War and the Louisiana Purchase. But the economic dislocations of 1806-1809 saw the debt burgeon. By the end of the War of 1812, it had grown to more than $120 million despite the imposition of new and onerous taxes.

At the end of Jefferson's second term, Madison reappointed Gallatin to the treasury in the new administration. Gallatin served actively into 1813, technically until February of 1814. He is, to date, the longest serving secretary of the treasury in American history.

For secretary of war, President Jefferson nominated Henry Dearborn. Among his assigned responsibilities was preliminary planning for the removal of various Indian tribes to the Trans-Mississippi West. It was Jefferson's policy to keep the army small and on a very limited budget. Obviously, it was Dearborn's responsibility to implement those plans.   Jefferson seems to have believed that natural aristocrats, of whom he was one, instinctively knew how to lead. As such they were likely to be a dominant element in any army. He was less sure that they could be trusted to be loyal to the government. He seems to have harbored concerns about a possible coup d'état. He also believed that non-aristocrats could be taught leadership skills and attributes. To that end, he embraced a goal of both Washington and Hamilton, the foundation of a military academy. It was also intended to fulfill a national need for engineers. No engineering school then existed in the United States. The end result, in 1802, was legislation authorizing the United States Military Academy at West Point, N. Y. This idea, too, was Dearborn's to implement.

President Jefferson chose Levi Lincoln to be attorney general. He was a

Harvard graduate, class of 1772, and a distinguished attorney and judge. He was serving in the Congress when nominated. He was attorney general from 1801-1804, when he resigned to return to Massachusetts. At the beginning of his term, he had also filled in as secretary of state because a death in the family and personal ill health delayed Madison's arrival in Washington.

Lincoln also served as a political guide for Jefferson, particularly in regard to how his New England constituents might respond to specific ideas or initiatives broached by the administration. On occasion his brief ran beyond the Northeast. For example, when Jefferson was preparing his directions for Lewis and Clark, he instructed them to seek a Northwest Passage. It was Lincoln who pointed out that if they were so instructed, and there was no passage to be found, the result might be to subject the administration to derision. Jefferson thereupon broadened the instructions to include a search for geographic and other forms of knowledge, such as the headwaters of rivers, and flora and fauna.

Lincoln's immediate successor was John Breckinridge, who then represented Kentucky in the Senate. He served only briefly, dying before the end of 1806. The last of the President's attorneys general, was Caesar A. Rodney of Delaware. A graduate of the University of Pennsylvania, he was admitted to the practice of law in 1793. A veteran of six one-year terms in the Delaware House of Delegates, he had been personally solicited by Jefferson to challenge Representative James A. Bayard for his seat in the House of Representatives. Rodney won by 15 votes. At the next election, Bayard closely defeated Rodney. It is pleasant, in our own day, to note that the two men, despite political differences and direct, vigorous political campaigns, remained friends. Becoming attorney general in 1807, Rodney not only served out the remaining years of the Jefferson administration but, like Gallatin and Secretary of the Navy Robert Smith, would go on to serve in the Madison administration as well. He finally left office in 1811 after failing to secure a nomination to the Supreme Court.

Smith, a Marylander, did not loom large at the time of his appointment, since the President's penchant for austerity – as well as his suspicion of the Navy as an inherently "aggressive" force – tended to keep the Navy on a budget perhaps slightly more penurious than the Army's. That tendency was, of course, negated by the necessity to bolster the Navy to wage the war in the Mediterranean.

Jefferson's style was, as we have seen, somewhat collegial, though he nevertheless, expected daily, written reports from each secretary on the business of the day. He, in turn, sought to reply on the same day. It seems a highly effective means of control. Taken all in all, the cabinet seems to have been excellent. Madison and Gallatin were clearly the stars, though Madison was, perhaps, underutilized.

The overall ranking seems judicious.

11. Overall Ability

When we addressed this question in the case of Franklin Roosevelt, we asked if a President needed to be "the smartest fellow in the room" to be awarded accolades. Perhaps that question has relevance here as well because Jefferson, who ranks first in intelligence in the 2002 poll, ranks only fifth in this category.

As we have seen, Jefferson brought unusual political skills to the presidency. His abilities helped to create his party and, indeed, the nation's first party political system. His social skills did much to bind his political colleagues in the Congress to his policies. By so doing, he fostered party unity. As we have seen, he was politically ready and willing, unlike his predecessors, even to personally recruit candidates to run for individual House seats. He was able to win and hold the affection and loyalty of a confidante as intelligent and wise as Madison. And, of course, he had unusual skills as a communicator outside the area of public oratory.

His organizational skills were also formidable. His style of governance was designed to appear simple and indirect. Like Eisenhower, however, there was much more direction and activity than was apparent at first sight. When we recall his near daily contact with the members of his cabinet, the requirement of daily reports and his frequent social interaction with the members of Congress, we can begin to understand that beneath the apparent simplicity of the casually dressed President, the man of the people, there lay a carefully constructed system by which his personality, intellect and policies could be carefully impressed on those who would be his agents of implementation.

His system seems to have worked well from 1801-1808, at least. It spoke to his strengths and it minimized his weaknesses. That is, for example, he was rarely called upon to directly deal with any political opponent. Overall, Jefferson's system strengthened the political unity of his party.

He was intelligent, and diligent, though he was not as driven as Adams. He had a clear set of goals, with the extinction of Federalism high on the list. Perhaps prime among those aims was the perpetual ascendancy of an improvable and improving citizen, defined best in terms of the yeoman farmer – the independent citizen, possessed of a competency, who would bring the ideals of the American Revolution to their final fruition.

12. Imagination

Once again, we find Jefferson in the top 10 per cent, in third place in imagination, behind Presidents Lincoln and Franklin Roosevelt.

The first question to be addressed might be: What constitutes imagination? All might agree that it consists of envisioning something that, at the moment, does not exist.

Was President Jefferson in such a sense an imaginative man and/or an imaginative President? If we examine his life and career, we can probably find examples to support either side of the argument. Given his complexity, it is certainly not a simple question. It is further complicated when we consider that as a public figure performing his duties there well may have been limitations imposed upon his ability to act freely.

The work that defined Jefferson was The Declaration of Independence. It is a powerful, carefully and beautifully crafted argument for the position of the revolutionaries in 1776. However, since it is, necessarily, derivative, it is not and cannot be an imaginative creation, other than in the superb use of language. Since the American Whigs – in pursuit of the "Rights of Englishmen" at first, and later independence – sought to prove by history and political theory that they were justified and the king and Parliament in error, it is reasonably logical to contend that none of the propaganda exercises, by Jefferson or anyone else, can be held to be original or imaginative.

Proponents of Jefferson's imaginative qualities might then point to his acknowledged prowess as an architect. Critics might respond by suggesting that as an architect he seems to have been rather slavishly devoted to the Palladian school, derived from the work of Andrea Palladio, and to intimate that he was not given to either innovation or experimentation. Proponents might rapidly shift gears and suggest that his ideas in regard to the creation and outline of the University of Virginia, right down to its "academical village," would certainly argue for an active and disciplined imagination.

Even in the greatest achievement of his presidency, the Louisiana Purchase, he can be said to have been conventional or conservative. When news of the Treaty of San Ildefonso arrived, he knew he must act, but did not choose a bold initiative. He sought only to acquire the port of New Orleans to provide market access for America's western crops. It was Bonaparte, determined to end his colonial misadventure, who made the great purchase possible.

It does seem to us that in his conception of American democracy Jefferson was highly imaginative. The Federalist felt that a self-governing state with elected representatives needed the guidance of the "better sort" as a type of balance wheel. That is, that the excesses of democracy, in the Aristotelian sense, could be avoided if the well born, the educated, and the wise acted as tutors or guides. The excesses of the French Revolution undoubtedly tended to confirm such views of the dangers of democracy and intensify the worst fears of the Federalists.

Jefferson, in his ideals, always tended to trust the common man. The word is used advisedly. While Jefferson admired women, he did not believe they had a role outside the domestic sphere. Once again, we find a Jeffersonian paradox. An aristocrat himself, he tended to find his closest friends and political associates among the members of the upper class. That did not, however, shake his faith in the common man. He seems to have either rejected or ignored all contemporary fears about the dangers or excesses of runaway democracy.

That argument has never ended. It resonates at some level in virtually every American national election and shows no sign of abating, even 200-plus years later. That Jeffersonian faith, evident before the close of the 18th Century, appears to us to be the strongest argument – the foremost evidence – in support of Jefferson as imaginative.

13. Domestic Accomplishments

This is a complex category in which to judge Jefferson. His goal on entering office was to diminish the role of the national government. To do so, by definition, would be to diminish the possibility of significant domestic accomplishments. There is no reason to believe that he was anything other than sincere in those plans. Despite, or because of that, he is ranked sixth overall.

Upon taking office, he began a series of symbolic gestures designed to visibly substitute the principles of Republican simplicity for what he saw as the unnecessary pomp and circumstance of Federalist ostentation. He walked rather than rode to his inauguration. Similarly, diplomats accredited to the United States were shocked by the lack of protocol that Jefferson assumed. Even state dinners appeared to be elaborately democratic, without attention to either decorum or rank. What was referred to as "the rule of pall mall" replaced a formal order of seating, for example. To what degree such symbolic statements or actions resonated with the general population is debatable, but they were important to the President and certainly representative of the nature of Americans.

The psychology of President Jefferson, once the elegant boulevardier of late 1780s Paris, now receiving British diplomats in slippers is a thought to contemplate. But the contrast can leave no doubt that the choice of costume, and therefore the act itself, was consciously chosen. Here stood the self-declared "man of the people."

At the same time, and for the first time in three administrations, the President began to guide the actions of the legislative branch. If Washington and Adams had scrupulously avoided active presidential intervention in the legislative function, Jefferson moved as both party leader and President. In this he set enduring precedents.

Federalist remnants, of which there were few, were addressed. As we have seen, the Alien and Sedition Acts had sunset provisions for 1800 and 1801. They had ceased to exist before Jefferson became President. The Naturalization Act was repealed, and the number of years of residence prior to citizenship was, once again, set at five. By 1802, even the excise tax on whiskey had been repealed to the delight of western Pennsylvanians and other frontier residents.

In 1803, the administration celebrated the greatest of all its domestic achievements – the Louisiana Purchase. It was an achievement notable in both domestic and foreign policy.

For a variety of reasons, France was ready to abandon her efforts in the Western Hemisphere by 1803. When James Monroe and Robert Livingston proposed the acquisition of the port of New Orleans, Talleyrand, the French foreign minister, countered with the offer of all of the Louisiana Territory.

For Jefferson it must have seemed like Christmas Day. Not only was his problem with the trans-Appalachian West solved, but he believed that the purchase also, because of the huge territory involved, would guarantee the survival and prosperity of that Jeffersonian ideal, the yeoman farmer, for centuries to come.

As a proponent of strict construction of the Constitution, Jefferson had suffered some qualms. There was, after all, no specific constitutional authority for the purchase. However, time and Napoleon both were pressing, and Jefferson's qualms were not enough to delay the act. In a wonderfully Jeffersonian locution, he urged his fellow Republicans to avoid "metaphysical subtleties" and to approve the purchase. Neither the Senate nor the House seems to have had any difficulty, and the ratification of the treaty and the authorization of funds proceeded. Though the term seems not to have been used, the Hamiltonian doctrine of broad or loose construction as to what was constitutionally "necessary and proper" was triumphant.

To intensify the irony, in a sort of act of political suicide, some Federalists chose this moment to come out as strict constructionists and oppose the treaty as unconstitutional. They did so in the face of an immensely popular action. Since that time, it would appear that those in power in the federal government tend to favor broad/loose construction while those out of power tend to find their true faith in strict construction. In any event, the Louisiana

Purchase qualifies as an immense accomplishment.

The Louisiana Purchase prompted Jefferson to send out the Lewis and Clark expedition to explore to the Northwest. Another expedition would be sent to the Southwest under Zebulon Pike. Both expeditions added greatly to the geographic knowledge of the continent and the country. That also significantly contributed to the knowledge about various trans-Mississippi Indian tribes and the flora and fauna of the United States.

Also connected to foreign as well as domestic affairs were the Non-Intercourse Act and the Embargo. In a complex and unanticipated way, each contributed to the industrial growth of the United States.

Merchant capitalists who normally invested in trade found that government actions, particularly the Embargo, impeded trade. They therefore began to make other investments. Many turned to industrial investment, particularly to the growing cotton mills. Continued uncertainty, which endured at some level or another until the end of the War of 1812, re-directed the flow of capital. That benefitted the growing industrial economy of the northern states, particularly the northeastern ones.

Though none of these activities were planned by the government, they nevertheless resulted from the actions of the government. It was an early and relatively benign example of the law of unintended consequences.

14. Integrity

As is true for Franklin D. Roosevelt, integrity is the category in which Thomas Jefferson achieves his lowest ranking. The historians and political scientists who responded to our 2002 survey have ranked him in 15th place.

Perhaps at the heart of this rating lies the enormous paradox, if not indeed hypocrisy, of Jefferson and slavery. George Washington, whose integrity ranks high, was also a slaveholder, but he freed his slaves. Jefferson, in his lifetime, freed only five slaves, all of whom belonged to the Hemings' family. Jefferson's apparent liaison with his slave, Sally Hemings, intensifies the issue. Recent DNA information coupled with his physical proximity at the time of her conceptions strengthens suspicions that he fathered one or more of her children. For a man who so eloquently wrote that "all men are created equal," this constitutes a seemingly grotesque hypocrisy – as perhaps does the fact that in 1803, he also would sign legislation to forbid free blacks from handling the United States mail.

To these contradictions, or paradoxes as they have been called, it is necessary to add others to the scale. Leonard Levy, as far back as 1963 in Jefferson and Civil Liberties; The Darker Side, undertook an examination of the relation between issues of civil and/or constitutional liberties issues and Jefferson's policies. Levy, for example, suggests that Jefferson was politically timid. He noted that while Jefferson was opposed to the Alien and Sedition Acts, his opposition was covert. He never publicly stood in opposition. Even his authorship of the radical Kentucky Resolutions was anonymous. Nor did the President's opposition to the Sedition Acts of the Adams years preclude him, when he was President, from suggesting to friendly state governors that at least some selective prosecutions under state sedition laws might have a beneficial political impact on Federalist opponents of the administration. Those seeking additional information might do well to consult Professor Levy's work.

His letters in defense of the excesses of the French Revolution may well be dismissed as hyperbole. It seems unlikely, however, that any American President since Jefferson has reached the level of attention to detail and direct coercion that Jefferson achieved during the worst days of the embargo. Indeed, no American President has ever been granted the power that Jefferson sought and received over the liberty and property of American citizens in the Embargo Enforcement Act. He did not hesitate to use those powers and to use them intrusively. The historian, Forrest McDonald, has summarized the President's position in regard to the embargo and its enforcement as a search for "broad and patently unconstitutional enforcement powers."

No human being has ever, always and without exception, behaved according to his announced principles. Political figures in power always behave differently than when out of power, if only because when they are in power they can have full faith in the morality and the motives of authority. Jefferson, whose commitment to abstract ideals tended toward the absolute, certainly leaned in a similar direction.

Clearly, however, he always had a penchant for the clandestine, perhaps the devious. It may well have been dislike of personal disagreement that drove him toward secrecy. He seemed to find it much more comfortable to urge Madison or another political ally to enter the lists against Hamilton. In such a circumstance, Jefferson could avoid confrontation and achieve the same ends. It was perhaps these characteristics that suggested to Joseph J. Ellis the title for his National Book Award-winning work on Jefferson and his character: American Sphinx: The Character of Thomas Jefferson, 1998.

15. Executive Ability

Trailing only Washington, Lincoln, and the two Roosevelts, Jefferson emerges in fifth place for executive ability. And yet....

It is almost a cliché to say that Jefferson's first term was replete with good fortune ranging from the Peace of Amiens to the Louisiana Purchase. It is equally true to state that his second term was beset with difficulty. Indeed, it reached the point that by 1809 he virtually had ceded his executive authority to Madison and Gallatin, with the exception of his almost obsessive effort to enforce the embargo. That effort would lead him far down the path toward egregious violations of the Bill of Rights.

Might we then infer that his executive style, which seemed to serve him so well in the first administration, proved to be inadequate in the second? Did the pressures of the office in the second term prove too much for him? Some would agree with this theory and relate it to his problems and reactions when he was governor of Virginia, arguably the worst moments of his political life.

In any event, looking at the overall achievements of the two terms, it seems clear that something was different. If it was not his management methods, then it might be that Jefferson's style was never adequate – at least not in times of stress.

He brought to office excellent communications skills and a real talent for dealing with politics and people. His failures inexorably are connected with the intransigent problems arising from the European war. These were problems that could not be solved by charm or mere economic pressure of the type the Non-Intercourse Act or the Embargo could exert on Britain or France.

President Jefferson did not seem able to grasp that, faced with the war with Napoleon, the British government felt that the stakes were too high to yield. Nor did he seem moved by the very real economic hardships he imposed on American citizens. In fact, he seemed willing even to run the risk of hunger and malnutrition for those citizens rather than reconsidering his policy. In short, his emotions seem to have been too heavily involved. For whatever reasons, the President moved inexorably forward, resolved in his determination to enforce and sustain the embargo. There seemed no cool and rational reassessment.

16. Foreign Policy Accomplishments

We think that his eighth place ranking here reflects some of the issues just addressed under executive ability. There were, from posterity's perspective, four significant foreign policy issues the Jefferson Administration confronted. They were:

1. Whether the United States should continue to pay tribute to the Barbary States to continue its trade in the Mediterranean region.

2. The events leading up to and surrounding the Louisiana Purchase.

3. The question of whether the United States should extend diplomatic recognition to the Haitian Republic as the second, revolutionary, post-colonial state in the Western Hemisphere.

4. Finally, there were the conflicts and causes that grew out of the resumption of the Napoleonic Wars after 1803, which – from the American point of view – primarily involved neutral rights on the high seas, the impressment of seamen and the seizure and confiscation of American flagged vessels by one or another of the belligerent powers.

The Barbary States of North Africa – Algiers, Morocco, Tripoli and Tunis – preyed upon merchant shipping of non-Muslim nations in the Mediterranean Sea. It was their official position that, as Muslims, they had a right and duty to do so and an entitlement to the plunder and slaves thus produced. European states paying an annual tribute were not molested.

In 1784-1785, after American independence had been recognized, American vessels began to be attacked. John Adams and Thomas Jefferson attempted a negotiation in 1785 but were rebuffed. Adams concluded that the United States should build a better Navy and then move against the pirates. Jefferson thought that America should defy the Barbary States instantly.

Under Presidents Washington and Adams, the United States paid the demanded tribute, which was sometimes quite onerous. When Jefferson took office, thanks to Adams, the country had a respectable Navy. Faced with a demand from Tripoli for Tribute, Jefferson refused. In May of 1801, Tripoli declared war on the United States. Jefferson sent naval units to the Mediterranean. The first combat took place in August. The war would last until 1805.

In October of 1803, the U. S. S. Philadelphia, one of America's strongest and most modern ships, ran aground in the harbor in Tripoli and was captured with her captain and crew. In February of the following year, a daring raid led by U. S. naval Lieutenant Stephen Decatur retook the ship. Unable to refloat her under bombardment, they burned her where she lay, and the raiding party withdrew.

By spring of 1805, an overland expedition of local auxiliaries and members of the United States Marine Corps captured the city of Derna in Tripoli and threatened the overthrow of the pasha, the ruler. At this point, peace was concluded, and American prisoners were returned, though the United States did pay a ransom of $60,000 for them. The policy, though expensive, worked reasonably well for the administration, at least temporarily, and redounded to the credit of the government. A second Barbary War would complete the task after the end of the War of 1812.

The Louisiana Purchase, while a stroke of good fortune, was an enormous foreign policy achievement. No matter how fortuitous, the importance of such an enormous accretion of territory to the United States cannot be overstated. Even contemporaries recognized that it rendered a significant increase in the stature and power of the United States a foregone conclusion. Barely 27 years had passed since Jefferson had labored over that founding document in Philadelphia when, as President, he signed the documents that extended the territory of the United States west to the Rocky Mountains.

Events in Haiti had much to do with making the Louisiana Purchase possible. There is, then, considerable irony in President Jefferson's refusal to extend diplomatic recognition to Haiti at almost the same moment he received Louisiana. Letters between Jefferson, Madison and Monroe make it difficult, if not impossible, to assign any rationale other than racism to Jefferson's failure to give any serious consideration to Haitian independence. In the presidencies of Madison and Monroe, too, Haiti would be thrust aside. In yet another irony, Haiti would be recognized only in 1862 by another President who represented another party that was also called Republican, although it was not the party of Jefferson.

The last problem was the most complex, and the only one in which the other parties to the issues could not simply be agreed with or, somewhat cavalierly, ignored. By 1803, the United States had become the world's largest neutral carrier of goods. Each of the warring powers, England and France, sought to retard U. S. shipping to the other.

Britain further irritated American sensitivities by continuing to impress seamen directly from American merchant ships, which were stopped on the high seas. This came to a spectacular head in June of 1807 with the Chesapeake Affair, which prompted Jefferson asked the Congress to pass the Embargo Act in December of 1807. It became a wildly unpopular law because of its negative impact on U. S. trade.

While the Republicans carried Madison's election in 1808 and even sustained their majorities in Congress, (though reduced) the 1808 elections politically were the death knell of the embargo. Indeed, though certainly reluctantly, Jefferson was forced by circumstances before Madison's inauguration to sign legislation repealing the embargo.

Fortunately for his reputation, little is remembered and less written about that element of his presidency.

17. Leadership Ability
Here, President Jefferson is ranked in sixth place among his fellows.
The ability Jefferson displayed in creating and wielding a political coalition

and keeping it together despite the vicissitudes of normal political life and dissenting elements, such as John Randolph of Roanoke, was no mean talent. (Randolph was a brilliant though highly eccentric Democratic-Republican party leader who represented an excessively puritanical view of the party philosophy. On a number of issues, he really sought to out-Jefferson Jefferson on issues of strict construction. One such issue was the embargo.) The fact that despite the complications and political negatives of the embargo the Republicans could still dominate the election of 1808 would certainly seem to illustrate the strength of that coalition and Jefferson as its creator and leader. In this area, we certainly must award accolades.

The first administration saw collegiality, cooperation and triumph and earned good marks. In the second administration little seemed to go well, and the President seemed almost a different man. The genial host and sophisticate virtually receded behind a curtain and a more driven personality appeared. High marks are more difficult to justify, suggesting a lower score.

Beyond that, we might consider saying of Jefferson, as we did of John Adams, that his talents might be seen as stronger in cabinet, committee and council than in the executive chair.

18. Intelligence

This is the one area in which the historians and political scientists virtually have enshrined Jefferson in first place. His intellect has long been extolled, but that admiration was significantly bolstered just about a half century ago. In April of 1962, at a White House dinner in honor of Nobel Laureates, the then President, John F. Kennedy, delivered an eloquent, perhaps hyperbolic, tribute to Jefferson when he said, "I think that this is the most extraordinary collection of talent, of human understanding, that has ever been gathered together at the White House, with the possible exception of when Thomas Jefferson dined alone."

Jefferson was insatiably curious. Indeed, he was nearly obsessive in his search for facts, whether it was keeping track of the cost of produce in the markets of Washington, D.C., poring over the journals of Lewis and Clark or his seemingly endless quest for data with which he could contest the views of the French naturalist Georges-Louis Leclerc, the comte de Buffon. Buffon offered the thesis that European flora and fauna brought to the North America tended to decay in the American climate. It was all grist for Jefferson's mill.

In passing, it is interesting to note that Benjamin Franklin, when he was exposed to adherents of Buffon contented himself with the humorous suggestion that the group all stand up and expose the theory to an analysis by eye. For Jefferson, who was not famed for his sense of humor, research on the topic went on and on.

We have already remarked upon his knowledge, interest and skill in architecture. He was also quite knowledgeable about music and was a skilled violinist. His well known interest in and affection for wine, together with his frequent and sophisticated purchases and the contents of his wine cellar, offer ample proof that he was a oenologist of note.

Perhaps no American President except Theodore Roosevelt has better credentials as a naturalist. Jefferson's quarrel with Buffon tended to dominate that element of his interests, as seen in his Notes on the State of Virginia and his excitement with regard to plants and animals in the reports he received from Lewis and Clark.

He was interested in what we would now call the science of agronomy, and he possessed one of the largest private libraries in North America. After the British burned Washington, Jefferson, facing economic adversity, sold his library to the federal government, where it became the foundation of the collection of the Library of Congress. While paying due deference to the intelligence of John and John Quincy Adams, Theodore Roosevelt and Woodrow Wilson, we still must note that the judgement of our experts is that no President has been more intelligent than Thomas Jefferson.

19. Avoid Crucial Mistakes

The panel of experts has placed President Jefferson in seventh place.

It would be difficult to point to any error in Jefferson's first term as even being serious. Certainly, none were critical. The second administration, however, offers a quite different perspective. The outbreak of war in Europe presented the President with a series of problems and crises to which there appear to have been no really effective solutions Indeed, after the Chesapeake Affair, there perhaps seemed to the President to be none at all, short of war. That would appear to have been what led, almost by default, to the Embargo Act.

Having said that, we are still left with the conclusion that if the embargo and its enforcement was not a crucial mistake it certainly was the next closest thing to one. The embargo left the economy nearly prostrate, and there seemed no sign that the policy had even tempted either Britain or France to review its policies. In fact there seemed to be no alternative, other than to declare the policy wrong and try again.

Indeed, from a French point of view, the Embargo was a wonderful policy. The United States essentially was blockading its own goods from England, something the French were not strong enough to do themselves. In short, the policy seemed to place stringent hardships on the American people and economy, while it did not achieve the goals for which it was intended. Politically it impacted adversely on both the President and his party.

Nevertheless, it was not crucial in two or three separate senses. First, the American economy was at that time sufficiently primitive, with many citizens still subsistence or near subsistence farmers, that it could withstand the blow. Second, it was not crucial in the way a major failed policy might well have been during the administrations of George Washington or Abraham Lincoln, when the fate of the republic was often in the balance. Third, we cannot imagine what might have occurred if President Jefferson had had two or three more years remaining in his term. What might have happened had the embargo been enforced for an additional year or two is unknown. Its relative brevity then may also have been a factor in keeping it from being crucial.

20. Present Overall View
The present overall view for Jefferson finds him ranked fifth, the precise equivalent of his averaged score.

Book III

Not So Prime Time Presidents

An examination of the Presidents of the United States in search of a group of consecutively serving presidents who might properly be labeled as failures or near failures proved to be less fruitful, yielding only one notable group. That group consists of the immediate pre-Civil War presidents – Millard Fillmore, Franklin Pierce and James Buchanan. Our criterion here consists simply of the fact that the separation of our first two notable groups consisted of only a 3-point variation from a total of 18 points: FDR at one, HST at seven and Eisenhower at 10, to a total of 21 points, Washington at four, Jefferson at five and John Adams at 12.

This triad, which totals 115 points, consists of Fillmore at 37, Pierce at 38 and Buchanan at 40. The next closest group, which would be Harding, Coolidge and Hoover, is separated by a full 18 points. There would seem then to be too wide a separation between them to consider any near equivalence.

The group consists of one Whig, Fillmore, who would in fact be the last Whig President, and two Democrats. We believe that, though the term is more usually applied to Democrats in the era, all three may properly be characterized as "doughfaces." In the political parlance of the 1850s a doughface was a northern man with southern sympathies or principles. The direct coinage seems to be a reference to the kneading or working of dough into various shapes – which is to say, they were, like dough, pliable in the hands of slaveholders.

Walt Whitman wrote a poem protesting compromise, which he saw as craven surrender to the slaveholders. The verses epitomize the epithet. It appeared in the New York Post in March of 1850, entitled Song for Certain Congressmen, later called The Dough-Face Song:… .

We're all docile dough faces
They knead us with the fist

They, the dashing Southern Lords,
We labor as they list;
For them we speak – or hold our tongues,
For them we turn and twist.

We join their howl against
Free soil and "abolition"
That firebrand – that assassin knife –
Which risk our land's condition,
And leave no peace of life to any
Dough-faced politician.

Principle – freedom – fiddlesticks!
We know not where they're found.

Beyond all such we know a term
Charming to ears and eyes,
With it we'll stab young Freedom,
And do it in disguise;
Speak softly ye wily dough-faces –
That term is "compromise."

All three presidents were at a disadvantage in that their terms of office followed the annexation of Texas and the Mexican Cession of the Treaty of Guadalupe Hidalgo. As a result, each found it necessary, at some level, to deal with the vexing issue of the extension of slavery into the new territories of the United States.

President Fillmore was confronted at his accession with the debate on the Compromise of 1850 and the Fugitive Slave Law. Pierce, many of whose problems were of his own making, had the Kansas-Nebraska Act, the Ostend Manifesto and "Bleeding Kansas," and Buchanan had the Dred Scott decision, the continued fallout over Kansas, John Brown's Raid and secession.

They entered the arena with enthusiasm – and, in Fillmore's case, with surprise – but none seems to have indicated any real reluctance. The issue of the hour, of the day, of the decade – the last decade of peace before the

180

Civil War – was slavery. What was to be done about the issue of slavery in the territories? Should slavery be allowed in the territories or should the provisions of the Wilmot Proviso, which barred slavery from all the new territories, be adopted? By common understanding, all recognized that the alternative to a successful solution would at least potentially involve disruption of the Union and, perhaps, civil war. All three wrestled with the question, and scholars, in our surveys and elsewhere, have found them wanting.

As with the previous two groups, we find numerous similarities within this group. Once again, they are generationally close. Only 13 years separate Buchanan, born in 1791, from Pierce, who was born in 1804; with Fillmore, born in 1800, in the middle. Buchanan and Fillmore were the last Presidents born in the 18th Century. As with the previous groups, they are, once again, all old stock.

All three were born in the proverbial log cabin, though both Pierce and Buchanan had economically successful fathers who moved up the social and economic ladders relatively quickly. Each, for example, would have access to a college degree – Buchanan from Dickinson College and Pierce from Bowdoin College.

The common historical experience that helped to shape our first two sets of Presidents was the American experience in World Wars I and II, as well as the Great Depression, in the case of the first set, and the American Revolutionary experience for the second. For this third group, their common experience involves political development during the formation of the second American political party system and then the disruption of that system. (See Appendix B.) Buchanan, for example, had started as a Federalist and then become a Democrat. Fillmore was an Anti-Mason, then a Whig, and ran for President in 1856 as a candidate of the American Party (the Know-Nothings). Pierce was a true-blue Democrat. All dealt with the turmoil of slavery and territorial expansion in American politics in the second quarter of the 19th Century and beyond.

All three seem to have failed to grasp an enormous change that had taken and was still taking place. The issues involving slavery were no longer simply political issues. When Henry Clay created the Missouri Compromise in 1820, they had been political, and it had been possible to "split the difference." That is, you could admit Missouri as a slave state and Maine as a free state, and most people could live with that. When Senator Clay could not secure passage of the Compromise of 1850 it was because this had now become an emotional and moral issue. That change probably was due to the vigorous propaganda activity of the religious abolitionists. For nearly a generation, they had inveighed against slavery as a moral evil. While their political impact had been negligible (that would come from free soil thought and activists) they had helped to redefine the argument. The North was also increasingly ashamed of slavery in the land of freedom. In the same period, for the South, slavery ceased to be simply an economic benefit, and even a faintly embarrassing one. It had become a "positive good" – good for the slave and master alike. Both attitudes at the start of this period were still developing, but soon they would be issues of principle, and neither side would be willing to concede any ground.

Significant elements of the apparent inadequacy of this group of Presidents lay in their inability to grasp that fact and their failure to conceive of a course of action to ameliorate the worst of the tension.

As we saw with our first two groups, these Presidents, too, had significant political differences. If there was a specific similarity among them, it lay in the deference shown by each, though with varying degrees of enthusiasm, to the expressed self-interest of slave holders and their polity. That, more than any other factor, was what led to the disruption of the second party system, the growth of free soil sentiment in the North, the emergence of the Republican Party and, ultimately, to the disruption of the Union and the Civil War. Somewhere in the course of the decade spanned by these three administrations, a tipping point was reached, and the American Civil War became inevitable.

Chapter 7 - Millard Fillmore – July 9, 1850 – March 4, 1853

"God knows that I detest slavery, but it is an existing evil, for which we are not responsible, and we must endure it, and give it such protection as is guaranteed by the constitution, till we can get rid of it without destroying the last hope of free government in the world."
– Fillmore to Daniel Webster, 10/23/1850, as cited in Robert J. Rayback, Millard Fillmore, Newton, CT., 1959, p. 271 n.)

1. Background (family, education, experience)

President Fillmore has garnered a rank of 38th among his peers in this category.

In terms of his family background and formal education, it would be difficult to quarrel with that judgment. Presidential biographies and appraisals often begin with a rhetorical trumpet blast, announcing that the President was "born in a log cabin" and worked his way out of poverty. Fillmore, however, was not only born in a log cabin in Cayuga County, N. Y., but his father's economic status thereafter declined to that of a tenant farmer. Millard (his first name was his mother's maiden name) at age 14, found himself apprenticed to a cloth dresser.

To that point, the limited schooling available on the New York frontier had provided him with basic literacy and little else. At 17 he purchased membership in a local circulating library. Then, at 19, taking advantage of slack time at the mill, he enrolled in a nearby academy. This experience at formal education led to intellectual growth and was an early sign of his dedication to self-improvement and to the advantages that learning might bring him. He also would fall in love with one of his teachers, Abigail Powers. She was 21 to his 19. Their affection and engagement would endure for seven years until their marriage in 1826.

At this point his father managed to arrange a trial period for him as a law clerk in a local judge's office. After the trial period, he taught school for a brief period to earn enough money to terminate his apprenticeship, after which he returned to the study of law. He later broke with the judge, who was more interested in his labor than his development. He then returned to teaching and to the study of law. He was admitted to the bar in 1823, after a very short period of reading law, and opened his own office in East Aurora, N. Y., just outside Buffalo.

He remained a serious student of the law. As his contacts and knowledge and experience grew, he prospered. East Aurora would not hold him long, but the Buffalo area would. His reputation, stature and public recognition grew, and so did his place in the surrounding community.

A series of events in the late 1820s brought about a near hysteria in the political atmosphere, associated with fear and suspicion of the Masonic order, which was perceived, due to its secrecy, as anti-democratic and elitist. By the end of the 1820s an anti-Masonic political party had formed and developed considerable strength in Western New York. Fillmore was approached and asked to run for a seat in the New York State Assembly as a candidate of the Anti-Masonic party. He accepted the nomination and, despite a statewide landslide for the Democratic Party, won election. He would serve three one-year terms in Albany. His signature issue in the Assembly was legislation to outlaw the practice of imprisonment for debt.

His constituents seem to have approved of his representation, since he was elected to the United States House of Representatives. After a brief hiatus, he was elected again for a total of four terms. In 1841, at the start of his fourth term, he was a candidate for speaker of the House. He finished second and served as chairman of the House ways and means committee, where he exercised considerable influence in the drafting and passage of the Tariff of 1842. Eight years later, when he found it necessary to assemble a cabinet, he would often turn to his former House colleagues. He did not seek reelection after 1843 and was defeated as the Whig candidate for governor of New York in 1844.

In 1847, for the first time, the New York state comptroller was popularly elected. Fillmore was the Whig candidate and won handily. His robust margin of victory, indicating his popularity in New York, may have well been a factor in the Whig decision to nominate him for vice president on the presidential ticket headed by Zachary Taylor.

He and Taylor were never close. Unknown to one another before the convention, some maintain that they never even met until after the election. Fillmore certainly never exercised much influence in the Taylor administration. Rather, he seems to have been outmaneuvered by the New York Whig Party boss, Thurlow Weed, and his protégé, Senator William H. Seward. Seward, via Taylor's brother, had great influence. Indeed, Taylor distributed patronage in New York not via Fillmore but through his rivals in the Whig party, Seward and Weed.

In short, from an exceptionally hardscrabble background and with very little formal education until his late teens, within 10 years Fillmore had studied and clerked, been admitted to the practice of law and been elected to a seat in the New York State Legislature. In just over another 20 years, at age 50, he also had served notably in Congress, been the Whig candidate for governor, carried a statewide election for the office of comptroller, been elected Vice President of the United States and then succeeded to the presidency.

As resumes go, while it certainly has gaps, it is not without merit. It is admittedly weak on family and on education, but it clearly finds strength in legal and political experience and is very strong on determination and perseverance and the respect of his legislative peers.

2. Party Leadership (political)

In addition to managing politics in both the state and federal legislatures, Fillmore was also an important regional political leader in western New York. His popularity as well as his reputation for intelligence and probity made him a force to be reckoned with.

To his disadvantage, first as an Anti-Mason and later as a Whig, his career overlapped that of the highly successful political leader/boss, Thurlow Weed. Weed's biographer, Glyndon Van Deusen, rather tellingly entitled the biography he wrote about Weed *The Wizard of the Lobby.* As he confronted Weed as a fellow party leader, so, too, Fillmore as a potential or actual candidate confronted Weed's protégé, Seward. From Weed's point of view, Seward was always the favored candidate and Fillmore often the sacrificial lamb.

As deft a political leader as Fillmore proved to be, he was rarely as deft as Weed. As successful a candidate as he was, he was not as successful as Seward, though Fillmore would attain the presidency and Seward would not.

In the area of party leadership, our experts rank Fillmore in 36th place.

We think it likely that his inability to overcome Weed's tactics and machinations played a large part in that determination.

Within a legislative chamber, committee or caucus, Fillmore seems to have initially devoted himself to learning the rules of the body in question and assessing its members. It also seems that he quickly earned the respect of his peers. In his three, single-year terms in the New York State Assembly, he had worked to pass legislation outlawing imprisonment for debt. The success of that effort seems to illustrate his political skills. The Anti-Mason/ Whig faction in Albany was a minority and could not pass the bill. However, the bill was not without public appeal, and there were Assembly Democrats who favored it. Fillmore worked at persuasion, but he also convinced the Democratic leadership to designate the legislation as non-partisan, meaning party loyalty did not bind a member to vote one way or the other. Once that parliamentary step was taken, he mustered enough votes from all parties to outlaw debtor's prison in New York.

He received less personal credit than he might have wished. In later years the Democrats claimed rather more than they deserved, but he did get the legislation through, and his constituents knew it. Ronald Reagan frequently quoted the old saw that it was astonishing how much a person could accomplish if he didn't care who got the credit. In this instance, as well as others in his career, Fillmore illustrated the adage.

3. Communications Ability (speak, write)

Placed at 35th, Fillmore finds that only 15 per cent of his peers are ranked lower than he. In this area, Fillmore probably suffers from the spotty nature of his early education, or the lack thereof. He was, however, a man of books throughout his life who labored to improve education and culture in Buffalo until the day he died. He was, in fact, very conscious of his lack of formal education and apologetic about it. While touring Europe after his presidency, he was offered an honorary degree by Oxford University. He rejected the honor, with gratitude, saying that he had not been classically educated and that a man ought not to accept a degree (inscribed in Latin) that he could not read.

His prose style was simple and straightforward in a day characterized by a more ornate, even florid style. His oratorical style also lacked the rhetorical flourishes of the age. In our judgment, while not striking or memorable, his communications were quite clear, reasonably concise and adequate to the purpose intended. No one has ever suggested that he was a Daniel Webster on the platform or competition for Jefferson as an author.

4. Relationship With Congress

Our panel has placed Fillmore in 31st place. One might have anticipated a higher rank for Fillmore. As a former member of the House, candidate for speaker and chair of the ways and means committee, he could be presumed to understand the working of the legislature. Certainly, in at least some ways, he seems to have done so. His views were not without influence. It must also be noted that he was, throughout his presidency, at a disadvantage in the face of Democratic majorities in both the House and the Senate. When President Pierce was inaugurated, he found a vacant Supreme Court seat waiting to be filled because the Democratic members of the Senate had refused to confirm a Whig appointee of Fillmore's, awaiting a Democratic appointee after the presidential election of 1852.

Unfortunately for his reputation, the great question of his presidency, which required an almost immediate resolution upon his accession to the office, was the Compromise of 1850. In this instance, the old political verities were no longer as reliable as they had once been. The issues were no longer Whig versus Democrat. They were now, increasingly, North versus South and/or slave versus free. Anti-slavery Whigs like William Seward would not vote for any fugitive slave law, nor would southern firebrands vote for the admission of California as a free state.

President Taylor had favored the immediate admission of California and New Mexico as free states, preferring to deal with other contested issues thereafter. Fillmore, probably as a result of the fear of secession, favored what would be called the Compromise of 1850.

The Compromise included the following provisions:

1. Admit California as a free state.
2. Decide the Texas-New Mexico boundary dispute in favor of New Mexico and pay Texas $10 million.
3. Organize the remaining territory from the Mexican Cession, Utah and New Mexico Territories, under "popular sovereignty" – that is, with no restrictions as to slavery as a precondition of admission.
4. Outlaw the slave trade, but not slavery in the District of Columbia.
5. Adopt a stricter fugitive slave law to protect property in slaves.

The broad outline had been presented to the Senate by Henry Clay in late January of 1850. Senator John C. Calhoun of South Carolina had signified the opposition of southern radicals in what was to be his last speech. He was already so weak that the speech had to be read for him. On March 7th, Senator Daniel Webster delivered one of his greatest orations in support of the compromise. This debate was, in a number of ways, the last stand of the great Senate triumvirate – Henry Clay of Kentucky, Calhoun and Webster of Massachusetts. Webster's former friends and admirers never forgave him for his Seventh of March speech, which was seen as treason to the antislavery cause.

As the debate wore on, it seems that Vice President Fillmore, as presiding officer of the Senate, may have been influenced by the argument, and his moderate anti-slavery position began to change. In any event, he came to believe that the acceptance of the compromise was the best course of action for the nation.

By September, despite the best efforts of Clay and Webster, the compromise – all of its provisions included in one so-called "Omnibus bill" – had failed. Clay withdrew to Kentucky in a state of near despair, and the baton of leadership passed to a new generation – into the hands of a young senator from Illinois, Stephen A. Douglas. By now, Fillmore had succeeded Taylor as President, and everyone knew he favored the compromise.

Douglas saw a mechanical solution to the problem. There were three factions in the equation – northern radicals, southern radicals and what some call the "national" faction. They were those who would vote for any and all measures to end the tumult to preserve the Union. Clearly, the first two were ideologically driven. For Seward, et al., slavery was a profound evil. They believed that free soil principles, as embodied in the Wilmot Proviso that barred slavery in the new territories, would provide the first step on the road to ending the evil. For Calhoun and his faction, slavery was no longer to be apologized for; it was a positive good and entitled to protection wherever the United States Constitution held sway. For the nationalists, perhaps for the most part consisting of the older generation who were not as driven by principles or ideology, any solution would be acceptable. Theirs was a pragmatic vision. Slavery was a problem to be solved, not an evil to be confronted. They – including a few younger men, like Douglas – would compromise. Fillmore cast his lot with them.

There was, then, no real compromise. There was no exchange of A for B; there was merely the mechanical structuring of votes. Overall, northern radicals voted aye for any measure that seemed to weaken slavery. The nationalists voted aye, the Southern radicals voted nay and, presto, California was admitted as a free state. Conversely, the southern radicals voted aye, the "nationalists" voted aye, the northern radicals voted nay, and the stricter fugitive slave law became the law of the land. There was no give and take. There was no true compromise. The result was mechanical, not collegial.

Fillmore certainly thought the problem had been solved. He always felt the Compromise of 1850 to be a permanent solution to the problem. He never seems to have grasped that in the Fugitive Slave Law the compromise contained the seeds of bitter dispute, the dissolution of the Union and Civil War.

5. Court Appointments
President Fillmore, who is ranked 36th in judicial appointments, appointed

only one associate justice to the United States Supreme Court, Justice Benjamin R. Curtis. Curtis, who was born in Massachusetts in 1809, was a Harvard graduate who practiced law in Boston and was a member of the Whig party. He served on the Supreme Court from September of 1851 to September of 1857.

Curtis' relatively short period of service was distinguished by two opinions. In the first, Cooley v. Board of Wardens, 1852, Curtis, writing for the court, held that the power to regulate commerce covers diverse subjects. He therefore stipulated that some topics require a single rule, covering all positions; other topics do not. Therefore, in the first type of instances, only Congress may legislate; in the latter the states may also legislate. The Cooley rule is still in effect.

The much better known opinion was a dissent offered in a much more significant and controversial case, Dred Scott v. Sanford, 1857. The Dred Scott case saw a court composed of seven Democrats, five of whom were from slave states, one Whig and one Republican ruling. Chief Justice Roger B. Taney, a Marylander, wrote for the majority. His opinion stipulated that no one of African descent could ever be a citizen, and that Congress, had no constitutional authority to bar slavery from any of the territories of the United States. The four other slave state justices agreed – as, after some arm twisting, did the two free state justices who were Democrats. The Whig, Curtis, and the Republican, McLean of Ohio, dissented.

Curtis' dissent directly and brilliantly contradicted Taney. It proved, conclusively, that at the time of the American Revolution there were men of color who voted, sued and were sued, served in the military and otherwise clearly fulfilled the legal functions of citizens — who had, indeed, been citizens at the ratification of the Constitution. Further, in contradicting Taney, he cited the Constitution itself (Article IV, Section 8) as giving to the Congress the authority "…to dispose of and make all needful and necessary Rules and Regulations respecting the Territory or other property … of the United States." He also stipulated eight separate instances between 1789 and 1848 when slavery had specifically been excluded from the territories. In six other cases, he noted, Congress had, equally specifically, recognized slavery in the territories. Curtis' logic, history and power of argument seemed to carry all before it. In northern opinion and, in general terms, Curtis seemed to have destroyed Taney's argument.

It may be argued that Curtis' dissent represented special pleading for the North, though such an argument certainly would be counterbalanced by raising the same point in regard to Taney's opinion. However, most realized that if Dred Scott stood then slavery, logically, could not be prevented anywhere in the United States. It wouldn't require a push to extend it into free territories, (and even states?), merely a nudge.

Curtis was clearly a brilliant appointment, recommended to Fillmore by his Secretary of State Daniel Webster. Based on this appointment alone, we wonder if Fillmore might not have deserved a higher ranking in this category.

6. Handling the U. S. Economy

The Siena Research Institute's experts have awarded Mr. Fillmore a rank of 26th in this category.

Overall, in terms of economic policy, Fillmore is probably best described as a Whig's Whig. He favored entrepreneurial activity and internal improvements, such as federal rivers and harbors bills. During his presidency, the first instance of a land grant to a state, Illinois, was passed to assist in railroad development. There were even preliminary discussions of the future need for a transcontinental railway.

The economy of the United States was booming in those years, as it would continue to do through the Pierce administration, bolstered by the discovery and early exploitation of gold in California, vast increases in railroad construction (from fewer than 3,000 miles in 1840 to 9,000 in 1850 to 18,000 in 1860) and the use of steamboats on the internal river systems. Greatly increased commercial activity on the Mississippi and Ohio Rivers, as well as others, led to increased urban development and commercial and industrial economic activity. The United States was also benefitting from dramatic increases in the use of steam power, with commensurate increases in mining and other activity, and from the initial application of mechanization to the agricultural economy, ranging from corn to cotton. Nineteenth Century America was witnessing the development of a burgeoning economic engine.

As a good Whig, President Fillmore also displayed considerable interest in overseas mercantile activity. That interest showed itself in attention to the possible development of an isthmian canal. Potential routes in Panama, Nicaragua and Mexico all drew at least some interest from both investors and the federal government. Even far distant Hawaii, long an important port of call for American whalers, drew new interest from the administration, which rather sternly warned France not to consider colonizing the islands.

Probably the best known indication of Fillmore's overseas interests was Japan. It was he who authorized the voyage of Commodore Matthew Perry to Japan to open Japan's markets to the United States. While Pierce would be the President when Perry returned, the mission was conceived and launched under Fillmore's auspices.

7. Luck

Our professors of history and political science have placed Fillmore in 27th place here.

In this category, for vice presidents succeeding to office, there is always a bit of discomfort in the analysis. What role did the death of the President's predecessor play in the judgment of our respondents? We are not prepared to offer any nearly definitive answer – merely to suggest that it was, in all likelihood, a factor.

Though wary of cries of superstition, we feel compelled to point out that Millard Fillmore also happens to have been the 13th man to assume the office of president.

It would not appear that luck played a large or beneficent role in his early life. As we have seen, his first 20 years or so were difficult ones. On the other hand, when he arrived in Albany in 1829 as an assemblyman, he certainly owed a debt to the highly emotional and unpredictable (as well as coincidental) rise of the anti-Masonic movement of the late 1820s, as well as to his talents as a young politician. Surely, luck must be assigned some role.

The dichotomy of good and ill fortune in his mature years might be, in part, attributed to the fact that Thurlow Weed and William H. Seward were his contemporaries and rivals, first in the Anti-Masonic party and later in the Whig party. That presented him with potent rivals in both public and internal political life, confronting him with political problems throughout his career.

On the other hand, his geographic location – western New York, in the 1820s, just as he was coming of age – surely constituted good fortune. He found himself, a bright and talented young man, in a bustling, quasi-frontier environment where he came to be seen by his constituents, as almost an extension of their own growth and development.

When luck is called into his career as a factor, we assume that the year 1847 must loom large. In that year, for the first time, the office of comptroller in New York State was to be decided by a statewide election. The Whig candidate, Millard Fillmore, won handily. As he settled into the comptroller's office in 1848, the Whig national convention nominated Zachary Taylor, hero of the early stages of the Mexican War, for President. Taylor was a national hero, but he was also a southerner (a resident of Louisiana) and a slaveholder. To the members of the convention, that made it self-evident that the vice presidential nominee had to be from a free state and should be able to command a large vote there. Fillmore was from New York, the largest of the free states, and had just won a convincing election there.

We also assume that the fact that he never was nominated for the presidency in his own right may be seen as evidence that he was not fortune's favorite. We know at the same time that he never seems to have wholeheartedly pursued the presidency. Indeed, in the late fall of 1851 he was prepared to announce that he would not be a candidate for the nomination in 1852.

Despite that, as 1852 loomed a coalition of Southern Whigs, who saw him as the only "safe" Northern candidate (from a slaveholding point of view) and some Northern Whigs who saw him as the only potential Whig candidate who was electable, seem rather to have driven him into a sort of half-hearted pursuit of the prize. After a series of ballots, Fillmore withdrew his name, with no noticeable anguish, and Winfield Scott became the nominee. As it turned out, Scott was not electable.

Whether the calculus of Fillmore's 1856 presidential candidacy as a candidate of the American Party, the Know-Nothings, should have standing in discussion of his good or bad fortune is a question that has troubled us. We are reasonably sure that he displays little evidence of any deep-seated nativism or anti-Catholicism. While he did before the 1856 campaign make the requisite pledges to the party, he rarely indulged in anti-Catholic rhetoric, and he had his daughter educated by nuns. It seems more likely that in a period of political flux, when it seemed as likely that the Know-Nothings would provide a new major party as that the Republicans would, Fillmore simply acted pragmatically to seize the party and use it as a "Union" party – that is, Union as opposed to sectional. In any event, we think that this association with nativism and religious intolerance, however intended, has been unlucky for him in that it has placed a stigma, deserved or not, on his name.

8. Ability to Compromise

Ranked in 18th place by the respondents, this is the highest rank he was awarded in any category. Given that his support for the Compromise of 1850 represents a total reversal of the position of Zachary Taylor, compromise may be said to be his major claim to fame. His relatively positive ranking here, then, would seem to be no more than recognition of reality.

It is in his support for the Compromise of 1850 and his dogged efforts to enforce the Fugitive Slave Law thereafter that we find justification for applying the term doughface to President Fillmore. Before his election as vice president, he was generally perceived as a moderate on slavery, but a moderate on the free soil end of the spectrum. Whatever had been the factors conspiring to change his mind, he arrived at a view that seemed to him to require a more sympathetic attitude toward the South and its position on slavery. Some suggest that it was as presiding officer of the Senate, listening to the debate over the compromise for month after month, that he was persuaded to adopt a pro-compromise position. Whether he was convinced by the force of the arguments or fear of secession and its possible results may be questioned. Others say that it was a matter of constitutional scruple. Slavery, after all, was recognized by the Constitution and was therefore entitled to protection. Still others believe it was as a result of his concern for the continued existence of the Whig party. If northern Whigs did not lend political protection to slavery, southern Whigs would cease to exist, being forced by concerns over slavery into the Democratic Party. Be that as it may, for whatever reason or combinations of reasons he came to support the Compromise of 1850.

We would note that Millard Fillmore always conducted his political career in a collegial fashion. Whether the issue was the effort to outlaw imprisonment for debt in New York in the early 1830s or the political challenges of drafting and passing the Tariff of 1842 in Washington, his political career had been one dominated by tactical machinations and maneuvers intended to bring sides together and insure the success of the political goals intended. It would not, then, be unnatural if, at a time of what he perceived to be a national crisis, he again turned to tactics that had always served him well.

9. Willing to Take Risks

In 36th place in this category Fillmore obviously seems to our experts to be risk averse. Certainly, in the light of his ranking, and our analysis of his ranking, this would seem logical.

Given that his presidency lasted less than three years (1850-1853) and that its most dramatic events took place between July and September of its first year we are left with little opportunity, other than his enforcement of the Fugitive Slave Law, for analysis of this characteristic. The quite dogmatic federal effort at enforcement certainly drew substantial ire north of the Mason-Dixon Line and might then be read as risky, which would continue to be true, but it was never really unmanageable. This judgment, while true in the political short run, does not take into account the influence of Harriet Beecher Stowe's Uncle Tom's Cabin. That work, published in 1852 – whether in serial form, novel, or play, based on her reaction to the Fugitive Slave Law – would do much to persuade the North of the corrupting effects of slavery. There is, however, no reason to postulate any immediate, direct impact, for better or worse, on Fillmore's presidency.

The greater question is probably a simple one. Should Fillmore have taken risks in this instance? What if he had opposed the Compromise of 1850? It would be incorrect to say that there would have been a substantial likelihood of secession and civil war. It would not be incorrect to say that such a possibility would have existed.

Objectively, it seems reasonable to suggest that if such a war had begun in 1851 rather than 1861, the South would have been better placed to win than it was a decade later. The great growth in railroads and industrial development in the free states would not yet have occurred. Therefore, the northern superiority in materiel would not have been nearly as great. The very significant growth in northern population as a result of immigration, especially from Germany and Ireland, also would not yet have reached its height. The burgeoning exports of northern agricultural products to Europe – which would in the early 1860s at least partially offset the impact of the loss of Southern cotton – had only begun. In short, conditions most favorable to the North in 1861 would have been fewer and much less thoroughly developed in 1851.

Perhaps the President's tendency to be risk averse was a stroke of good fortune for the Union.

10. Executive Appointments

Finding himself once more in 36th place pushes President Fillmore well down the scale in this area.

The vice president had little influence in the Taylor Administration. In addition, Fillmore's position on the compromise opposed the President's. Taylor favored the immediate admission of California to the Union as a free state and similar treatment for the New Mexico Territory. This position was anathema to the South, which saw it as a triumph of free soil principles effectively denying the South any opportunity to establish slavery in the new territories. The vice president was prepared to ease the South's fears by the adoption of a pro-compromise position, which he did in July, 1850, when Taylor's death brought him to the presidency. Their positions were so diametrically opposed that, upon Taylor's death, all cabinet members tendered their immediate resignations, which Fillmore accepted with equal celerity. Fillmore asked that they remain in office a month to give him time to construct a cabinet. They agreed to remain only a week. The cabinet the President constructed would be distinguished by the previous service of its members and by the presence of a number of prominent figures. It would not be notable for particular actions, activities or policy initiatives.

In another footnote to history, we might note that Fillmore alone, among

Presidents succeeding to office after the death of their predecessors, was immediately required to replace every single sitting cabinet member.

There were at this time seven cabinet positions. As secretary of state, Fillmore nominated Daniel Webster. Then a senator, Webster had supported the Compromise of 1850 in his immortal Seventh of March speech and thereby forfeited most of his popularity in free soil Massachusetts. He resigned his Senate seat, and Fillmore sought him out for the state department. In addition to their hearty support for the compromise, the two men also both vigorously supported the Perry mission to open trade with Japan. Webster was often unwell during this, his second, stint, as secretary of state. Fillmore, however, frequently acted as his own secretary of state. Nor had Webster abandoned his almost perpetual quest for the presidency, though that seems to have created no friction with the President. When Webster resigned to seek the 1852 Whig nomination for President, against, among others, Fillmore, Fillmore appointed Webster's longtime friend, supporter and state department assistant, Edward Everett, of Massachusetts, to replace him.

To the treasury department, Mr. Fillmore summoned Thomas Corwin, United States senator from Ohio. A noted orator, Corwin would have liked to provide the United States with a protective tariff, something of a Whig shibboleth. However, with the relatively recent Walker Tariff of 1846 in place and a Congress under Democratic control, that was simply not likely. He served as secretary until the conclusion of Fillmore's presidency.

Charles Magill Conrad of Louisiana was the President's selection as secretary of war. He had served both in the House of Representatives and the Senate, and Fillmore had found him a solid Whig who had proven both co-operative and skillful on the Senate side, in the passage of the Tariff of 1842. He was also a reliable supporter of the Compromise of 1850, which was a litmus test for the President. He did not want sectional Whigs in the cabinet, but national Whigs. We note in passing that Conrad served as a delegate to the Provisional Confederate Congress and, from 1862-1864, as a Louisiana representative to the Confederate Congress.

The sitting governor of Kentucky was selected as attorney general. John J. Crittenden was an alumnus of William and Mary who had served in the Kentucky House of Representatives before the War of 1812. He served in that war, returned to Kentucky, was speaker of the Kentucky House and was sent to the United States Senate no fewer than four times by the Kentucky legislature, serving roughly 20 years. He was the 15th and 22nd attorney general of the United States, the first time for William Henry Harrison, the second for Fillmore, and presented a brilliant résumé. When invited by the President, he resigned as governor and joined the cabinet.

Fillmore, despite his support of the compromise, was uncomfortable with the Fugitive Slave Law and asked Crittenden for an opinion on its constitutionality. Crittenden replied that it fulfilled the direct constitutional obligation that runaway slaves be returned. Reassured, Fillmore signed the bill into law.

William Alexander Graham was the administration's first secretary of the navy. He served roughly two years, from August of 1850 to July of 1852, when he resigned to become Winfield Scott's running mate on the Whig presidential ticket. Before entering the cabinet, he had served in the North Carolina House of Commons, including two terms as speaker, had been a United States Senator and had served as governor of the state. After his cabinet service he served briefly as a senator of the Confederate States of America.

Graham was succeeded by John Pendleton Kennedy of Maryland, who served just over seven months. A combat veteran of the War of 1812, he is best remembered as a literary figure, though he was an active Whig who had thrice been elected to the House of Representatives, where he had worked with Fillmore. He had also served as speaker of the Maryland House of Delegates. Kennedy was one of those who enthusiastically urged the Perry mission to Japan and also was an ardent supporter of the exploration of the Arctic region. His literary output included novels, biography, sketches, and political satire. He was also an early and enthusiastic promoter of the work of Edgar Allan Poe.

For postmaster general, President Fillmore turned to his former law clerk and partner, Nathan K. Hall. Hall, like the President, was a resident of Buffalo, N. Y. He had held local offices in Buffalo and Erie County and had served in the New York State Assembly and in the House of Representatives. While he was certainly a trusted confidante of the President, there seems little reason to believe that he wielded the potent patronage power of his office in any unusual or even significant way. Indeed, Fillmore seems strangely pacific in his use of, or failure to use, patronage against his political enemies.

Quite late in the administration, Fillmore nominated Hall for a federal judgeship in the Northern District of New York. Just before Hall mounted the bench, he resigned as postmaster general. He was succeeded by Samuel Dickinson Hubbard of Connecticut, who served from August 31, 1852 until March of 1853. A Yale graduate, he had after about 15 years of practicing law become an industrialist. He, too, had served in the House of Representatives.

Fillmore also appointed the second and third secretaries of the interior. The second was Thomas McKean Thompson McKennon. An attorney from Pennsylvania, he, too, had served in the House of Representatives. Though he was reluctant to accept the appointment, his friends persuaded him. Having second thoughts, he resigned only 11 days after taking office. McKennon was replaced by a Virginian, a graduate of the University of Virginia, Alexander Hugh Holmes Stuart. He, too, had served in the House with Fillmore and was a national Whig. He proved an able administrator and served as a conduit of information about the views of the southern firebrands for the President.

11. Overall Ability

Mr. Fillmore achieves another ranking of 36th.

There can be no doubt that the ranking reflects the record of the administration as seen by scholars. We think, though, that it may reflect the fact that the record seems so dire in light of events of the ensuing decade, that the ranking may have underestimated some real talent.

Perhaps the major problem Fillmore confronted was that he was trying to compromise viewpoints that were, in fact, not open to compromise. Indeed, the Compromise of 1850 was not really a compromise but a technical or mechanical rearrangement of points of dispute. There was, however, still a genuine desire to avoid confrontation. As a result, in the months after the passage of the legislation there came to be a grudging acceptance of the result. It clearly was seen as a last resort, a sort of "thus far and no farther," but an acceptance. It could be and was used by moderates in both sections and both parties to control more radical proposals and actions. Could it have provided for a longer term solution if left in place? Would that have altered scholars' view of Fillmore's abilities? We will never know. At best we can offer the old verdict of Scottish law, "not proven."

It did prove almost at the outset of the administration that the President was decisive. He was for the Compromise, and he would continue to support that position throughout his presidency.

He was also a man capable of humility. There is evidence to sustain the view that, early in his administration, he concluded that the nation would be better served if he did not seek election in his own right and – though a certain erratic behavior arose, primarily from those outside the White House – he was prepared to act upon that conclusion.

It seems that he could work with strong personalities and egos both within and across party lines to achieve specific goals. One need only cite his association with the Democratic Party's senator from Illinois, Stephen A. Douglas, not only on the Compromise of 1850, but also on the use of land grants to states as subsidies for railway development. Similarly, when

Webster ran for the Whig nomination for President in 1852 directly in competition with Fillmore's rather reluctant candidacy, the President seems to have not only displayed no anger but not even to have shown a touch of pique.

He drew men to him and held their loyalty. By way of illustration, most of his cabinet served until the end, or the last few months of the administration, and there was little or no unseemly bickering or backbiting.

He was well read and intelligent and known for his ability to research and quickly grasp knowledge in areas new to his experience. It appears, then, that he combined people skills with a good intellect and a willingness to work.

Certainly, even those most cynical about Fillmore's motives in espousing the compromise would find it impossible to dismiss the notion that, to at least some significant degree, his motives involved his devotion to the Union.

12. Imagination
Ranked at 37th in this category Fillmore is fifth from the bottom trailed by only Pierce, Harding, Buchanan and Andrew Johnson.

The fact that all three Presidents in this group fall into the bottom five in the 2002 poll, the first Siena College Research Institute survey of the 21st Century, suggests strongly that our experts view the question of imagination as reflecting on their inability to avoid the Civil War. Certainly, that and its ramifications were the issues of that decade.

In that regard, it seems to us that there are two questions to be considered. One, was that outcome preventable? Two, did their actions make that outcome inevitable or did those actions slow or accelerate the movement to disruption and war?

The first, of course, belongs to the "if school" of history/ "If" A had taken place, would B then have evolved differently? Such questions are not imponderable but they are unanswerable. In any event, there is little in his career to suggest that Fillmore was likely to think outside the box. On balance, we would be inclined to say that the Compromise of 1850 did delay the oncoming tide of secession and war by about a decade.

We might further suggest that, like a physician taking the Hippocratic Oath, he did try, first of all, "to do no harm." His successors seem less benign. When we look at the Ostend Manifesto or the Kansas-Nebraska Act, it seems more like Pierce taking a lit torch into a powder magazine than anything else. Buchanan seems more prone to dither than decide, while also being too pliant – as, indeed, all of them were in the face of Southern demands.

Fillmore alone among the three – at some price, personal and political – seems to have been trying to put the genie back into the bottle. It may be argued that the instrument chosen was insufficiently imaginative, but it was also the instrument at hand when Taylor died, and one that could not be ignored. It professed to be evenhanded, and the President certainly tried to implement it in that fashion. Of the three, Fillmore alone seems to have had sufficiently imagination to understand where the ongoing chaos was likely to lead and sufficiently thoughtful to attempt to restore order to his political universe. However, as we pointed out earlier, such a position failed to take into account the moral dimensions of the slavery issue and their impact on the political process.

Nevertheless, we would probably rank him somewhat higher here – not in the upper echelon, but perhaps somewhat closer to the middle.

13. Domestic Accomplishments

Respondents to the SRI 2002 poll, ranked President Fillmore at 31st in this category.

As we have noted from the outset, the Compromise of 1850 is the domestic accomplishment of Millard Fillmore's presidency.

The annexation of Texas and the Mexican Cession of 1848 had awakened the dormant issue of whether slavery would be permitted in the territories of the United States. The Missouri Compromise of 1820 had disposed of the question for a generation. Now, with the addition of the new territories, the old question roared back into life. The South, still apologetic about slavery in 1820, was in some quarters already in full cry about slavery as a positive good 30 years later. In the North, even some Northern Democrats felt themselves abused by the increasingly shrill southern demands and rallied behind the so-called Wilmot Proviso. Named for the man who proposed it, David Wilmot, Democratic member of the House of Representatives from Pennsylvania, the Proviso sought to forbid the presence of slavery in any territory acquired as a result of the Mexican War. This either/or proposition rather upped the ante in the high stakes game of "what shall we do about slavery in the territories?" The entry of the Wilmot Proviso's free soil proposition into the game was particularly dangerous for the South. Abolitionism, the mot feared prospect of Southern radicals, was potentially less damaging than free soil because of the intrinsic racism that was dominant at the time.

Southern propagandists, to discomfit Abolitionists, had created a new fear, amalgamationism, a forerunner of miscegenation. If blacks were free, would they not enter into competition for white women and thus bring about the amalgamation of the races? A white farmer who loathed blacks did not want to compete economically against slave labor, nor did he care to think about a black son-in-law. But free soil skipped both abolition and amalgamation. If the new territories were organized on the basis of free soil, our white farmer would have to worry about neither. Effectively, blacks would be proscribed. Free soil principles, it seemed, were as or more detrimental to slavery in the territories than was abolitionism.

The issues Fillmore confronted in the summer of 1850, then, with a form of the compromise already under debate, were highly volatile. Indeed, he was made aware that secession was in the air after the resignation of the United States attorney in Charleston, S. C. The search for a successor proved nearly futile because, as it turned out, the firebrands had determined that it would be more difficult for federal authorities to respond to secession or its threats if the principal federal law enforcement office in the state was vacant.

This certainly represents a close approximation of the view of the perils the nation faced as President Fillmore saw it when he assumed office. It may be, in whole or in part, why he set aside the moderate anti-slavery view that most contemporary political figures had ascribed to him and assumed a new role as champion of the Compromise of 1850.

Whatever else may be said, it was at least a temporary success, and it probably enabled the nation to continue its development for an additional decade before the Civil War.

14. Integrity

Here we find President Fillmore in 32nd place. While not an accolade by any means, it does find him ranked above such modern Presidents as John Kennedy, Lyndon Johnson, Richard Nixon and William Clinton.

In this category it seems to us that Fillmore's flirtation and association with the Know-Nothings has probably weakened his standing. No matter how half-hearted his acceptance of their ideological views, no matter how pragmatic his use of their political operatives and machinery, the fact remains that he did, to whatever degree, associate the prestige of the presidency with a nativist group that decried immigrants. Nor should we forget that he, himself, at least once, intimated that major political offices should be reserved for the native born. It was not only unseemly, but it also lends weight to the arguments of those who theorize about his possibly cynical motives for other actions, up to and including his support for the Compromise of 1850. It weakens any claim to the moral high ground.

Nevertheless, it does not appear that his flirtation with the American Party – the Know-Nothings – endured after his candidacy in 1856. We should also note that other political entities, including the embryonic Republican Party, also flirted with the Know-Nothings, hoping, as did Fillmore, to gain access to the political energy and machinery as well as the voting base of that party.

Overall, it seems safe to say that Fillmore in the course of his public and professional life had been honest, trustworthy, discreet and even amiable. The fact that integrity marks one of his most favorable ratings, as low as it is, appears to us to be appropriate.

15. Executive Ability

Here we find Mr. Fillmore in 35th place.

It is obvious that he possessed drive and clarity of purpose. His immediate declaration of purpose in regard to the Compromise of 1850 and the obvious clarity of intent in the formation of his cabinet makes that abundantly clear. The drive for the compromise found a parallel in his drive to staff the cabinet with national Whigs. The corollary was obvious. The administration would not lean North or South but to the Union. Members might be northern or southern Whigs geographically, but not philosophically. They must cherish the Union if they were to join the administration.

He also illustrated the Whig bent toward commercial activity. This was most clearly seen during his presidency in his interest in developing trade with Asia and Asian markets and best demonstrated in his interest in and support for Commodore Perry's mission to Japan. In a similar fashion, while not an imperialist, he was aware of American overseas interests, whether in Hawaii, Latin America or elsewhere, and was prepared to announce those interests to potential or actual rivals strongly and clearly.

In these instances, as in those relating to political problems, his demeanor was always calm and his approach rational with no trace of jingoism evident.

We think, once again, that the overwhelming and perhaps insoluble problems of the era result in relatively low scores for what otherwise might have been seen as at least a moderately successful administration. He was neither a bad administrator nor a weak executive, but the problems he faced were immense and his political resources few.

16. Foreign Policy Accomplishments

President Fillmore occupies 37th place in this category.

Clearly, the historical significance of the Fillmore years lies primarily in the realm of domestic policy. Given that reality, it is rather surprising to see how many foreign policy issues occupied the President. Certainly his attitudes toward the development of domestic commerce – rivers and harbor legislation, benevolent attitudes toward canals and railways – had their counterparts in foreign affairs. He favored expanding overseas trade, too. Whether it was a matter of coaling stations for the new steamships, of island ports for whalers or for general commerce, or canals or railways to link the Atlantic and Pacific Oceans as a sort of bridge across the Isthmus of Panama to more easily reach the new West Coast state of California; it found some degree of interest and/or favor with the President. None, it should be noted smacked of empire building or of new territorial acquisitions. Perhaps recent events had sated any delight he might have ever had in that regard. In any event, it had never been a Whig issue.

Matters of foreign affairs involved several discrete areas of activity. For purposes of simplicity we may categorize them as European, Asian/Pacific and Central American/Caribbean. In the last category we can include issues relating to filibustering expeditions and Cuba.

In Europe, the President early on found himself facing a potential diplomatic confrontation with the Hapsburg Empire. In 1848, Hungary had risen in revolt against Austrian rule. The leader of the revolt was Louis Kossuth. President Taylor was intrigued by these events and had appointed an agent empowered to enter into a commercial treaty, and perhaps more, with the Hungarians. By the time the emissary arrived, the revolt had been quelled and Kossuth, in flight, had been placed under arrest in Turkey. Austria, learning of Taylor's scheme, was angry and complained. Taylor thereupon, in early 1850, sent all the correspondence to the Senate and condemned Austria. Austria now formally addressed its complaints to the United States government. At this point Fillmore came into office. The President and the state department issued a rather belligerent note in response, probably at least in part to fan the flames of American nationalism and union in the face of the crisis over slavery in the territories.

At America's behest, the Ottoman Empire freed Kossuth and sent him to the United States, where he was greeted by enthusiastic crowds, feted and made much of. He seems to have interpreted the public approval as a sign of American support for the Hungarians.

President Fillmore, to prevent misunderstanding, informed Kossuth that while he personally was sympathetic to Hungary's plight American policy flowed from Washington's Farewell Address, so Hungary could expect neither aid nor recognition. Gradually the bout of Kossuth mania withered and died.

Much more urgent issues flowed around Cuba. The 90-mile distance between Cuba and America had created a specious claim by some of U.

S. possession by proximity, even though the island was Spanish property. The fear of a slave rebellion, `a la Haiti at the end of the 18th Century, set off southern apprehension. That combined with the spirit of adventure allied with acquisitiveness had sparked quasi-invasions of the island, called "filibustering expeditions." (Filibustering in this context has no reference to parliamentary delaying tactics. Instead, it is military adventurism in which irregular military forces seek to seize, occupy and govern a relatively weak foreign state).

One conspicuous leader of such expeditions was a Venezuela-born Cuban expatriate named Narciso Lopez, who, using New Orleans as a point of departure, was planning yet another filibustering expedition into Cuba. On learning this, President Fillmore alerted the forces of the United States to keep him from sailing. Fillmore's efforts failed, and in August, 1851, the Lopez expedition sailed. Landing in Cuba on August 11th, the forces of Lopez were defeated by August 24th. Summary executions followed, including that of Lopez. Among those executed were American citizens.

Outrage resulted, particularly in the South. Fillmore avoided any appearance of making political capital of the moment. He decried the expedition and disclaimed any connection between the United States and Lopez. He even publicly agreed that Spain had done no more than exercise her rights under international law.

France and England reacted, seeing the incident as a possible preliminary to an American effort to annex Cuba, and sent naval forces into the region. Fillmore then sent American naval units into the Caribbean and dispatched diplomatic protests to Paris and London. The state department informed London that the President believed that Cuba was an American concern, not a European one.

These events coincided with the delivery to Congress of the President's annual message, and Fillmore took the occasion to draw some of the sting from his diplomatic notes by a formal disavowal of any American designs on Cuba. (The American ejection of Spain from Cuba would wait for another 50 years, until the Spanish-American War.)

In another area of the world, the growing interests of the United States in Asian trade made Hawaii, long an important site for American whalers, increasingly important as a coaling station and a resupply point. To that end, the United States early on had recognized the independence of the Kingdom of Hawaii. British and French interests in the islands had been diplomatically rebuffed.

During Fillmore's term, renewed rumors arose that the French were pursuing their own interests in Hawaii. In 1851, the French made demands upon the King of Hawaii that threatened to reduce the kingdom to a French dependency. Secretary of State Webster thereupon informed Paris that Hawaiian independence was to be preserved, unless it was to become part of the United States. The French, shortly thereafter, withdrew their demands.

Just as the Asian trade, at least in part, drove American interest in Hawaii, so, too, – along with the need to communicate with California – it was a driver for the interest of the nation in an isthmian canal. A quick route from the Atlantic Coast of Central America to its Pacific Coast, whether via Panama, Nicaragua or Mexico, by sea or by rail, was in the interest of the United States. Once again, in this instance, we see Fillmore carefully avoiding overreaching or the appearance of imperialism. Various crises, real or imagined, were handled with vigor and dispatch, but also with tact.

Finally, in this mixed series of initiatives and responses unified by a constant desire to have access to the potentially lucrative Asian markets, was the dispatch of Commodore Perry to Japan.

Overall, Fillmore's record in foreign policy seems relatively moderate, even benign by 19th Century standards. While we see no evidence of objective error in the survey, we also do not believe that a slight upward adjustment in his ranking in this area would constitute objective error.

17. Leadership Ability

President Fillmore has been assigned a ranking of 37th place in this ranking barely ahead of his cohorts in this section, Buchanan and Pierce.

Few would crown Fillmore with laurel based on his leadership. He was by temperament and experience a man who valued accommodation and compromise. His was another example of a legislative style of leadership rather than an executive one.

Forcefulness characterized his presidential leadership only in relation to the Compromise of 1850. That measure alone, which he regarded as essential to the preservation of the Union, fully engaged his intellect and spirit. He persistently held to the idea that it was and needed to be the final political solution to the issues of slavery, the territories and the Union.

In a presidential mixture including Washington and Lincoln, Theodore and Franklin Roosevelt and so many others, it would be difficult to suggest that this ranking, though low, is in any way inappropriate.

18. Intelligence

Only in the area of communications does Fillmore receive a lower ranking than in intelligence, where he is accorded 38th place.

Certainly he was poorly educated. Equally certainly, he had educated himself well in the law, where he appears to have been an able and talented attorney with a busy and lucrative practice. He was also, it seems, an avid reader, with a significant library at home to which he almost obsessively added. He and Mrs. Fillmore were the originators of the White House library. It seems to us that each of those factors might well be said to argue for intelligence.

At the same time, it must be recognized that much of his legacy, like the Compromise of 1850, was largely the work of other men and that no great state paper or oration exists to argue a stronger case for him.

19. Avoid Crucial Mistakes

In 28th place here, Fillmore has his fourth highest ranking.

This placement would seem to argue that the experts show some significant agreement with Fillmore's assessment that the Compromise of 1850, warts and all, was probably the wisest course of action available at the time. There really was no other action of sufficient significance undertaken by the President to fall under this heading. The fundamental issue remained – what to do about the issues of slavery and territorial expansion?

The Compromise of 1850 did not resolve the dilemma. It did, however, provide at least an additional decade of peace. That was a decade in which, by all quantitative measures, the forces that ultimately would preserve the Union and end slavery burgeoned as the North grew much more rapidly than the South.

Fillmore might have been disposed to argue that, had his immediate successors been wise enough to leave the Compromise undisturbed, more might have been achieved. Whether that is so we cannot know. If that view is correct, it might well have meant that slavery in the United States could have been sustained into the 20th Century.

In any event, in a time of real crisis, he managed to avoid crucial errors, though he never seems to have realized that the compromise was a palliative and not a panacea.

When the Civil War came, he was an unabashed supporter of the Union. However, unlike most of the old northern Whigs, he never was able to bring himself to support Lincoln. In 1864, Fillmore counted himself an adherent of George B. McClellan for President.

20. Present Overall View

When it comes to this category, Fillmore has gained one place and is ranked 37th, rather than 38th.

Chapter 8 - Franklin Pierce – March 4, 1853 – March 4, 1857

"One thing must be perfectly clear to every intelligent man – this abolition movement must be crushed or there is an end to the Union."
– Franklin Pierce to John P. Hale, Mar. 5. 1836, as cited in, Peter A. Wallner, Franklin Pierce, New Hampshire's Favorite Son, Concord, NH, 2004, p. 67.

The policy of my administration will not be controlled by any timid forebodings of evil from expansion. Indeed, it is not to be disguised that our attitude as a nation and our position on the globe render the acquisition of certain possessions not within our jurisdiction eminently important for our protection, if not in the future essential for the preservation of the rights of commerce.
– Franklin Pierce, Inaugural Address, March 4, 1853 as cited in Michael F. Holt, Franklin Pierce, NY, 2010, p. 53.

Franklin Pierce is the second in this set of Presidents and the youngest of the group. He was born in a log cabin in New Hampshire in 1804, the first American President to be born in the 19th Century. He died on October 8, 1869. In a list of presidential footnotes, he would command a relatively exalted position as the only President to date who did not swear an oath at his inauguration but rather, as the Constitution allows, affirmed. In our age of ubiquitous teleprompters, it is also noteworthy that he delivered his entire inaugural address, which exceeded 3,000 words, from memory. He is also the only President who never needed to replace a single cabinet member; all served from beginning to end.

It is to be regretted that his list of policy successes and triumphs of leadership are not nearly as notable.

1. Background (family, education, experience)
In this first category, the 2002 SRI Presidential Tracking Poll places

Franklin Pierce in 35th place. That is, only 15 per cent of his peers are ranked lower than he.

While Pierce was born in a log cabin, unlike his predecessor, Fillmore, his father was a successful small town entrepreneur and politician who would rise both economically and politically. Benjamin Pierce would serve in both houses of the state legislature, as sheriff, and, indeed, occupy the governor's chair. He was a dedicated member of the Democratic Party and was prepared to grapple with its opponents whenever and wherever possible. Pierce's own fierce loyalty to the Democratic Party is seen by his biographers as owing much to his father's example.

Franklin's father was a veteran of extended service during the Revolutionary War. He entered the army immediately after Lexington and Concord and served to the end of the war and beyond. He rose from private into the commissioned ranks, becoming a company commander before his discharge. In his post-war political and militia career, he would rise to the rank of brigadier general of the New Hampshire militia. Franklin Pierce was exceptionally proud of his father's military prowess as well as the military experience of his older brothers. They fought in the War of 1812 and then, remaining in the army, in the Seminole Wars as well.

As a boy, Pierce was reasonably well educated by the standards of the day and place. In 1820, his parents enrolled him in Bowdoin College in Maine. Geographically, Dartmouth might have seemed more logical, but Benjamin, as a good Democrat, believed that Dartmouth was tainted by Federalist elitism while Bowdoin was more thoroughly Democrat.

Certainly, though the student body was small, it was talented. In Pierce's years there, in addition to men who would serve in state and national offices up to and including the Senate of the United States, the college was also graced with the presence of Henry Wadsworth Longfellow and Nathaniel Hawthorne. The latter became a close friend of Pierce, who, in later years, frequently sought out one sort of federal sinecure or another for him. The student body, of course, also contained one future President.

After his graduation in 1824, Franklin read law, as was the custom of the day. He was admitted to the bar in 1827. Two years later, at age 25, he was elected as a Democrat to the New Hampshire legislature. He served in that body until 1832, rising to speaker during the last half of his service. From 1833 to 1837, he was a member of the U. S. House of Representatives, entering as its youngest member.

That portion of his political experience ended after his second term with his election to the United States Senate by the New Hampshire legislature in 1836. Once again, he entered the chamber as its youngest member.

His service in Washington was neither particularly meritorious nor notable. He was, in general, a reliable Democratic vote. His most significant role may have come in the mid-1830s when, as a member of the House, he mildly resisted the demand of southern members that anti-slavery petitions be rejected without even being formally received. Pierce maintained that the proposal violated the right of petition as guaranteed by the Bill of Rights. Instead, he suggested that such petitions be received and immediately tabled. Most might suggest that this was a distinction without a difference, since in either case the petitions would not be subject to either discussion or action. His proposal of December, 1835, was what ultimately became the "gag rule" with which the House would muffle anti-slavery opinion until 1844. In any event, his career in the national legislature does nothing to refute the charge by practical political figures of the day that Pierce was a doughface.

He resigned from the Senate in February of 1842 with slightly more than one year remaining in his term. Speculation about his resignation seems to center on two themes. The first focuses on his problems with alcohol. This speculation suggests that he found it difficult to control his drinking when Mrs. Pierce was not available to support him. She detested the political society of Washington and preferred not to go there. Pierce seems to have stopped drinking, with some success, around 1840-41. Indeed, he became the head of the temperance movement in New Hampshire. When Jane, who was often in poor health, found it impossible to join him in Washington in that heavily masculine, hard drinking society, he felt it impossible to cope with the social customs of his colleagues and, therefore, resigned.

The second theme focuses on the fact that Pierce had never before the election of 1840 served in the minority at any level of government. In this scenario, he decided that after a year of minority status he had all that he cared to tolerate.

After his resignation, he returned to New Hampshire and his law practice, though he remained both highly visible and active in state Democratic Party politics. In that role, he continued to display his antipathy to abolitionist views and, indeed, to free soil opinions. On at least two occasions, he convened special meetings of the state Democratic Party to withdraw previously awarded nominations to candidates who had broken with the party's national position on slavery and/or slavery in the territories. In addition to controlling the New Hampshire Democratic Party he also enhanced his decade out of office (1842-1853) with his very successful and lucrative law practice and by his service in the Army during the Mexican War.

At the time of the Mexican War, Pierce was called on by President James K. Polk, whose candidacy he had supported and whose election New Hampshire had bolstered, to raise a regiment of troops. Having raised the troops, Pierce took command as colonel of the regiment. He then was promoted to brigadier general to lead a brigade of troops to join General Winfield Scott's Army in Mexico. He led his force from the Mexican port of Vera Cruz to the rendezvous with Scott in an exemplary manner, successfully fighting a number of small engagements and favorably impressing Scott.

Thereafter, he was less fortunate. With their leader hampered by dysentery and an early injury, which resulted in a bad leg, his men often found themselves led into battle by other commanders. The result included rumors, probably scurrilous, of cowardice. There were also instances, and more rumors, which would indicate that the army, like the Congress, was not an environment particularly conducive to temperance pledges. The two circumstances were, in all likelihood, conflated.

While Scott and other officers such as Pierre Beauregard of Louisiana were well disposed toward Pierce, which would seem to argue at least competency, the war was a mixed experience for him. It did enable him to share the military heritage of his much admired father and of his brothers. It also would add a useful line to his campaign résumé in 1852. On the other hand, it also would be a source of slurs. There was a sort of tag line, perhaps begun in Mexico and certainly often used in 1852 – perhaps as a way to introduce his problem with alcohol – to the effect that General Pierce was the hero of many a hard fought bottle.

In any event, this was the background that Pierce's supporters would offer to the Democratic National Convention in Baltimore in 1852.

2. Party Leadership (political)

Despite his political experience, including his longtime leadership of the Democratic Party in New Hampshire and his lifelong and unquestioned loyalty to the national party, the experts polled by the SRI have accorded Mr. Pierce only a ranking of 38th place.

It seems evident to us that the experts have defined their terms quite narrowly in this category, limiting the analysis and ranking to the years 1853-1857. While Pierce should not bear all the blame for the chaotic era – certainly Senator Stephen Douglas and many southern solons deserve their full share – the fact is that in those four years a political firestorm took place. In 1852, Pierce captured 51 per cent of the popular vote. His opponent and old Mexican War commander, Winfield Scott, commanded only 44 per cent. Pierce carried 27 states, Scott won only four. By 1856, the Whig Party had collapsed in the wake of, and as a result of, Pierce's presidency. The modern Republican Party had been born as an avowed free soil party, the Democracy was weakened and Millard Fillmore garnered more than 20 per cent of the popular vote on a Know-Nothing platform. The political arithmetic of the 1856 election was also highly encouraging to the Republicans as they looked forward to the election of 1860.

The Republicans had carried 11 states in 1856, and the political picture was clear. If they could hold those 11 states, which some scholars call the "Upper North," and carry Pennsylvania and either Indiana or Illinois, the presidency was theirs. There were other possible combinations as well, but this was the least complex.

These changes, as well as the congressional disaster of the 1854 election, were responsible for Pierce's fall from political grace – not only in the 2002 SRI poll of academic experts but also in the brutal political fact that he was to become the only elected President who sought re-election but was denied re-nomination by his party.

Pierce's errors, which would undermine the President as well as his party, operated at two levels. We will examine each. The historically more important of the two was at the policy level. That was the Kansas-Nebraska Act of 1854.

The Compromise of 1850, so dear to President Fillmore's heart, had, by 1852, come to be seen as a permanent position. Political leaders who had opposed it and still found it distasteful, had come to accept it as a settled matter. It seemed to resolve the issue of slavery in the territories once and for all. The Kansas-Nebraska Act that specifically declared the Missouri Compromise null and void reopened the whole question of slavery in the territories, which had threatened disunion only three years earlier. Moreover, the act carried additional sting for the North by opening as possible slave states territories where slavery had been forbidden for a full generation. President Pierce had given assistance as well as his full approbation to Kansa-Nebraska. Radical southerners were delighted. Freesoilers were appalled.

Within six years, the specter of secession and civil war, which the Compromise of 1850 had done so much to quiet, would once again confront the nation. The palliative of the Compromise of 1850 was washed away in the flood of violence generated by the Kansas-Nebraska Act.

At a less significant administrative and political level. But stemming from the notion of strengthening and uniting the Democratic Party, President Pierce set out to create a "balanced" administration. His effort appears to have boomeranged in that it tended to strain and fragment the party rather than unite it. He determined that his administrative appointments, cabinet and subcabinet, would be offered to all factions of the party. Somehow, he felt, this would make all loyal to the administration and supportive of the

Compromise of 1850 and the other elements of the Democratic platform. A significant number of contemporaries saw the flaw almost at once.

Those who had kept the faith during the struggle over the Compromise of 1850, particularly southerners who had worked for its goals in the 1852 campaigns against the southern radicals, saw themselves or their friends passed over. Radicals like Jefferson Davis, who had reprobated the principles of the compromise, were appointed to office and virtually begged to join the administration. Northern Democrats, who had argued against Northern freesoilers, saw the freesoilers rewarded while they were not.

Less dramatic and, indeed, less important than Kansas-Nebraska, this policy tended to operate against the best interests of the party, however appealing it might sound in the abstract. If disloyalty was to be rewarded equally with loyalty, then why remain loyal? It is surprising that as thoroughly seasoned a political operative as Pierce failed to perceive his error.

3. Communication Ability (speak, write)
In this category, we find President Pierce, once again, ranked at 38th.

In his day, Pierce was admired as an orator of considerable talent. His ability as an attorney to move a jury or to sway a crowd as a political speaker was legendary. His fellow advocates frequently are cited as admirers, nearly devotees, of his oratorical style and ability. The products of his pen are less frequently lauded. Virtually no one, however, speaks or writes of his breadth of vision or of the depth of his thought.

In his lifetime, people were wont to speak frequently and admiringly of his warmth and amiability. He was a man often spoken of as charming. His depth of courtesy is cited over and over.

Perhaps in this way his visible public attributes may be said to parallel his abilities as a communicator. It seems that there was much to admire, but that, on examination, there was a sense of facility rather than good judgment. He seems then to have enjoyed a reputation as a highly effective speaker, but one for whom there seems to exist no quotation encompassing any great thought or emotion.

Certainly, he had warmth and charm and courtesy. But when he allowed his hat to be thrown into the presidential ring in 1852 there is no evidence that he even consulted his wife, whom he knew hated Washington and political life perhaps above all things. It might then seem that there is something of a contradiction evident. Where is the courtesy?

We believe that our experts have ranked him so low in this area because they see him as essentially superficial.

4. Relationship With Congress

Once again, we find a ranking of 38th.

If we accept as a given the rather cynical idea that nothing is as important to a sitting politician as personal reelection, we can gauge Pierce's impact with a few numbers. When he was inaugurated, there were 158 Democrats, 74 Whigs and five "others" among the members of the House of Representatives. Democrats controlled two-thirds of the group. Two years later, when the 34th Congress assembled, there were, in round numbers, 80 Democrats, 50 Know-Nothings, 100 "opposition" members and a few "others." The Democratic caucus had fallen from a two-thirds majority to just above one-third, and the Whigs – formally at least – had disappeared. Definitions also become problematic between Democrats, Independent Democrats, Anti-Nebraska Democrats and others.

A bitter quarrel over the speakership further discouraged any remaining vestiges of collegiality. The lines between the increasingly radical South (as old Whigs either vanished or adopted increasingly sectionalist views), and an increasingly freesoil North were more tightly drawn. The North not only felt betrayed by the Kansas-Nebraska Act but also resentful of partisan Democratic claims that the recent election, with its Democratic Party debacle, had somehow validated and confirmed Kansas-Nebraska. That boast seemed insult added to injury.

Pierce meanwhile had negotiated the Gadsden Purchase with Mexico to acquire land for the railroad right of way into Southern California. Despite the fact that it encompassed land essential for the quite popular transcontinental railway, Congress insisted on reducing the size of the acquisition to illustrate its displeasure with any issue of new territory and anything beneficial, even potentially, for the South.

5. Court Appointments

Ranked at 37th, Pierce made only one appointment to the Supreme Court, Associate Justice John Archibald Campbell of Alabama.

Campbell had graduated from the University of Georgia in 1825, when he was 14 years old. He then was appointed to West Point, but withdrew after three years when his father died. Shortly thereafter, he moved to Alabama, where he married and began the practice of law. He served in the Alabama State Legislature and was twice offered and rejected appointment to the Alabama Supreme Court.

He is usually described as holding moderate states rights views and being opposed to violence. Nonetheless, he appears to have regarded most northern views as inimical to southern interests. He would, once secession came, resign his seat on the Court (1853-1861), go south and serve in Jefferson Davis' war department throughout the Civil War. In an interesting irony, Campbell's resignation enabled President Lincoln to appoint his 1860 campaign manager, Judge David Davis, to the Supreme Court – probably not the outcome that Justice Campbell would have preferred.

When Pierce was inaugurated, an appointment was waiting. The Democratic majority in the United States Senate had refused to confirm any nominee of Fillmore's, preferring to await the arrival of a Democratic president and his nominee. In a most unusual circumstance, the entire United States Supreme Court, including Chief Justice Taney, suggested Campbell's nomination to Pierce. His nomination was unanimously confirmed by the Senate on the day it was submitted.

When, a few years later, the Court issued the Dred Scott Decision, Campbell's concurrence was, if anything, stronger than Taney's majority opinion – though, here again, his proponents point out that he was not a strong advocate of slavery. Without question, he was an intelligent advocate and wise interpreter of the law, though clearly biased in his views on the rights and entitlements of the South's "peculiar institution."

6. Handling of the U. S. Economy

Our panel has awarded a placement of 32nd to President Pierce on the economy.

As had President Fillmore before him, Franklin Pierce was fortunate enough to serve during a period of peace and prosperity. Whether one sang of California gold or stood prepared to claim that "cotton was king," the United States was in a period where everything seemed to be working well. Further, Pierce and the Democratic Party platform of 1852 proclaimed that the Compromise of 1850 had put the issues of slavery and territorial expansion to rest permanently. There seemed little to threaten the plans and hopes of the administration, unless the administration chose to create it.

Like virtually all administrations of the era, the government did little to interfere with the economy. The promise of a smooth journey for the Pierce administration proved to be fleeting and false, but the economy would not prove to be the cause of the failure.

7. Luck

Here, again, we find Pierce in 32nd place.

President Pierce's career, from his early years until his election as President, seems to offer evidence of good fortune in the public areas of his life, amply leavened by private misfortune.

Born to Benjamin and Anna Kendrick Pierce, he greatly admired his father, who was, by all accounts, outgoing and gregarious. Benjamin was an avid Jeffersonian Democrat and a highly skillful and successful Democratic Party political leader. Less is known of Franklin's mother, of whom he had virtually nothing to say.

His birth in a log cabin was a stroke of good fortune. In the post-Jacksonian era of the "common man" a log cabin birth was a selling point for presidential aspirants. This was emphasized, perhaps, for Pierce, whose father's success in life represented another element of good fortune. It enabled Franklin to obtain a much better than average education, including a college degree. It also offered him ready access to the legal profession and entrée to politics.

His father's political background and undoubted influence also represented a stroke of good fortune for the young man. Certainly, having served in the state legislature, including as speaker, and arriving in Washington at 29 as the youngest sitting member of the House, represented something more than mere strokes of extraordinary luck. It would be ingenuous to fail to give consideration to his father's status in New Hampshire politics.

Franklin Pierce's career had been exceptional. From its earliest days, he had enjoyed major public success. Then, for whatever reasons, he resigned from the U. S. Senate in 1842 with just over a year to go on his term. He returned to New Hampshire, the practice of law, virtual dominance of the state Democratic Party and, later, service in the Mexican War.

He had married Jane Appleton in November of 1834. She was of a very well-to-do Whig family and strenuously disliked politics and the society of politicians. They seemed something of an odd couple, he gay and gregarious, and she, pious and aloof. Jane would bear three children, all boys, none of whom would live to maturity. The last, Benjamin, would die, horribly, in the presence of his mother and father, in a train derailment shortly before Pierce's inauguration. One result would be that throughout Pierce's presidency his wife would be a virtual recluse, retiring to the White House family quarters and remaining there.

It would be unfair to label the marriage as bad fortune for Pierce. The couple seems to have been genuinely attached. Nevertheless, it seems unavoidable to suggest that he probably would have benefited greatly from the strength of a more outgoing and resilient woman. Having said that, we note that it omits what appears to have been her clearly salutary influence upon his ability to refrain from alcohol.

His Mexican War service with its suspected recurrence of his drinking seems also to have been a mixture of good and bad luck. He successfully raised and commanded a regiment and then a brigade. He took his troops to

Mexico and seems to have done well. Thereafter, a series of misadventures, injuries and infections plagued him, and no tint of battlefield glory attached itself to him.

There was a balance of good and bad luck to this point in his career, with the good luck primarily in public life and the bad in his personal life. His presidency saw his luck turn virtually universally bad, though a case can be made that much of that was primarily of his own doing.

His attainment of the nomination as an underdog, while a triumph of planning by his political friends, also required a modicum of good luck, and that was perhaps the last scintilla of good fortune he was to see.

The 1852 Democratic Platform was pledged to uphold the Compromise of 1850 as permanently having put to rest the issues associated with agitation and tension over slavery and territorial expansion. Pierce clearly was pledged to that faith. And yet, even in his inaugural address he refused to shy away from the possibility of further territorial acquisitions, claiming even that some might become necessary. That rhetoric seems already, in light of the political turmoil of the previous three years or so, to be pushing his luck.

He did make genuine efforts to curb filibustering, though they were far from uniformly successful. Those failures distressed northern freesoilers fearful of possible doughface efforts to acquire more territory as possible slave states. Those fears were heightened by the Ostend Manifesto – a document written in 1854 that described the rationale for the United States to buy Cuba from Spain or to seize it militarily if Spain refused to sell. The Kansas-Nebraska Act would come to symbolize the fulfillment of that apprehension and would bring the whirlwind around Pierce's head, momentarily shatter his Democratic Party and drive him from the political stage. Its origins were as follows.

The growth of the idea of a transcontinental railroad had been launched and well received among the American people. It was also common knowledge that it could not be built without a federal subsidy, which would be in the form of land grants.

The proposed southern route, running roughly from New Orleans to Southern California and on to San Francisco, lay entirely through slave states and organized territories. In those cases, lands could readily be surveyed and specific land grants provided. A more northerly route, due West from Chicago, ran through unorganized territory, including what would be the Kansas and Nebraska Territories. Unorganized territory was not subject to survey until after it was organized. Therefore, no immediate prospect of the necessary land grant subsidy for a northern route was available.

Senator Douglas of Illinois, chairman of the U. S. Senate Committee on

Territories, championed the more northerly route. The fact that its Eastern terminus was to be in Chicago may well have played a role in Douglas' enthusiasm. In 1853, he proposed to organize the Kansas Territory. Southern senators proved recalcitrant. This might be done, they said, but only with concessions to the South. What ultimately would be demanded was a specific guarantee that effectively would repeal the Missouri Compromise. That, in turn, would open territories to slavery that by law had been denied slavery since 1820. That quite incendiary notion appears to have presented neither Douglas nor Pierce with any warning of a formidable political problem.

The southern Senators and Douglas also insisted that the President be a party to the deal. Pierce not only agreed, he wrote the most significant portion of the death knell of the Missouri Compromise in his own hand. In effect, the ploy was to specify that the Compromise of 1850 superseded the Missouri Compromise and it was, therefore, null and void.

Whether these events qualify him as naive, stupid or just unlucky, they certainly were unfortunate for Pierce, the Democratic Party and the United States. Seven more years would pass before the Civil War would erupt, but it seems likely that these actions set events in motion that made war virtually inevitable.

8. Ability to Compromise

At 31st, this constitutes the highest ranking that President Pierce attained. It is ironic in that Pierce's willingness to compromise probably marked the first evidence of a lack of wisdom in his policy.

He had determined that Democratic Party unity was to be the bedrock of his administration. To that end he proposed that his appointments – cabinet, subcabinet, at whatever level – would be equally composed of all sections of the party. It was clearly an exercise in futility.

The 1852 party platform had stressed the centrality of the Compromise of 1850. Yet, to achieve his quite ephemeral goal of unity Pierce would shoulder aside moderate southerners who had formed "Union" parties in the South to labor against the Southern radicals and for the Compromise. Instead, he favored the radicals. Men like Davis, who had reprobated the compromise and even had characterized it as a potential reason for secession, would be favored, even courted, by Pierce. Thus, he persuaded a reluctant Davis to become his secretary of war and one of the most influential members of the inner circle. Meantime, moderates like Robert Toombs and Howell Cobb in Georgia, who had labored on behalf of the compromise and the Union, were largely ignored. It seemed almost from the beginning that Pierce's appointment policy was better designed to disrupt than to strengthen the

Democratic Party.

On the other hand, Pierce had quickly bought into the Kansas-Nebraska Act. He steadfastly opposed any criticism, making a test of party loyalty. One academic hypothesis suggests that the President thought that the position would strengthen Democratic Party unity by a battle against the Whigs, who, it was assumed, would vigorously oppose Kansas-Nebraska in the 1854 election cycle. Whatever Pierce's motives, the political results in the 1854 cycle were disastrous.

Overall, as we examine Pierce's record on when to compromise and about what, we feel constrained to suggest that, at best, he had a marked propensity for choosing the wrong course of action.

9. Willingness to Take Risks

This represents the nadir for Pierce, his lowest ranking, which he would attain in four categories, 39th. At one level, we are tempted to conclude that the question may be moot. Might it not be enough to conclude that his level of the awareness of risk was so inadequate that he may very well have rarely been aware of the presence of danger, political or otherwise?

On the other hand, when the Kansas-Nebraska Bill was being drafted and amended and subsequently passed in 1853-1854, a great many supposedly sophisticated politicians, notably Douglas, also seemed quite cavalier about its potential ramifications. Nor were the southern senators so insistent on the repeal of the Missouri Compromise able to see anything daunting in their futures as a result of these activities.

Here, it seems clear to us, the logic of the then-current events yoked to a rather complete failure of imagination blinded the principal actors in this drama to the hardly unforeseeable results of their actions.

In any event, we find nothing in this category that would be beneficial to any assessment of Pierce's presidency.

10. Executive Appointments

The 2002 SRI poll places Pierce at 37th in this category.

Pierce's cabinet in one instance was unique. It was and remains the only cabinet in United States history to have served unaltered throughout an administration.

Its members were Secretary of State William Marcy of New York; Secretary of the Treasury James Guthrie of Kentucky; Secretary of War Jefferson Davis of Mississippi; Attorney General Caleb Cushing of Massachusetts; Secretary of the Navy James Dobbin of North Carolina, Postmaster General James Campbell of Pennsylvania and Secretary of the

Interior Robert McClelland of Michigan.

Three represented slave states, and four represented free states. Of the four, however, Cushing was perhaps the most thoroughgoing doughface of his time. A few years later his support of the Dred Scott Decision was so vigorous and effusive that Chief Justice Taney personally wrote him a letter of thanks.

In line with Pierce's policy, Cushing had been a vociferous proponent of the Compromise of 1850, while Jefferson Davis had been equally vehement in his opposition. Secretary Marcy was an enemy of New York Senator Daniel S. Dickinson, who had ardently adhered to the Compromise. Secretary of the Interior McClelland of Michigan was a supporter of Senator Lewis Cass and thus aligned as a pro-compromise man. Secretary of the Navy Dobbin had been influential in Pierce's nomination but had opposed the compromise as insulting to the South. At the request of Polk's former secretary of state, James Buchanan of Pennsylvania, Pierce appointed James Campbell, another Pennsylvanian, as postmaster general. Secretary of the Treasury Guthrie was essentially unknown to Pierce but was well regarded as a businessman.

Taken all in all, the cabinet functioned reasonably well. There were no significant scandals in any of the departments. Some cabinet members, notably Davis, did yeoman-like work in their departments. In his late 60s, Marcy perhaps was beyond his most vigorous days, but Pierce, who foresaw major foreign policy activity during the administration was quite happy to act on his own.

When we turn to the advisory role of the cabinet or its individual members, the scholarly consensus seems to be that Davis and Cushing exercised a sort of malign, pro-southern influence on the policies of the administration, with or without the influence of Douglas and a small bloc of southern Senators. McClelland, Marcy and Guthrie seemed to have formed the more moderate core of the cabinet, but their role is seen as less influential than that of Cushing and Davis.

11. Overall Ability

For the fourth time, Pierce is ranked at 38th.

Franklin Pierce was a fine attorney and a highly successful politician. He was genial and affable, and most people who met him were charmed by him. He was quite capable of mixing with and even captivating people whose political views differed from his own. As a student and an attorney he gave every indication of possessing a good intellect, especially when he was motivated and disciplined.

On the other hand, he does not seem to us to offer instances of a particularly analytical mind. Most of his political experience had taken place in New Hampshire, where the Democratic Party dominated the state. Pierce was from early on a sort of political golden boy and later the dominant figure in the state party. In that environment and in that experience, the unity and triumph of the party might well appear to be a be all and end all. It simply may be that when he left the parochial politics of New Hampshire he was unable or unwilling to learn any new lessons. Perhaps he was just intellectually lazy.

Whatever the cause, it is clear that his abilities simply seem not to have grown after he left his native heath.

12. Imagination

This category yields another ranking of 39th. Only five per cent of his 41 peers are ranked lower. When Pierce was inaugurated, he chose not to take an oath of office but simply, as the Constitution provides, to affirm. Rather than place his hand on a Bible, he placed it on a law book as he affirmed. That symbolic act may have been the most imaginative action of his entire administration.

The possible impact of his lack of imagination may be discerned by examining about one half a decade.

The Mexican War and questions about slavery and territorial expansion arising from the Mexican Cession had convulsed the nation and raised questions about secession and possible civil war. That near political paroxysm had quieted only in the wake of the Compromise of 1850. Originally scorned by many, it had by 1852 become a central plank in the platforms of both political parties. It became a sort of ultimate fallback position, so much so that Pierce was pledged to prevent it from being disturbed. It was, initially, assumed to be sacrosanct.

However, by 1853, within six months or so of his inauguration, he already had pledged himself to the Kansas-Nebraska Act, which promised not only renewed agitation but specifically would repeal the Missouri Compromise, which had denied the possibility of slavery in those territories for a generation or more. The President, in the face of these simple facts – not to mention their symbolic and emotional contents – seems to have been incapable of assessing the likelihood for damage, even disaster, in the new realities. He committed not only his administration, but also insofar as he was able, his party to the issue.

It is our belief that the accumulation of errors that followed, leading ultimately to the Civil War, was primarily due to the inability of the nation's political leaders to foresee the birth of new realities. For many political leaders, things had always worked in this fashion – threat, counter-threat, compromise. That had been the pattern at least since the Nullification Crisis of the early 1830s in which South Carolina had challenged national tariff laws; therefore, it always would be. The notion that at some point one or both parties really would mean what they said and either carry out their own threats or defy the threats of the other group seems not to have occurred to anyone.

The growing intensity of conviction regarding slavery simply seems not to have registered on many of the era's major political leaders. One result was that within eight years of Pierce's election the Whig Party would be dead, and a brand new party, the Republican Party, would elect freesoiler Abraham Lincoln President, leaving the nation on the brink of dissolution and civil war.

Pierce seemed particularly resistant to change. He remained even during the Civil War at best ambivalent about the Union cause. In this, he was unlike his successor, Buchanan, whose support for the Union was absolute and Fillmore, who bore Lincoln no love but stood staunch for the Union. When Jefferson Davis' plantation was seized by the Union Army correspondence from Pierce was discovered that seemed to many to be overly sympathetic to Davis and to the Confederacy and its woes. Pierce's letters to Davis seemed notably cool to the Union cause.

13. Domestic Accomplishments

Our experts, once again, have placed President Pierce at 39th. Since the Kansas-Nebraska Act in American history is rather akin to the opening of Pandora's Box in classical mythology – and it is the major piece of domestic legislation to receive President Pierce's signature – the rating is not surprising.

If we examine the world Pierce inhabited on March 4, 1853, and the one he left to Buchanan on March 4, 1857, we initially see a political world in some sort of balance, if rather tenuous, followed by one skating on the edge of chaos.

Americans in 1852 had voted for the stability they believed the Compromise of 1850 promised. Those who had supported the compromise were elected or reelected. Even in the deep South compromise opponents had learned that overly vigorous criticism could bring political punishment. With Kansas-Nebraska, Pierce had had shattered the illusion of balance.

As Buchanan sought office, new terms had been or were being added to the American political lexicon – terms such as "border ruffian" and "Bleeding

Kansas." Newspapers reported further violence in Kansas, where John Brown murdered five pro-slavery men on the banks of the Pottawatomie Creek. So too, the country would learn that on the floor of the United States Senate Representative Preston Brooks of South Carolina had taken his cane and beaten Senator Charles Sumner of Massachusetts into insensibility as a result of an anti-slavery speech Sumner had made.

Pierce's beloved Democratic Party would rally to elect Buchanan in 1856, but the outlines of a free soil electoral victory were clearly delineated in the 1856 electoral returns. More ominously, the threat of southern secession loomed should the North legitimately elect a free soil candidate.

Five more years would see the specter assume a grim reality.

14. Integrity

In integrity, Mr. Pierce receives a ranking of 36th.

We think that some clarification may be called for in analyzing Pierce's placement in this category. During his presidency no defalcations of funds, no scandalous shenanigans, and no betrayals of state secrets were brought to light. In short, there was no misfeasance or malfeasance of office. Whether, or to what degree, his drinking problem entered into the equation is unknown.

In Pierce's case, we think the issue of integrity is probably wrapped up in the failure of imagination to which we already have alluded. A President who was pledged to upholding the status quo in relation to slavery and the territories entered office with an inaugural address that already showed him casting his eyes outward in an imperial manner. If it did not speak of manifest destiny – the 19th Century conviction that the United States was destined to enjoy dominion over all of North America – it surely whispered of it. He promised to resist any "timid forebodings of evil from expansion." He called upon all to recognize that America might have a legitimate need to acquire "… certain possessions not within our jurisdiction … ."

This rhetoric harkened back to the glory days of manifest destiny with no recognition of the tumult that had resulted – ranging from the annexation of Texas and the Mexican War and Cession to the ensuing political and sectional turmoil that followed. It made no mention of that turmoil that Pierce had pledged had been permanently settled by the Compromise of 1850. Depending upon the auditor, it might also be heard as a harbinger of the acquisition of Cuba and/or other interests in the Caribbean and Central America, perhaps with an eye to acquiring territory useful to slave-owning interests.

Further doubt as to Pierce's commitment to his public pledge to uphold the party platform on the Compromise of 1850 seemed also close at hand. The ease with which Douglas and the southern senators brought Pierce to agreement on the Kansas-Nebraska Act, even to effectively standing as "Godfather" to the explicit repudiation of the Missouri Compromise, did not seem to suggest a man whose pledged word could be trusted under all circumstances.

Finally, in this regard, it is difficult to understand the degree of deference he seems to have accorded southern men and southern views. While he did try to prevent filibusterers from leaving American ports, in most major matters he seems to have been in the southern camp.

Cuba always hovered in the background. President Polk had offered to buy Cuba from Spain, though the offer had been rejected. It remained a sticking point between the two nations. Spain, though facing bankruptcy, was unwilling to let the island go. The United States coveted the island. The South saw it as a new slave state, and also feared that a slave insurrection there might unleash terrors akin to those of Haiti at the end of the previous century. It had been and was the preferred target for numerous filibustering groups. In all these ways, it created tension and aggravated diplomatic relations between the two nations as well as roiling already turbid domestic waters.

Pierce thought to pressure Spain to sell. He thought her weak economic status might add to the pressure and asked the American ministers to London, Paris and Madrid to meet and prepare an internal memorandum for the state department on what to do about Cuba. Meeting in Ostend, Belgium, in October of 1854, quite unsurprisingly the ministers foresaw possible circumstances under which the United States might be forced to intervene in Cuba. They suggested that a revolt in Cuba might make such an intervention both inevitable and appropriate.

The so-called Ostend Manifesto did not demand that Spain sell Cuba under threat of American assault. It was simply an exercise, and the document itself broke no new ground. It became public in 1855. Coming, as it did, however, in the wake of the Kansas-Nebraska Act, May 30, 1854, it seemed to fulfill the darkest fears of the freesoilers. The Missouri Compromise had been repealed, and territory barred to slavery for more than 30 years had been made available to slave owners. Yet still the "slave power" was not satisfied and wanted to acquire Cuba. One did not need to be a public relations genius to make this piece of propaganda seem likely.

It may be argued that this does not really speak to Pierce's integrity. Perhaps it only indicated that he was naïve or overly pliable. Nevertheless, in the political world of the 1850s an increasingly large number of free state residents felt themselves betrayed. True or not, their suspicions did not seem unreasonable.

15. Executive Ability

President Pierce ekes out still another placement at 38th.

Franklin Pierce brought no executive experience to the presidency. His legislative experience, outside that of his brief, youthful service as speaker of the New Hampshire legislature, had brought no notable recognition of ability from his fellows. He did bring to his presidency personal charm, collegiality and some reputation as an orator.

His cabinet was not untalented, especially considering the peculiar base upon which it was created. The grief felt by the President over young Benjamin's death must have dogged Pierce as he recruited for the cabinet. Jane's withdrawal surely constituted a strain upon him as well. For all that, however, his cabinet members seem to have developed a liking, even affection, for him and he for them, and all members served throughout his term. It was perhaps that affection that would later cause him to write to the then president of the Confederacy, Davis, Pierce's former war secretary. That correspondence, which expressed some sympathy for Davis and his cause and lamented the war, would cause some contemporaries to excoriate Pierce.

Pierce's most basic flaw was his seeming inability to separate the significant from the mundane. That inability may point to Pierce's fatal shortcoming as President – his inability to subject ideas, his own as well as those presented to him, to any sort of rigorous analysis. If an idea seemed attractive and feasible he was likely to embrace and pursue it, especially eagerly if it had the imprimatur of individuals he trusted. In any event, there seems always to have been a slightly superficial quality to Mr. Pierce, something of the lightweight. He had a tendency to embrace or resist ideas or plans based more on emotions or personalities than thought and planning.

It is difficult to illustrate specific strengths for the President in this category.

16. Foreign Policy Accomplishments

No new ground is broken here, with Pierce, once again, relegated to 39th place.

Diplomacy was an area in which Pierce had expected to shine. The administration opened with a bang with the return of Commodore Perry's mission to Japan, complete with colorful costumes and exotic individuals.

The idea of manifest destiny had not lost all its charms for Americans, least of all for Franklin Pierce. Even his selection of the aged William Marcy as secretary of state was, at least in part, premised on the notion that much of the foreign policy initiative of the day would pass through the President's hands. Marcy was happy to welcome a presidential initiative, but not prepared to become a puppet.

Three nations and their attendant problems would vie for Pierce's attention. They were, Spain – and, with Spain, the Cuban issue – Britain and Mexico.

With Spain, came those diplomatic issues centered on Cuba. The President sent Pierre Soule of Louisiana to Madrid as the minister from the United States. This was arguably the worst appointment that Pierce made in his entire presidency. If the term "loose cannon" ever was properly applied it was in Soule's case. In virtually no time, by the summer of 1854, Soule had fought a duel with the French minister to Spain and been expelled from the country by the Spanish government because he had been urging the overthrow of that government. Whether any other minister might have succeeded, per Marcy's instructions, in purchasing Cuba for $130 million seems quite problematic. The likelihood of Soule succeeding at anything in Spain seems impossible.

The end result of all of the diplomatic flailing about was to be stalemate with Spain, more American meddling in Cuba and the ill-advised and largely futile exercise known as the Ostend Manifesto. The manifesto would serve only as a cudgel with which suspicious Northern freesoilers could beat the Pierce administration and an inducement to southern radicals to demand further territorial aggrandizement.

After much effort Pierce had succeeded in persuading Buchanan to agree to represent the United States in London. His primary assignment was to persuade Britain to accept the American interpretation of the Clayton-Bulwer Treaty of 1850. That treaty specified that any projected isthmian canal (British or American) was to be neutral, and each power was pledged to keep it so. That pledge included the rejection of fortifications and territorial control. Britain preferred her own interpretation, which allowed her to keep British dependencies in the region. They, she insisted, antedated the treaty and were therefore not covered by it.

Buchanan was hampered because Pierce, in another ill-conceived appointment, had saddled him with Daniel Sickles as his secretary of legation. Sickles, a hothead and later a highly controversial Union general in the civil War, was only marginally more diplomatic than Soule and quickly alienated British opinion. To assist Buchanan, Pierce in December of 1855, in the President's annual message, forcefully articulated the administration's position. At the same time, the Crimean War, which had begun in 1854, removed Russia as a main foreign source of wheat for the British market, leaving Americans virtually a monopoly in that area. In, around and through all of these complexities, Britain increasingly found the American interpretation more palatable.

Simultaneously, in negotiations conducted in North America, Marcy had worked out acceptable accommodations between the United States and Canada in regard to contested issues, which involved the north Atlantic fisheries and a reciprocal trade treaty. Both had been resolved by 1854.

James Gadsden, a South Carolina railway organizer, was sent to Mexico to seek modifications to the Treaty of Guadalupe Hidalgo of 1848. His mission was to negotiate the purchase of land in northwestern Mexico for construction of a transcontinental railroad from the southwestern territories of the United States into southern California and on to San Francisco. The Gadsden Purchase, as it was know, completed the growth of the contiguous United States. Pierce seems not to have fully grasped the depth of the nation's emotional turmoil till the Senate refused to ratify the Gadsden purchase until the extent of the land purchased was negotiated downward.

The Gadsden Treaty and the settlements with Canada were the administration's most significant foreign policy successes. The Perry mission and relations with Japan are normally assigned to the credit of the Fillmore presidency.

Even here, though, we perceive a taint. Due to bad luck or lack of imagination and/or planning, the Gadsden mission's success ended up lending impetus to the fast tracking of the Kansas-Nebraska legislation.

17. Leadership Ability

President Pierce is again ranked 39th.

Merriam Webster's On Line Dictionary defines leadership as, "1. the office or position of a leader; 2. The capacity to lead; 3. The act or an instance of leading." In our case, Pierce fulfills definition number one by virtue of occupying the office of President. It is difficult, as the ranking of the experts indicates, to offer credible evidence of his fulfilling either definition two or three.

He could and did, both in New Hampshire and as President, use power and patronage to force people into line and to deliver votes. Such tactics, however, while useful, have never been perceived as anything more than ancillary to genuine leadership.

18. Intelligence

Here we find that the academics have assigned him a ranking of 36th among America's Presidents.

Pierce, after a rocky start at Bowdoin, disciplined and applied himself to compile a good academic record. He was a highly successful attorney and advocate, which certainly argues in favor of an adroit intelligence.

On the other hand, unlike many of his predecessors and successors, nothing in his career, including his post-presidential years, argues in favor of his pursuit of the life of the mind. It was said of Pierce's immediate predecessor, Fillmore, that whenever and wherever he traveled he always returned to Buffalo with packages of books. Similarly, while Mrs. Fillmore is usually given most of the credit, the White House Library dates from the Fillmore years. In retirement, it was the University of Buffalo and other educational institutions which formed a very important part of his activities. There are no parallels in Pierce's career.

Here, as so often seems to be the case, Franklin Pierce's gifts seem shallow and facile rather than substantive. A reasonable summary might be that he was bright, but not thoughtful.

19. Avoids Crucial Mistakes

Ranked 34th, this represents his fourth highest score. To some it may appear overly generous.

It would be both cynical and flippant to say simply that Franklin Pierce never met a crucial mistake he failed to embrace. On the other hand, it would take a veritable Pollyanna to fail to acknowledge that the Kansas-Nebraska Act, which he so enthusiastically supported, did much to launch the United States on the path to disunion and civil war.

Kansas-Nebraska was what the United States Army calls a "force multiplier." The Ostend Manifesto, which became public the following year, was most definitely not a demand that Spain sell Cuba to the Americans – with the implication of at least one more slave state being added to the country – or that the Americans would be justified in seizing the island by war. In the wake of Kansas-Nebraska and the turmoil in "Bleeding Kansas," however, it did not require a genius to create that impression.

His appointment and patronage policy was not what caused the Democratic Party's debacle in the 1854 elections, but it surely helped fragment the party and, with the Kansas-Nebraska Act, paved the way for the rise and triumph of the Republican Party. That party went from non-existence in 1853 to controlling the Congress in 1859 and winning the presidency as well as both the House and Senate in 1861.

Few Presidents, barring major economic collapses, have produced so much change, or so much mischief, in so little time as Franklin Pierce.

226

20. Present Overall View

In the 20th category, present overall view, Pierce retains the 39th place ranking, which the averaging of the other 19 categories had already established.

Chapter 9 - James Buchanan – March 4, 1857 – March 4, 1861

"If you are as happy entering the White House as I shall feel on returning to Wheatland, (Buchanan's Pennsylvania home), you are a happy man indeed."
– James Buchanan to Abraham Lincoln on the occasion of Lincoln's inauguration, March, 4, 1861.

The last president in this set is James Buchanan of Pennsylvania. He is the oldest of the three Presidents in the group, born in 1791. He is also the only President to have been a lifelong bachelor. Like the other members of the trio, he was born in a log cabin, as was his successor, Abraham Lincoln.

1. Background (family, education, experience)
This is the category in which Buchanan achieves his highest score, ranking 26th.

Few candidates for President have ever presented a more impressive résumé to the American people. While he was born in a log cabin, like Pierce, Buchanan's father, too, was upwardly mobile and successful. Therefore, unlike Fillmore and Lincoln, he would have available the resources necessary for educational opportunities. He matriculated at Dickinson College, where he proved an excellent student despite being briefly suspended for overly exuberant behavior. After readmission, he graduated in good standing in 1809, at age 18.

As we have seen in a number of cases, he, too, "read the law" with a distinguished attorney and began practice in 1812. During the War of 1812, he served briefly in a local volunteer militia unit at the time of the British campaign in the Baltimore/Washington, D.C. area.

In this period, he also became a Mason and served as a Federalist in the Pennsylvania Legislature from 1814 to 1816. His law practice flourished, and he prospered. In 1821, still a Federalist, he was elected to the House of Representatives and served in the House for a decade. In his last term in that body, by then a Democrat, he was the chairman of the house judiciary committee.

By that time the Federalist Party was virtually moribund. Buchanan, however, managed to continue in office as he transitioned from Federalist to Democrat by joining with the movement to elect Andrew Jackson president. In 1828, he ran for the House and won as a Democrat, while ostensibly representing a fusion or confederation of Federalists and Jacksonians. He was never really close to the seat of power in the Jackson years, though he was seen as an important power broker in Pennsylvania politics.

His style of politics, best described as slow and patient, was developed during those years. That style sought to avoid confrontation and political donnybrooks. He was loath to hold grudges and rarely gave offense. His campaign style tended to emphasize the role of his friends. It was most often surrogates who touted his abilities. He rarely appeared on the hustings. The letter rather than the speech was his preferred form of communication, and tight reasoning and civil argumentation his chosen mode.

When his last term in the House expired in 1831 he already had chosen not to seek reelection. In that term, he fought a significant battle on the House floor defending the independence of the judiciary, which he won handily. He also served as the principal manager in the successful impeachment of Judge James Peck of Missouri, though the Senate failed to convict.

By June of 1831, Buchanan already had agreed to accept an appointment from President Jackson as the United States minister to Russia. He served briefly, from January 1832 to August of 1833, but he did well. He negotiated the first commercial treaty between the United States and Russia. His appointment was seen as successful.

After his return, in 1834 the Pennsylvania Legislature elected him to the U. S. Senate. There he would serve for 11 years when he resigned to enter the cabinet of President Polk as secretary of state, 1845-49. When, during that time, Polk offered him a seat on the Supreme Court, Buchanan declined because he was engaged in on-going negotiations with Great Britain over the settlement of the northern boundary of the Oregon Territory.

On that issue, Buchanan had differed sharply with President Polk. Buchanan pointed out that all American Presidents since Monroe had been prepared to settle the boundary at 49 degrees north latitude. Polk, in his inaugural address, had taken a stronger line, echoing the "fifty-four, forty or fight" rhetoric of the 1844 campaign. After much discussion and pulling and hauling, Polk was persuaded, and the ensuing treaty accepted the 49th parallel, ending the issue amicably.

In later years, northern freesoilers would point out that the expansionists of the era were prepared to go to war with Mexico for new territory that might become slave but prepared to compromise with regard to northern territories likely to become free states.

During the Pierce administration, the President persuaded a reluctant Buchanan to agree to serve as the American minister to Great Britain. In that capacity he again proved successful despite having to deal with the fallout created by aggressive American expansionists like Sickles. Buchanan was also one of the principals in the drafting of a controversial document called the Ostend Manifesto, though not one of its originators. That document sparked fears of an American takeover of Cuba and the addition of another slave state to the union.

Buchanan did not, at the time, realize how fortunate, politically, he was to be abroad at that moment. That fortunate circumstance meant that he did not have to stake out a public position on the Kansas-Nebraska Act. It did much to improve his prospects for the Democratic nomination for President in 1856 and to enable him as a candidate to appear to both sides of that quarrel with clean hands.

Throughout virtually all of these years, certainly since the 1830s, Buchanan had always been at the head of one faction of the Democracy (the colloquial name of the Democratic Party) in Pennsylvania. Sometimes his group was dominant, or nearly so; sometimes it was significantly outweighed by another, such as the Family Party, centered in Philadelphia. Even in the midst of infighting, however, he seems always to have kept one eye on the necessity of Pennsylvania's Democrats uniting to maximize the state's leverage with the then current Democratic administration in Washington.

He also seems to always have kept an eye on the presidential nomination of the Democratic Party. At a minimum, his name was in the mix from 1844-1856. The nomination finally came to him in 1856, when he was 65 years old. The only two Presidents who had been about as old as he, William Henry Harrison and Zachary Taylor, had died in office.

His résumé amply validates the rather unfortunate nickname he seems to have given himself when he spoke of himself as the "Old Public Functionary." In the last years of his presidency, the "OPF" epithet was often used as a term of derision. Certainly, however, Buchanan had given good, even distinguished, service to the republic in a variety of capacities.

2. Party Leadership (political)

In our 2002 SRI poll, Buchanan was accorded only a rank of 39th in this category.

Buchanan began his political career as a Federalist, and not until after a decade or more of public service in Pennsylvania did he formally become a Democrat, though he had been known as an Andrew Jackson supporter much sooner. Indeed, it was President Jackson who appointed him to his first diplomatic post as minister to Russia. During most of his political career, the Pennsylvania Democratic Party was divided into factions and, in spite of his best efforts, he was unable to unite it. That failure may have played a significant role in the failure of his efforts to attain the Democratic presidential nomination in 1844, 1848 and 1852.

Whether his close-to-the-vest style of politics played a role in the failures is unclear. Perhaps a leader more given to public appearances and oratory and less to the use of correspondence and surrogates might have been more successful. We can never know.

In 1856, Buchanan's time came. It probably was influenced, at least in part, by the fact that his residence in London in 1854 and after kept him clear of any known public position on the Kansas-Nebraska Act. Regrettably for both the nation and James Buchanan the party and country had been so split by the furor over the Kansas-Nebraska Act and its aftermath that Buchanan would once again find it impossible to unite his party.

Still reeling from its rout in the 1854-1855 elections and facing a fresh and energized political coalition rising from the ashes of the pre-Kansas-Nebraska political system, particularly in the North, the Democracy soon found itself in further flux and turmoil. President Buchanan and Senator Douglas of Illinois found themselves at such loggerheads that by 1859 the clearly pro-administration members of the party found themselves representing no more than 30 per cent of the House of Representatives. Surrounding them were former Whigs, anti-Nebraska Democrats and Republicans. The following year, of course, the Republicans would elect Abraham Lincoln as President and control Congress as secession stalked the nation.

While it may be fair to say that it is unlikely that anyone else could have done better, the fact seems to be that there seems little to show for Buchanan's efforts that did not exacerbate the country's difficulties. Northern Democrats increasingly dismissed him as a doughface while southern Democrats sought to require more of him than he could give.

3. Communications Ability (speak, write)

The professors who comprised the 2002 SRI respondents have placed him at 40th.

We have already stipulated that Buchanan preferred to avoid the kind of political oratory that was characteristic of the period. Indeed, it often seems that he was loath to appear in public except when he deemed it a true political necessity. There seems to be no particular reason for this attitude other than personal preference.

We know, for example, that he was a successful litigator, which requires some facility in speech. Accounts of his forensic feats, though, do seem to stress his use of logic and specifics. That might be taken to indicate that, for non-litigators, there may have been some sense of repetition and tedium in his oratory. In any event, there seems to be no contemporary evidence which would argue substantial talent as an orator.

We also know that much of his business, personal, political and commercial, was carried on by letter. (That was true for many, if not most, public figures of the era.) Specific examples frequently cited tend to be quite precise and even overly detailed. Our tendency is to conclude that, here too, little was present to engage the imagination or brighten the spirit.

As with Pierce, it seems difficult to find a record of enduring wit or wisdom shining through the mountain of workmanlike presidential prose.

4. Relationship With Congress

Here we find Buchanan in 39th place.

It would be logical to assume that a President who had served with success in both the House and the Senate as well as Minister to Tsarist Russia and to Great Britain – with honor in both instances – as well as serving a full term as secretary of state, would have done well with a Congress in which his party at the beginning of his term had control of both houses.

Unfortunately for Buchanan, the political trauma of the Pierce administration, reflected in the heavy losses in the elections of 1854-1855, had not been healed by 1856-57. While the Senate was comfortably Democratic, enjoying a roughly 2-1 majority over the rising Republicans when he took office in 1857, the House showed much narrower margins with disgruntled Democrats and Know-Nothings frequently determining outcomes. Nor do bare numbers account for party strife resulting from Buchanan's quarrel with Douglas. In his last two years, the Republicans would come into control of the House. As secession began, the Senate would become theirs as well.

The whirlwind in the Democratic Party, which began to stir with the Mexican War and the Mexican Cession, had gained velocity in the North with the Fugitive Slave Law of the Compromise of 1850. It was further energized by the Kansas-Nebraska Act of 1854. It then would find greater energy with the ongoing violence of Bleeding Kansas, the Dred Scott Decision of 1857 and the Lecompton Constitution, a proposed framework for the admission of Kansas to the Union as a slave state. Written entirely by the pro-slavery faction, it ultimately was rejected by Kansas voters.

Buchanan has been seen by many historians, perhaps most notably Allan Nevins, as a sort of prototypical doughface – a tool in the hands of stronger, southern men who dominated him. Indeed, Nevins spoke of Buchanan's cabinet, together with a few southern members of Congress as a "Directory" exercising control over him.

Philip S. Klein, a modern Buchanan biographer, has challenged that characterization. Klein suggests that rather than a doughface Buchanan saw himself as a sort of slave to the law. In this sense, the President, who genuinely disliked slavery, operated in a specific context.

Slavery was legal and constitutional. Since that was true, Buchanan reasoned, the South was entitled to the protection of the law and to equality before the law. Since the Kansas-Nebraska Act was legal, proslavery elements in Kansas who drafted the Lecompton Constitution were entitled to full protection of the law. The Topeka government in Kansas was a mere faction, composed of the anti-slavery settlers, who had organized in opposition to the proslavery settlers at Lecompton, the tiny town that had been the territorial capital when the proposed pro-slavery constitution was drafted. In this context, the Topeka government was illegal and without standing.

Thus, in Klein's view, the President was constrained to support the Lecompton faction to which Pierce had given the legal recognition of the federal government. To a large degree, other than as it affects a view of Buchanan's temperament, this seems to us to represent another distinction without a difference, since the end result, regardless of motivation, would appear to be the same.

When the Lecompton government petitioned for the admission of Kansas to the Union as a slave state under the so-called Lecompton Constitution, Buchanan essentially offered his support. The Topeka government had boycotted the voting process on the draft constitution, because they thought that the referendum would be rigged. For Buchanan the boycott was their problem. The duly constituted government had held a legal election. That process was then legally valid. He was, therefore, prepared to submit the Lecompton Constitution to the Congress for a vote on the admission of Kansas as a slave state.

It was this decision that brought the President into direct political confrontation with Senator Douglas of Illinois, who was arguably the most popular Democratic leader in the country. Ironically, Douglas, the initiator of the Kansas-Nebraska Act, was now politically required to oppose its result. Douglas had surrounded the legislation with the cloak of "popular sovereignty." The idea was simple: Congress would say nothing about slavery in the territories. The residents of the territory would decide the issue of whether the new state would be slave or free. His constituents, the small farmers, had wanted no part of competition with slave-based agriculture. Douglas and others had reassured them that their votes would prevent it. Now, as a result of both chance and chicanery, it seemed they might not. For Douglas, that created a political imperative.

Douglas faced reelection in 1858, and the Lecompton controversy was blossoming just about a year before that campaign. He wanted to be President, and opposing Lecompton would hurt him in the South. However, if he were not reelected in Illinois in 1858 he had no chance of being nominated at all. He had to oppose the Lecompton Constitution.

The direct confrontation between Douglas and the President was intense but accomplished nothing except straining the party. The issue would occupy political leaders for most of the year. Buchanan was forced to pull out all stops, using patronage both positively and negatively just to avoid a humiliating defeat. It is interesting to note that President failed to draw any lessons from getting very few northern Democrats to vote with him because they feared electoral defeat in 1858. At last, by the vote of the speaker of the House, the President got a compromise bill (the English Bill) through the House, which ostensibly accepted the Lecompton Constitution. The bill, however, provided for a referendum in Kansas on the draft constitution, and, as all knew, it ultimately would be rejected by the people of Kansas.

The deciding factor in Douglas' efforts had been the 1858 elections. Virtually all scholars agree that the northern Democrats simply did not dare to run with the tag of being pro-Lecompton hanging around their necks. Buchanan, in short, had won a battle, but it was the Republicans who gained the most from the intramural Democratic war. This struggle and the results are, we believe, a useful metaphor for Buchanan's strained relationship with Congress.

5. Court Appointments

For the second time, Buchanan appears in 40th place.

Nathan Clifford of Maine was James Buchanan's only appointment to the United States Supreme Court. Born and educated in New Hampshire, Clifford moved to Maine where he began the practice of law. After serving in the Maine Legislature for four years, the last two as speaker, he went on to serve as the State's attorney general from 1834-1838. In 1838, he was elected to the U. S. House of Representatives as a Democrat. He did not seek re-election after his second term.

In 1846, President Polk appointed him attorney general of the United States. He held that office for about a year and a half, until 1848. During that period, he and Buchanan had been cabinet colleagues. He was then appointed minister to Mexico (March, 1848-September, 1849). In that role, he was a principal in the Protocol of Queretaro, which provided for minor modifications in the Treaty of Guadalupe-Hidalgo, which had ended the Mexican War. After leaving Mexico, he resumed the practice of law in Maine until December of 1857, when the President nominated him as an associate justice of the Supreme Court. In the climate of the day and the growing ascendancy of the Republican Party in Congress the nomination of another northern Democrat seen as a doughface was controversial. Clifford was only narrowly confirmed in early 1858. He served nearly a quarter century on the court until his death in 1881 and was the author of nearly 400 opinions during his years of service.

In an interesting footnote to his service on the court, in 1877, Clifford was chosen to serve as president of the extra-constitutional electoral commission established to determine the contested results of the Hayes-Tilden presidential election of 1876. His vote, unsurprisingly, was cast for the Democratic candidate, Tilden. The commission, equally unsurprisingly, awarded the presidency to Hayes.

6. Handling of the U. S. Economy
This is Buchanan's third ranking at 39th.

Not quite six months after taking office, Buchanan would be confronted with the Panic of 1857. In late August, New York financial houses began suspending specie payment. They would not or could not redeem their bank notes with gold. By September/October, most banks had experienced "runs" – large numbers of depositors all demanding to withdraw the money from their accounts at the same time, straining the bank's financial resources. The causes of the Panic were multiple, including over-speculation in railway stocks in the United States as well as rising interest rates in European markets. Those interest rates not only caused fewer Europeans to invest in American markets, but, in some cases, led to the recall of European monies from the American markets for investment in Europe.

The impact would be relatively brief. It was probably the mildest financial panic of the 19th Century, but its effects would be notable. Within six months, stronger banks had resumed specie payments. By 1859, most normal economic activity largely had resumed. One thing, however, seemed obvious to all – the southern states, most particularly the cotton-producing states, had not suffered from the Panic to the same degree as the northern states. Cotton, southerners proclaimed, was "King!" The North, with its banks and railroads and factories, was an economy built on sand, they argued, while the agricultural economy of the South was solid. From the point of view of history, this was perhaps not the ideal moment to boost southern self-confidence. The resulting attitude would in 1860-1861 strengthen the southern radicals as they contemplated secession.

As was the norm for that day and age, the administration took no steps to modify or ameliorate the economic circumstances. The economy corrected itself quite quickly.

7. Luck

In this category, Mr. Buchanan occupies his third best ranking, at 37th.

We have already seen that Buchanan's appointment as minister to Great Britain was an excellent piece of luck for him. His absence during the political frenzy over the Kansas-Nebraska Act effectively had insulated him politically. As a result, he came to the 1856 presidential season as a blank slate, tied to no specific position. Therefore, he had no group of enemies based on the issue.

Nevertheless, that controversy and the issues that surrounded it – Bleeding Kansas, the Dred Scott Decision, the Lecompton Constitution and the issue of statehood for Kansas – were to dog his presidency. The climax came in John Brown's raid on Harper's Ferry in 1859 and/or the beginning of secession in the waning days of his term.

In 1857, Buchanan had to face not only the Kansas issues and the Panic of 1857, but also the so-called Mormon War. While the conjunction of problems may be ascribed to bad luck, the Mormon War was clearly an avoidable problem that Buchanan chose to meet head on.

Relying on an anti-Mormon report from three federal judges in the Utah Territory, all with known anti-Mormon propensities, the President sent the army to Utah as well as a new, non-Mormon governor to replace Brigham Young, the Mormon religious leader whom Fillmore had appointed governor. The Mormons, who had been driven to remote Utah by religious persecution further east, were offended and frightened by Buchanan's action.

The result was not really a war, but Young's vigorous guerilla activities – denying U. S. troops provisions, stampeding their cattle and other tactics – nearly crippled the 2,500 troops while avoiding any large scale confrontation.

Buchanan finally sent a sympathetic envoy to Utah. Negotiations resulted in a full pardon for the Mormons, the transfer of Utah's governorship from Young to non-Mormon Alfred Cumming and the peaceful establishment a U. S. Army military presence in Utah. While tension remained, a functional arrangement was created between the Mormons and the federal government.

Perhaps Buchanan's ultimate piece of bad luck was that he had missed becoming President in the three previous elections. By 1856, the prize was really, for someone like Buchanan, a poisoned apple. To a time that called for bold, visionary leadership, Buchanan brought caution, legalism and vacillation. Even elements that in other times might have been his strengths, like his respect for the law, now worked against him. Instead, Buchanan's instincts produced a sort of narrow legalism that came to be seen by many, both then and now, as fundamentally pro-southern.

8. Ability to Compromise

At 35th this is the President's second highest ranking.

There would seem to be a sort of ultimate irony in this ranking since throughout his career compromise had been virtually Buchanan's stock in trade. From the earliest days of his career, he accepted political defeat and/or compromise with equanimity. His transition from an effectively moribund Federalist Party to the Democracy was made so smoothly, for example, as to be nearly invisible. He often urged his colleagues and confederates to put intraparty defeats behind them and to unite with the victors to strengthen the party and look for the next opportunity for victory. As a successful diplomat, he certainly had learned that give and take, compromise, was necessary for any significant achievement. And yet, we find, our experts believe that only 15 per cent of all American Presidents were less able to compromise than James Buchanan.

Certainly the President's confrontation with Senator Douglas over the Lecompton Constitution and its bitter, angry tone of threats and recriminations did not seem to lend itself to a climate of compromise. Only after a long and acrimonious struggle with Douglas was the administration able to salvage even the appearance of a victory, with the compromise known as the English Bill. All knew that it was merely a face-saving gesture, one which neither the President nor the senator would have accepted at the onset of the quarrel. Indeed, Douglas would feel compelled almost immediately to take issue with it.

Similarly, in the House of Representatives seated after the 1858 elections, the strength of the Republicans allowed that party to defeat all of Buchanan's foreign policy initiatives, including another proposal to seek to purchase Cuba. The President in his turn regularly vetoed important Republican initiatives, such as a proposed Homestead Act that would provide land ownership to small farmers for little or no money. Some of these Republican initiatives seem to have been proposed specifically to generate a veto that could form campaign fodder for the Republicans in 1860. On the other hand, since it was clear that the southern radicals would not tolerate the passage of such legislation and would demand a veto, the Republicans were free to initiate such proposals with political impunity.

Some scholars feel that the Homestead Act veto, in particular, helped to elect Lincoln by weakening Douglas, clearly the Democrats' strongest potential candidate, with his core constituency of farmers. It made the Republicans appear to be the champions of the free small farmer and, by stressing the opposition of southern Democrats to the needs of the small farmer, seemed to show the Democratic Party as opposed to such needs.

9. Willingness to Take Risks

In this category, for the first of five times in the 2002 survey, James Buchanan is ranked 41st, dead last among all American presidents.

We believe the issue for the experts was simply that President Buchanan never seems to have sought a solution other than those that immediately appeared to him based on his personal experience and/or through a narrow, legalistic lens. Metaphorically, having been dealt a bad hand, it never seems to have occurred to him to have sought a different game or a new deal.

In Kansas, the pro-slave settlers already were in control of the levers of power when the free soil settlers began arriving. The immigrant freesoilers thought it necessary to boycott political processes they believed were rigged against them. To Buchanan the issues of fairness and equal electoral opportunities were of minor importance. President Pierce had recognized the legitimacy of the pro-slave Lecompton territorial government. If that government held a census or an election, it was automatically legal. If the resident freesoilers in Topeka, whose political arrangements had no legal recognition, boycotted or cried foul, it was a matter of no consequence. They could have voted, but they chose not to. Therefore, they had no valid complaint. While such views might have been technically and/or legally correct, in a time of near hysteria and heightened emotions they were so politically insensitive as to be incendiary.

His apparent concessions to southern interests were cut from the same cloth. Slavery was legal; therefore Southern interests were entitled to equal protection, even equal opportunity under the law. What the President saw as equal protection or equal opportunity often appeared to northerners to constitute special interests or special protection for the South.

Nor did Buchanan ever take his position to the public. He never articulated his vision for the country to its people. He did, on the other hand, at least on occasion, indicate to his southern friends that he hoped to eliminate from the political landscape groups arguing against slavery.

In short, it seems that Buchanan defined the issues and circumstances very narrowly and then acted almost purely legalistically within those narrow confines. It is in this context that we find ourselves agreeing fully with this ranking.

10. Executive Appointments

The 2002 poll, once again, finds Buchanan ranked 39th.

Seven cabinet positions existed. State, the most prestigious, was given to Lewis Cass of Michigan. Treasury went to Howell Cobb of Georgia and the war department went to John B. Floyd of Virginia. Buchanan's old friend from Pennsylvania, Jeremiah S. Black, was seated as attorney general. Isaac Toucey of Connecticut took the navy department and Jacob Thompson of Mississippi became secretary of the interior. Aaron V. Brown of Tennessee was appointed postmaster general.

The template for analysis of this cabinet is the role it played, or didn't play, in the increased North-South tension of the period.

Freesoilers would have been quick to note that four of the seven positions were given to the slave states and that two of those, interior and the post office, were the cabinet posts with the most patronage to distribute. Of the three members from free states, Cass, who was in his mid-70s, had just been denied reelection to the Senate. He was unlikely to prove contentious, nor did he until the very end of Buchanan's presidency. Toucey was known to have favored rigorous enforcement of the Fugitive Slave Law and to have been a proponent of the Kansas-Nebraska Act. Before he left office, the legislature of his native state was sufficiently angered by his doughface propensities that it ordered his portrait removed from the state's portrait gallery of former governors. Black seems to have been the only northern man strong enough to stand up to the southern wing. A doughface himself, he was at first acquiescent to Buchanan's southern bent, but as the crisis approached he would emerge as a bulwark for the Union. Cass, too, eventually would protest by tendering his resignation.

As a cabinet, their credentials were fairly standard. Cass had been governor of the Michigan Territory, minister to France, secretary of war, senator and president pro tempore of the Senate. Cobb had been a member of the House of Representatives and speaker of the House, as well as governor of Georgia. At the war department, Floyd had served as a member of the Virginia House of Delegates and governor of Virginia. In the latter capacity he had asked the Virginia Legislature to place an import duty on goods entering Virginia from states that had failed to vigilantly enforce the Fugitive Slave Law.

While the suggestion was of dubious constitutionality, it offered astonishing clarity as to Floyd's political views. For reasons unknown, he seems to have been something of a personal favorite of Buchanan's who, while forced to correct him with some frequency, seems never to have lost confidence in him.

Black was undoubtedly better known to Buchanan than any of the others. He was a distinguished attorney, who had served six years on the Supreme Court of Pennsylvania, half that time as chief justice. A fairly enthusiastic doughface, much opposed to the so-called "Black Republicans," the attorney general was, when push came to shove, a thoroughgoing Unionist. Toucey had served in both houses of the Connecticut Legislature as well as in the U. S. House of Representatives. He also had been Connecticut's governor, though failing to win reelection. He had served as Polk's attorney general and had had a five-year term in the Senate, declining to seek reelection. Jacob Thompson had represented Mississippi in the House of Representatives for a dozen years. Aaron Brown also had served in the House of Representatives, and had been elected the governor of Tennessee. An upholder of southern rights, he had been a member of the Nashville Convention of 1850, which had given some early credibility to the idea of secession. He served in the cabinet for only two years, dying in office. He was succeeded by Joseph Holt of Kentucky. Holt had been serving as commissioner of patents, when in 1859 Buchanan nominated him as postmaster general.

The cabinet was not without talent and ability. Even Cobb's enemies, for example, would have found it difficult to fault his stewardship at treasury, where his regime was characterized by integrity and efficiency.

Floyd represents the exception to the rule. His administration of the war department is notable for its scandals, which would play a significant role in the 1860 Republican campaign. The Covode Committee of the House of Representatives, headed by Pennsylvania abolitionist John Covode and charged with investigating Buchanan's possible impeachment, would use Floyd and other less well known scandals to fasten the label of corruption on the already badly wounded and divided Democratic Party in the 1860 election.

In the wake of the Republican victory in 1860, the beginning of secession, and the seizure of military posts and equipment of the United States in the southern states, the cabinet disintegrated. Bolstered by Black, Buchanan was forced to create a new cabinet. By December of 1860, frustrated by what he saw as Buchanan's supine acceptance of southern aggression, Cass resigned, and Black was moved to the state department. Black urged Buchanan to take a stronger line.

Cobb, too, resigned in December. Indeed, within two months he would emerge as a leader in the secession movement and the speaker of the Provisional Confederate Congress. He would later serve as a general officer in the Confederate Army, as would Floyd. Treasury was now given to Philip F. Thomas of Maryland. Thomas served only two months. When a treasury bond issue released by Thomas failed to sell, no great surprise given the chaos caused by secession, he resigned and was succeeded by John Adams Dix of New York, (January 15-March 6, 1861). Dix, rather famously, was prepared to shoot anyone who sought to haul down the American flag. A former professional soldier, he would serve the Union as a major general of volunteers.

Floyd also resigned in December, using the confusion of the time to somewhat mask the issue of war department financial mismanagement on his watch. At his resignation, he claimed that his honor had been impugned. Joseph Holt of Kentucky took his place. After the Civil War had begun, Holt would serve the Union Army as a colonel, and was appointed by Lincoln in 1862 as judge advocate general of that army. In that capacity he would preside over the trial of the Lincoln assassins.

When Black ascended to the state department, Edwin M. Stanton of Indiana was nominated as attorney general (December, 1860-March 1861). Less than a year later, Lincoln would choose him as his secretary of war. Jacob Thompson resigned in January of 1861 and would become the inspector general of the Confederate States Army. Toucey served until the end of Buchanan's term.

As we have seen, Holt had replaced Brown as postmaster general. When Buchanan moved Holt to the war department to replace Floyd, he also appointed Horatio King of Maine, who was serving as an assistant postmaster general, as postmaster general. He served a day or two over three weeks until Lincoln replaced him. Living until 1897, King has the distinction of being the shortest serving but longest surviving member of the Buchanan cabinet.

In effect, Buchanan had two cabinets – one from 1857 until late 1860 or so, and the other, with Toucey and Black as bridging elements, for the last three or four months of the administration. Of the original group, the three slave state members, Cobb, Floyd and Thompson, all served the Confederacy in high political and/or military positions. That record, correlated with Buchanan's known close relationship with such southern leaders as Senators John Slidell of Louisiana and James Murray Mason of Virginia, as well as Governor Henry Wise of Virginia, has done much to persuade contemporary scholars that the label of doughface was, and is, properly applied to the President.

11. Overall Ability
Here, for the third time, Buchanan is assigned 40th place.

Like his predecessor, President Pierce, Buchanan was a noted lawyer and successful political leader. His personal skills seemed to work most effectively with individuals or small groups. Until his presidency, he seems to have borne political setbacks with patience and tact. Once again, like Pierce, as President he seems to have taken the absolute necessity of political unity within the Democratic Party as an ultimate principle. This may be seen most clearly in the struggle with Douglas over the Lecompton Constitution and the issues of popular sovereignty. Indeed, though he later somewhat moderated his position, initially he rather overtly threatened Douglas with political destruction. To reach such a point with a figure as politically potent as Douglas reflects a failure of political rationality. In a number of ways, in Buchanan's presidency that seems almost to become a theme.

Buchanan appears to have been unable to accurately assess the mood of the country. That might have been because as a doughface he was dominated by more aggressive southern leaders or because his respect for law seemed to him to have required him to take the positions he did, or some combination of the two. It often seems as if he took southern recalcitrance and/or threats at face value. At the same time, he seems consistently remained deaf to, or contemptuous of, the increasingly restless and angry mood in the free states. To be politically tone deaf in such a major area of public interest certainly indicates the shortage of a crucial talent in a political leader.

As an administration, Buchanan's presidency displays failure, most notably in his seeming tolerance of Floyd's ineptness at the war department but also elsewhere in the administration. Developed and manipulated by the Republican-dominated Covode Committee, those failures would provide the Republican Party with effective campaign material for the 1860 election.

In practice, Buchanan's gifts seem to have been highly limited. Even his patronage policies were often erratic. For a leader with more than 40 years' experience, some of his actions seem baffling unless he was simply overwhelmed by the difficulties he faced. Talents and abilities that must have been perceived in him by the Democratic National Convention of 1856 came rather quickly in ensuing years to prove to be merely illusions.

12. Imagination
Here, for the second time, Buchanan is ranked last at 41st.

We would not quarrel with this ranking. Obviously, from the perspective of the 21st Century, we have the advantage of knowing where each successive step would lead – right up to what we consider to be the inevitable firing by Confederate troops on Fort Sumter. Equally obviously, these steps were, to Buchanan, a series of contingencies leading to an unknown future. He gave no sign, nearly the end, that he ever saw civil war coming.

Compounding the feeling is that contemporaries seem, with no real difficulty, to have seen farther than the President. When Lincoln spoke of "the house divided" in 1858, he certainly saw more than Buchanan did. In that same year, Jefferson Davis spoke of the necessity of secession if the Republicans elected a president in 1860. He indeed, foresaw civil war where Buchanan could not. Buchanan, in fact, seems to have been completely oblivious to the locomotive of revolution racing down the tracks at him.

When he hoped, and believed, that the Dred Scott Decision would settle the issues that agitated the country, once and for all, he appears almost to have been in a different world. To believe that a Supreme Court decision – one that sweepingly denied that Congress had any power over slavery in the territories, denied popular sovereignty, and said that persons of color had never been and could never be citizens, a decision made by five slave state justices with two, cosmetic, free state Democratic party justices in concurrence – would be upheld with docility by the inhabitants of the free states beggars the imagination. Instead, a torrent of criticism swept over the decision and the Court.

Buchanan and the court must not have considered that the decision denied the very purpose of the Republican Party and its adherents. The decision virtually compelled them to resist it. It also ran contrary to the ethos of 19th Century western civilization in regard to slavery.

At bottom, perhaps the President was incapable of grasping how the world had changed during the preceding 20 or 30 years or that it was changing still. His inability to grasp the true nature of the world around him betrays a failure of imagination of such magnitude that it may be said to have played a central role in the failures of his presidency – perhaps the central role.

13. Domestic Accomplishments

This marks James Buchanan's third 41st place finish.

Given the turmoil surrounding the issue of slavery in the territories and its various elements – ranging from the Dred Scott Decision in 1857 through the Lecompton Constitution to John Brown's raid at Harper's Ferry in 1859 – the President's failure to articulate and propose significant domestic programs is, perhaps, not difficult to understand.

To that, however, we need to add President Buchanan's concept of the presidency. For him, the idea of a chief executive was quite literal. It was the President's duty to execute – to carry out the laws and policies enacted by Congress. That conventional view of the role of the President was, of course, entirely inadequate to the perils the nation confronted.

As a Democrat, he was at a marked disadvantage. The party, largely driven by its southern wing, was opposed to most popular programs. It opposed internal improvements at federal expense and it opposed what, in Republican hands, would become the Homestead Act. Since it opposed federal aid to private enterprise, it was, of necessity, not in a position to fully support a transcontinental railroad. Strong supporters for all of these ideas existed within the party, but as long as the southern wing was dominant the party would stand in opposition. Its traditional position opposing protective tariffs committed it to a low tariff policy, another key element for the South. Low tariffs after the Panic of 1857 were not well received by the northern working class. That group had been convinced by Republican arguments that higher tariffs would have saved their jobs during the Panic.

As an executor, then, Buchanan had little room to display initiative outside the realm of foreign policy, and he did not do so. In effect there is no record of domestic accomplishment, outside those issues relating to slavery in the territories.

14. Integrity
Here President Buchanan gains three places to 38th.

This category probably needs to be considered under three separate headings. The first would be the President's personal integrity. The second would be the administration considered as a whole, and the third would involve integrity as related to the issues of secession and civil war.

In the first instance, there would seem to be no serious accusations leveled against the President personally. There were, in fact, during the Civil War, a variety of scurrilous charges raised, but none appears to have any real substance. Given what we know of Buchanan's attention to financial detail throughout his life it seems unlikely that any questions regarding his personal financial probity would stand scrutiny.

In the second instance, we have already alluded to issues involving possible fraudulent financial schemes involving Secretary Floyd and the war department. These, indeed, even impinged on the interior department, though Secretary Thompson seems to have been unaware of them, and his fury when he discovered Floyd's gambits seems genuine. Debate over these matters split the cabinet just at the time that the 1860 election, secession, and Fort Sumter were under review.

Some recent historical work has suggested that Secretary Floyd was not engaged in fraud, but rather "robbing Peter to pay Paul" by manipulating funds to cover deficiencies in congressional appropriations for the army. In this interpretation, Floyd, it is theorized, anticipated supplemental appropriations, which would enable all manipulations to be covered and the troops paid and fed. Be that as it may, it was a financial scandal of considerable magnitude which, but for the coming of the war, might well have led to impeachment and indictments.

As to the third area, secession and war, Buchanan appears to have been dazed and bewildered. As the situation deteriorated, he tried to conceive of measures to palliate anger and to slow the pace of secession. He was hoping for time – which, he prayed, would allow cooler heads to prevail. Or, perhaps, he was praying for just enough time for his term to end. In these vague and vain hopes, he was not much different than Lincoln's secretary of state-designate, William H. Seward, who was also seeking solutions, but mostly hoping for them during much of the same time.

Buchanan, then, can be held guilty of being unimaginative, even obtuse. He can be charged with failing to understand the minds, or at least the psyches, of men like Howell Cobb, who had been among his closest advisors and who, by the autumn of 1860, saw secession as not only legitimate but necessary.

Buchanan's personal integrity – as opposed to his sagacity, however, seems unimpeachable.

15. Executive Ability

Again, Mr. Buchanan registers a 40th place finish.

As we have tried to indicate, President Buchanan's understanding of the role of the presidency acted to limit his vision, and his lack of imagination undoubtedly diminished the scope of any actions he might have seen as available to him. A dynamic executive in the mold of, say, Andrew Jackson, might well have resorted to a call for something like Jackson's Force Bill (1833), the first piece of legislation to publicly deny individual states the right to nullify a federal law. Its approval meant that, at least for President Jackson, the federal government was superior to that of any state. Such an action by Buchanan would have indicated clear opposition to the possibility of peaceful secession. Whether that would have proven effective we cannot know. What we do know is that Buchanan, despite the fact that he had lived through the events of the 1832-1833 crisis over South Carolina's efforts at nullification with its implications of secession, and the Force Bill, seems not even to have thought of any strong executive action. He did speculate about the notion of a national constitutional convention, though not at his initiative.

Ultimately, we are left to cite, as so many others have done, the famous, oxymoronic statements of his last message to the Congress, in which he stated his convictions that (A) no state had a right to secede from the Union, but that (B) he had no right to prevent such an action.

In terms of his executive ability, and imagination as well, we need do no more than contrast those concepts with the words of his successor in his first inaugural address. Abraham Lincoln said:

"In your hands my dissatisfied fellow countrymen, and not in mine, is the momentous issue of civil war. The Government will not assail you. You can have no conflict without being yourselves the aggressors. You have no oath registered in heaven to destroy the government, while I shall have the most solemn one to 'preserve, protect and defend it.'"

Where President Buchanan could find no authority to act, Lincoln finds an imperative in his very oath of office.

16. Foreign Policy Accomplishments
This is his fourth ranking at 41st.

Like Pierce, Buchanan had hoped to make his mark in foreign affairs and, given his résumé, perhaps no President since John Quincy Adams seemed as well qualified as he did in 1857. Again, like Pierce, Buchanan's inaugural address had more than hinted at further American expansion, clearly with an eye turned toward Central America and the isthmus. Britain quite quickly signaled a willingness to accept some sort of American protectorate in the region. England's goal was commerce, not colonies.

While relations with England flourished and some progress was made regarding the Central American republics, Republicans in Congress were not anxious to provide Buchanan with foreign policy laurels. That was true especially as they came to control in the middle of his term. They would not provide him with votes necessary for treaty making.

Certainly, Buchanan, if only to forestall European intervention in Mexico, sought to increase American influence in the region, perhaps even by further land cessions or a protectorate. The President also, with characteristic tone deafness to northern opinion, sought congressional authorization for up to $30 million for the acquisition of Cuba from Spain. That had been a goal of Buchanan's for more than a quarter century. All of the President's plans involving the spread of American influence in the Caribbean or Central America, which might have done well had he been elected in 1844 or 1848, failed because they ran afoul of the suspicion and cynicism that had grown

246

between 1849 and 1857.

A minor success attended the naval expedition he sent to Paraguay in 1858. The affair began with the killing of an American sailor in Paraguay in 1855. The United States demanded damages. In 1858, Buchanan sent a large naval force to Paraguay to enforce the claim. The fleet awed the Paraguayans. They agreed to apologize and to pay the damages sought, $10,000.

The administration entered in 1857 into talks with Russia to purchase Alaska. The talks occurred at the behest of the Russian minister to the United States. The President seems to have at least considered Alaska as an alternative to Utah as a refuge for the Mormons. When he made an offer in 1859 the Russians rejected it as too low. Buchanan, knowing he would not get Congressional approval for a larger amount, then withdrew from the negotiations.

Succinctly put – other than with Great Britain, which had concluded that if the United States wished to spend the time and money to bring order to the Caribbean region, it would be in Britain's best interests to allow her to do so – Buchanan's foreign policy was a failure. That was true even though Buchanan was more imaginative in that area than in any other aspect of his administration. His foreign policy actions carried with them the scent of manifest destiny and possibly additional slave states. Free soil principles would stymie all efforts to extend American authority.

And so, as with domestic accomplishments, we once again conclude that there were no significant foreign policy accomplishments for Buchanan.

17.   Leadership Ability

For the fifth time, Buchanan is again last, at 41st. It is difficult to grasp how a man who had a stellar career in politics for over 40 years could reach the pinnacle of his profession and career only to prove an abject failure. Yet it is so.

His subordinates, as exemplified by the members of his cabinet, were men of reasonable talent and ability. They were able, at least until near the end, to get on well with one another and with the President. Perhaps they were too much alike and too much like the President. Some of his defenders have argued that his cabinet was not a "Directory" driving Mr. Buchanan, but rather a coterie of men chosen by the President because he was comfortable with their thinking, and they, with his. Though this posits a narrow, southern-oriented view of the events and currents of the period within the administration, it is certainly arguable. Undoubtedly, he was comfortable with them. He so liked and trusted Howell Cobb, his treasury secretary, that when Mrs. Cobb was in Georgia Buchanan had Cobb live in the White House. Jeremiah Black, Buchanan's political ally who was attorney general and then secretary of state, though he had had no strong objections to the courses pursued until the crisis loomed, became a pillar of strength for Buchanan as his world collapsed in 1859-1860.

None of them, however, seems to have tried to turn Buchanan's eyes toward the new, emerging reality until disaster was upon them. All seem to have had, like their master, a peculiarly narrow vision that did not allow them to see that the comfortable verities of the previous decade or two were verities no longer. The fault, of course, was Buchanan's. He had sought and won the mantle of leadership. Unfortunately, it did not fit him very well.

Possibly, the comfort provided by the fact that they thought so much alike prevented them from becoming alert to the dangers awaiting them until few courses of action remained. Conformity, perhaps, stifled imagination and initiative. It was very late before they realized the dangers confronting the administration and the nation.

Presidential leadership is not only different from that needed at other levels but infinitely more difficult. That may be particularly clear in Buchanan's case. The reality seems to have been that while problems compounded – while actual fist fights took place on the floor of the House, while many members of Congress came to Capitol Hill armed each day – Buchanan came to the cusp of the disruption of the Union without seeming to have fully grasped the problems he faced. When daring and imaginative leadership might have offered the nation a warning, if not an alternative, he presented only the staring eye of his self-awarded nickname. He was, indeed, no more than the "Old Public Functionary."

18. Intelligence

Our experts, in this instance, have placed Buchanan at 39th.

When we wrote of Franklin D. Roosevelt, we quoted Mr. Justice Oliver Wendell Holmes that FDR possessed "a second class intellect, but a first class temperament." We allude to that now because the issue of presidential intelligence does not, we think, reference SAT or GRE scores, but the ability to understand and communicate with the nation. Presidential intelligence entails grasping both the perils and opportunities faced and the policies to be pursued or abandoned in the best interests of the country.

In that sense, we believe that President Buchanan's rating in this category is fully justified.

Obviously, he was not stupid. At a fundamental level – in college, as a lawyer, legislator, diplomat and cabinet member – Buchanan, who prided himself on his intelligence, was a very bright man. As President, in a time of growing tension and crisis, he is rather reminiscent of Neville Chamberlain and Edouard Daladier at the 1938 Munich Conference with Hitler. Blinded by the experience and the trauma of World War I, they blundered into the betrayal of Czechoslovakia – hoping, in vain, that the policy of appeasement would prevent another world war. So too, Buchanan was a captive of his own experience and was unable to search outside that experience for solutions to the problems the nation faced. Indeed, it sometimes seems that he did not even understand that a crisis was upon him.

Thus it appears that Buchanan and those around him were unable to distinguish between previous southern threats of secession and the much greater intensity present in the years 1858-1860. Similarly, the growing anger in the free states failed to make an impression as to just how much more threatening the moment was. When circumstances forced the President to address the major issues, he continually offered or referenced narrow legislative or legalistic remedies. He failed to grasp that what had been a legal or political issue at the time of the Missouri Compromise – and even, to some degree, at the time of the Compromise of 1850 – had now become a moral and emotional issue. It was as a result far less open, if open at all, to compromise.

Had he sought to impress upon the slave states that secession would mean a hard war and bloodshed, as Jackson had in 1833, might that have made a difference? Clearly, we cannot say. We can, however, fairly confidently stipulate that it seems unlikely that such a warning could have made matters much worse.

Buchanan, charitably, seems to have displayed little intelligence during the crisis years. He merely parroted legalisms and old formulas. He was inept.

19. Avoid Crucial Mistakes
In this, the last category, we find him ranked once again, at 39th.

Like his predecessor, Buchanan seems to have been almost enamored of the opportunity to make or to compound critical errors.

To illustrate:

A. Though his duties in England had insulated him from the political effects of the passions created by the Kansas-Nebraska Act, he had had the time and the opportunity to see and analyze its impact. Nevertheless, he seems to have wholeheartedly embraced it.

B. He failed to understand that rather than settling the issues of slavery in the territories the Dred Scott Decision had merely increased passions and stoked volatility.

C. It seems almost incomprehensible that he threw the whole weight of his administration behind the Lecompton Constitution, even to the point of rupturing his relations with Senator Douglas and creating a major rift in the Democratic Party.

D. He seems to have been unable to realize the degree of hostility and suspicion with which still another effort to acquire Cuba would be received in the North.

When the rupture came and secession was no longer theoretical, he was unable to choose a course of action that offered some possibility of preserving the Union. His alternatives seemed to be drift, indecision and confusion.

After the war came, unlike Pierce, he was a wholehearted supporter of the Union, but until then he seemed like a deer in the headlights, frozen and incapable of useful action.

It is exceptionally difficult to assign a motive for his behavior other than citing the oldest one proposed by both his contemporaries and historians. He was, in fact, a dough- face whose closest advisors were southerners – men whose advice and company he valued. His position was one which to a large degree had been the position of the Democratic Party for a generation or more – Buchanan's generation.

Perhaps, at the end, he at least partially realized his weakness. On January 8th, 1861, in a special message to Congress, with less than two months of his presidency remaining, President Buchanan wrote what might be said to be his political epitaph: "… I have often warned my countrymen of the dangers which now surround us… I feel that my duty has been faithfully, though it may be, imperfectly, performed, and, whatever the result may be, I shall carry to my grave the consciousness that I at least meant well for my country."

It would seem to serve as a summary of his presidential career that even he could find nothing more positive to say about his stewardship.

20. Present Overall View

In ranking him in the last category our experts have dropped him another notch, placing him last on the list of Presidents through the end of the second millennium in 41st – and last – place.

Book IV   Not Three in a Row: But One of a Kind

Contemplating a decade of difficulty culminating in the election of Abraham Lincoln, it seemed to us virtually churlish, as well as a disservice to the reader, not to recognize the contrast between Lincoln's administration and that of his immediate predecessors.

Having determined to add Lincoln to the book, we realized that in discussing him, FDR, Washington and Jefferson, we had dealt with four of the five men who always appear among the top five Presidents in every survey conducted. Only Theodore Roosevelt would be excluded.

When we began this exercise in tracking polls, we had not realized that there was a statistically significant difference between the top five Presidents and those Presidents who occupied places six through 10. In the 2002 survey, President Franklin Roosevelt had the top overall score, at 88.9. In fifth place, Thomas Jefferson scored 81.4. The total variance between 1 and 5 is a total of only 7.5 points, less than two points per place. The sixth place finisher, Woodrow Wilson, was scored at 72.7, which represents a variation of 8.7 points between fifth and sixth.

In the light of that large difference, we thought it advisable to include Theodore Roosevelt as well as Lincoln so that all of the most significant Presidents would somewhere be included in this effort.

Chapter 10 - Abraham Lincoln – March 4, 1861 – April 15, 1865

"I am loath to close – we are not enemies but friends. We must not be enemies. Though passion may have strained, it must not break our bonds of affection. The mystic cords of memory, stretching from every battlefield and patriot heart and hearthstone, all over this broad land, will yet swell the chorus of the Union, when again touched, as surely they will be by the better angels of our nature."
– Abraham Lincoln, First Inaugural Address, March 4, 1861.

Like his three immediate predecessors, Abraham Lincoln was born in a log cabin. In the SRI 2002 expert opinion tracking poll, he was ranked second, just after Franklin Roosevelt. The 16th President was surely, with the possible exception of Fillmore, the most poorly educated President. By his own reckoning, he had only about one year of formal education. He did not even "read law" with an established attorney, as Fillmore had done. Rather, he simply acquired law books and studied the law, as he had studied surveying, and then persuaded the necessary judges to acknowledge that he was fit to practice law in Illinois. His study habits seem to have consisted of multiple readings, considerable memorization and the reduction of significant elements onto paper until he was sure that he had fully grasped the thought. Lincoln was almost entirely self-taught..

Born in Kentucky in 1809 to Thomas Lincoln and Nancy Hanks Lincoln, he was the scion of a family that could be traced back to the Puritan migrations to Massachusetts in the first half of the 17th Century. For a time, Thomas Lincoln did well in Kentucky, where he had taken up residence, but his prospects were diminished, if not ruined, by the ubiquitous problem of defective land titles. The same problems had forced Daniel Boone out of Kentucky. In 1816, Thomas Lincoln moved his family to Indiana. There the family eked out a living, and young Abraham, as he grew older, seems to have resented his father's lack of success, his own paucity of education and the lack of opportunity he found available. In 1830, the Lincolns moved to Illinois. The following year, having attained his majority, young Lincoln left the family home and moved to New Salem, Ill. He proved to be popular and developed a reputation as an honest and intelligent young man, though not necessarily an industrious one. Clearly, for Abe, the years of working with farm equipment, axes and wedges in rail splitting and other endeavors may have created respect for manual labor but apparently not affection.

In 1832, only one year after coming to New Salem and at the age of 23, he offered himself as a candidate for the Illinois State Legislature. That year he also served briefly as a captain in the state militia during the Black Hawk War. He lost his first political race, though he did manage to gain an appointment as postmaster in New Salem. It was in this period that he taught himself to be a surveyor and functioned, apparently with considerable success, in that capacity.

In 1834, unabashed by the 1832 result, he again ran for the legislature, and this time he was victorious. He would represent Sangamon County for four terms, and he was a leader in the effort to relocate the Illinois state capitol to nearby Springfield. The Sangamon County delegation clearly recognized the advantages of possessing the State Capital, and they moved effectively to secure it. Lincoln's leadership in this process, while still in his 20s, marked him as a comer in the Illinois Whig Party. Unfortunately for Lincoln, the Whig Party was a distinct minority in the state, with virtually no prospect of carrying any statewide election. Indeed, his own congressional district was, normally, the only one in the state the Whigs were likely to carry.

As a devoted Whig and a great admirer of Henry Clay, the Whig leader, Lincoln would carry on and fight the good fight for Whig principles. The fight, however, offered few opportunities until the disruption caused by the Kansas-Nebraska Act of 1854. That was when the logic of the political situation would necessitate for Lincoln, as for many northern Whigs, movement into the new Republican Party.

After his fourth term in the state legislature, he chose not to seek reelection. Instead, he concentrated on developing his law practice, though his interest and participation in politics never waned. Nor was he ever without influence in Whig circles.

In 1846, he was elected to the House of Representatives, where he served a single term. The practice in Lincoln's congressional district was to rotate the office, with each candidate elected then serving a single term and then being succeeded by the next candidate in line. Once again, he returned to the practice of law.

It was the Kansas-Nebraska Act that brought him back into active politics. His opposition to the extension of slavery into the territories of the United States, as well as his ambition, caused him to seek the support of the Whigs in a run for the United States Senate seat to be chosen by the Illinois legislature in 1855. Ultimately, though he had more votes, he threw his support to Lyman Trumbull as the only way in which the seat might surely be kept in the hands of freesoilers. After his election, and for the next few years, Trumbull would become one of Lincoln's staunchest supporters.

Lincoln also was influential in bringing the old Whigs into the Republican Party. Partly as a result of his recruiting efforts, he was that party's candidate for the Senate against Stephen Douglas in 1858. Once again he was defeated, but his campaign and the clarity of his positions, particularly during the Lincoln-Douglas debates, made him a national figure. The debates, looking ahead to the 1860 presidential election, also seriously weakened Douglas in the South. The 1858 campaign and the debates formed the springboard for Lincoln's presidential race.

Approaching the 1860 campaign, Lincoln's resumé was thinner than those of his predecessors. While he had always been a leader, it was often in lost causes and, not infrequently, behind the scenes. Nevertheless, his guidance and advice always had been sought in matters ranging from the mechanics of election races and elections to the clarity of his enunciation of free soil principles.

By all accounts, when he was on his game, he was one of the greatest political orators of his day. Even opponents like Douglas, no mean orator himself, were prepared to acknowledge that in facing Lincoln they faced a daunting challenge. When he was at his best he brought a conjunction of clarity of thought, self-deprecating humor, the telling use of simile and metaphor and a crowd-pleasing personality to the platform. Most of his more effective speeches have been in print constantly from his day to our own, and all seem to withstand the test of time. His correspondence too, offers clarity, humor, concise organization and, frequently, a very human touch.

As American Presidents are measured, we think it arguably correct to stipulate that, as a communicator, he has few if any peers, and no superiors. This is emphasized when it is recalled that, unlike modern Presidents, Lincoln wrote his own speeches.

Lincoln's relationships with Congress were, in some ways, unique. Driven by the exigencies of the Civil War, he would prove to be one of America's strongest chief executives. The Republican Congress was, virtually always, prepared to sustain him, as, for example, it did when it retroactively approved his suspension of the writ of habeas corpus, thereby legitimizing his executive suspension of the writ in the early days of the war.

On the other hand, outside the vast area encompassed in the term "waging the war," he was very deferential to the Congress. Like a good Whig, and not unlike Buchanan, he was not disposed to suggest new programs to Congress – the Homestead Act, for example – but rather to leave such initiatives to the legislative branch, which often found its inspiration in the Republican platform of 1860. So, the President did not need to propose the Homestead Act, only to sign it.

Since the principal work of the Lincoln administration was the prosecution of the war – and since, at root, the causes of the war involved the very rationale for the Republican Party's formation – there clearly were strong forces tending to unite the legislative and executive branches in those years. This is not to say that peace and harmony reigned, but rather to suggest that when problems arose – as with the Joint Committee on the Conduct of the War – Lincoln was prepared to meet with the members of Congress involved. He was prepared to seek common ground on topics such as how to deal with General George McClellan, who would become Lincoln's 1864 presidential election opponent. He then was wiling to move on. Nor would we suggest that the President was exempt from criticism.

Unusual circumstances, events, and a series of coincidences gave Lincoln a nearly unique opportunity to influence the judicial branch. He appointed no fewer than five justices to the Supreme Court.

The death of Chief Justice Taney in 1864 gave the President the chance not only to appoint a new chief justice but also a means to quietly remove secretary of the treasury Salmon P. Chase from the cabinet. Chase had been prepared earlier in 1864 to contest the presidential nomination with Lincoln. The appointment meant that the President would not have to risk alienating the more radical wing of the Republican Party, as the mere removal of Chase would surely have done. Chase took his oath as chief justice on December 15, 1864.

When Lincoln took office, there was already one vacancy on the Court. Then Justice John McLean died and Justice John Campbell resigned to "go South." Next, the Congress, very briefly, created a 10th seat on the Court, for the West Coast (1863-1866).

First, President Lincoln appointed Noah Haynes Swayne of Ohio, installed in January of 1862. Born in Virginia, his move to Ohio had been at least partly motivated by his opposition to slavery. Just before his death, Justice McLean had recommended Swayne as his successor. Next, in July, 1862, came the appointment of Samuel Freeman Miller. He, too, was a southern-born man, from Kentucky, where he was also raised and educated. He was a doctor as well as a lawyer. His discomfort with slavery had sent him from Kentucky into Iowa. Third among the associate justices Lincoln would appoint, in December of 1862, was Lincoln's campaign manager, Judge David Davis of Illinois, before whom Lincoln had often argued cases. Last of the four associate justices, in March of 1863, was the 10th Justice, Stephen J. Field of California.

As a group, they are noted for long service. Chase served for about nine years until his death, The others served from just over 14 years to 34 years.

Most of them had significant impact. Swayne, the first, was the least distinguished, though he did generally and strongly support the President, as he did in Ex parte Milligan. In that case Justice Davis wrote the majority opinion.

Justice Miller also upheld the President's war measures, such as the executive suspension of habeas corpus. In his nearly 30 years on the court he seems to have been a sort of wheel horse, writing about twice as many opinions as did any of his colleagues. He was so well thought of that when Chase died many members of both bench and bar urged President Grant to appoint Miller in his place. Grant chose otherwise.

Stephen J. Field, Lincoln's last appointment, is most famous for his early espousal of the doctrine of "substantive due process," a guarantee against unreasonable legislative interference with private property in the so-called Slaughter House Cases. Field was then in the minority, and the doctrine was not established until later. In any event, as a class they seem to have functioned at a reasonably high level.

The American Civil War placed extraordinary pressures on the American economy and financial system. The government needed to raise enormous amounts of money. In this area, the President was well served by his three treasury secretaries – Chase, William Pitt Fessenden of Maine and Hugh McCulloch of Indiana. Chase was an excellent treasury secretary. He established the base for a stable national banking system and began the issuance of paper money. In co-operation with Jay Cooke and Company, he managed successful bond drives to subscribe large loans. Fessenden left the Senate, where he chaired the Finance Committee and backstopped Chase and Lincoln, to replace Chase. As secretary, he moved to limit the inflation caused by paper money and, in the absence of subscribers for renewed large loan drives, began marketing the loans in smaller denominations. That action opened an entire new market of subscribers for the government. Finishing the work he deemed necessary, he returned to the Senate in 1865 and was succeeded by McCulloch, the comptroller of the currency who had overseen the National Banking Act of 1864. He would continue in office under Andrew Johnson.

The war years also saw two tariff acts become law, which increased federal revenue. More importantly for the future, the first income tax, the Revenue Act of 1861, was initiated, as well as its successor, the Revenue Act of 1862. The rest of the economic needs imposed by the war for goods and services were provided by the actions of the market and the spur, sometimes conducive to corruption, of profits from government contracts. In any event, from "Greenbacks" to gunpowder, from hardtack to horseshoes, from shoes to swords, all that was needed was provided with the usual profligacy of government in wartime. In the context of 19th Century government the economy functioned well.

The question of luck or good fortune and Abraham Lincoln is difficult. When applied to an historical figure who was assassinated, luck seems an implausible consideration, though it remains relevant. A number of instances of good fortune accompanied Lincoln to his inauguration.

Largely forgotten now is that Stephen Douglas, realizing early that he would not become the next President, spent much of his campaign warning the South against secession. The very fact that Douglas campaigned around the country was itself unusual. Candidates in those days customarily remained at home and awaited events.

Nonetheless, Douglas traveled heavily in warning the South that the northern Democracy would not tolerate secession and that secession would not be a peaceful event. When secession began, Douglas pledged his loyalty to the Union. Not only was he seated on the platform for Lincoln's inauguration, he – in what now seems a deeply symbolic act – held Lincoln's hat for him while he spoke.

Nor was Douglas alone. There were, to be sure, any number of "Peace Democrats" who would complicate Lincoln's life and work. But there were also the "War Democrats," for whom the Union was more important than party. They would, for the most part, support Lincoln's policies, at least in regard to the restoration of the Union.

Jefferson Davis would, ironically, function as a source of good luck for Lincoln. First, the new Confederate government allowed emotion to triumph over reason and fired upon Fort Sumter, a Charleston fortification that Lincoln could not assist and that both Lincoln and Davis knew could not hold out longer than six weeks. Thereafter, Lincoln could simply point to that action to prove that the South had been the aggressor.

Similarly, the Confederacy decided to withhold the cotton crop from the world market in an effort to use cotton to blackmail the European powers into recognizing the Confederate government. The naval blockade that Lincoln had declared was, at that point, beyond the Union's capability to enforce. Davis did it for him and thereby deprived the Confederacy of a significant supply of hard money that otherwise might have purchased arms and munitions and other strategic goods.

On the military side of affairs, Davis found Robert E. Lee relatively early in the war, while Lincoln bore the weight of McClellan and John Pope and Ambrose Burnside. Davis, however – and seemingly willingly – bore the weight of Braxton Bragg to the detriment of his western forces and campaigns. Ultimately, Lincoln would be able to trump Lee's military leadership with Ulysses S. Grant, William Tecumseh Sherman, George Henry Thomas and Philip H. Sheridan.

The President's greatest military luck was probably the institutional existence of the United States Navy as an organized force. Under the leadership of Secretary of the Navy Gideon Welles the navy emerged as a highly professional organization, possessed of a knowledge of tactics and operational skills, but still open to enough innovation as to see the rapid emergence of the U. S. S. Monitor and other ironclads on one hand and the equally rapid construction of the armored river gunboats on western rivers on the other. In modern terms, a "blue water" navy rapidly developed a "brown water" capability. Both redounded to the success of Union arms.

While the list might be extended, we will conclude by noting that the very act of secession by the Confederate States was, in a left-handed way, fortunate for Lincoln's presidency. The withdrawal from the Congress of its southern members acted as a force multiplier for the Republicans, providing the party and the administration with much larger legislative majorities than they could otherwise have claimed.

The bad fortune is, of course, obvious. Lincoln was called upon to direct a terrible civil war in which tens of thousands of soldiers would be killed and wounded and incalculable economic damage done, especially to the seceded southern states. Yet, even there, if we accept Lincoln's definition of slavery as a "scourge," there was good fortune among the bad since the war enabled the country, once and for all, to rid itself of that scourge.

As President, Abraham Lincoln's talents would prove to be highly adaptable and open. He also was capable of "eating humble pie" when he found it useful or politic. In the period between his election and inauguration, a number of schemes and scenarios were advanced in search of a compromise to hold the Union together. While he displayed no enthusiasm for any of them, he was prepared to allow surrogates to consider them, providing they did not lose sight of principle. He very clearly stipulated that no compromise would be considered acceptable if it promised even a scintilla of acceptance to any growth to slavery in the territories of the United States. That was a basic principle of the Republican Party on which he had campaigned and won, and it was sacrosanct.

When, early in the war, the radical wing of the Republican Party urged him to pursue an abolitionist course, he temporized and held them off because he believed the policy of war for the restoration of the Union offered a wiser course of action. Once convinced that there were no significant Unionist elements in the Confederacy as a whole, and once the border states seemed no longer likely to secede, he began to prepare for the Emancipation Proclamation. (The border states were those slave states – Delaware, Kentucky, Maryland and Missouri – that had not seceded.) His course of action in this period may seem somewhat serpentine, but it illustrates his rationality, his ability to compromise and his willingness to take risks by altering course when useful.

That willingness to compromise was, or seems to have been, present at all times, though not at a visceral level. He could and would compromise when there was a goal to be attained, or when necessity dictated, but he never seems to have seriously considered compromising principle.

We can illustrate that point by referencing the issue of the exchange of prisoners in the latter stages of the war. From the beginning of the war, prisoner exchange and/or parole of prisoners had been commonplace. After the Emancipation Proclamation, when the Union began to recruit and deploy black soldiers, the Confederacy balked. It was announced that they would exchange only white prisoners and that captured black Union soldiers would be "returned" to slavery.

The Union thereupon halted all prisoner exchanges on the ground that skin color did not make a Union soldier; the uniform did. The new policy worked direct and severe injury on prisoners on both sides in hellish prison enclosures such as Andersonville, Ga., and Elmira, N. Y. It also worked to the direct military disadvantage of the South, which could have used as many exchanged prisoners as possible. Despite repeated Union requests for an alteration in the policy, the Confederacy never altered its position. Even as distinguished a soldier as Robert E. Lee formally rejected such a change. Lincoln, moved by the suffering, agonized over the issue but in the end upheld the principle.

Perhaps the most difficult line to draw about a President is the line between his ability to compromise and his willingness to take risks. In Lincoln's case the line is very closely drawn, with perhaps a slight edge to the risk-taking side. This was a man, who, one year after arriving in New Salem, Ill., "threw his hat into the ring" by announcing his candidacy for the state legislature at age 23. Two years later, he won the seat. In 1854 and 1858, not having held office for a number of years, he contested for a Senate seat. Two years after that, not having held a political office in a dozen years, and having lost two consecutive contests for the Senate, he sought and won the presidency.

In a similar but nobler vein we can examine those years in light of the Kansas-Nebraska Act. It was in response to that act that Lincoln returned from a political semi-retirement. He may have hoped for, but he certainly could not then have known, the triumph to which his vigorous espousal of free soil principles would carry him. It certainly must have appeared a risky proposition, though one he was willing to take for conscience sake.

During the war, when Grant's 1863 campaign against Vicksburg saw him cross the Mississippi River into enemy territory and march his army off on a campaign, abandoning his supply lines, Lincoln, though anxious, remained supportive, and, at last on July 4th, 1863, Vicksburg fell. Similarly, the following year, when Grant moved against Lee and the Army of Northern Virginia, fighting from the Wilderness down to Petersburg with tremendous casualties, seemingly imperiling the cause and Lincoln's re-election, Lincoln again accepted the burden. That is, the President bore the political and emotional pressure of casualty lists, of plummeting northern morale and the apparent failure of the northern armies, while sustaining Grant. Arguably, only Admiral David Farragut's victory at Mobile Bay in August, 1864, the fall of Atlanta to Sherman in September, 1864, and Sheridan's destruction of the Confederate forces in the Shenandoah Valley between August and October, 1864, made possible Lincoln's reelection.

As a point of interest, we might also take note here of the soldier vote. The Civil War marks the first time that soldiers, away from home, got to vote. Some states provided for absentee ballots. For states that did not, in many cases leaves were granted so troops could get home and vote. The soldier vote broke overwhelmingly for Lincoln.

In a quite different sense, Lincoln's selection of the members of his cabinet must have appeared to involve risk taking, too. Overall, the members of the cabinet brought much better political resumes to the table than did the President. Seward, at the State Department, had served as governor of New York and completed two terms in the United States Senate. Chase, at Treasury, had been governor of Ohio and served in the Senate; Simon Cameron, the first secretary of war, had a checkered political past. He had been both a Whig and a Democrat before becoming a Republican. But, he, too, had served in the Senate and he was known as a master political manipulator. His successor, Edwin Stanton, was a Democrat and had been Buchanan's last attorney general. Secretary of the Interior Caleb Smith of Indiana had served multiple terms in the Indiana legislature as well as several in the House of Representatives. He had been an early and enthusiastic

Lincoln backer. He would later be replaced by Assistant Secretary of the Interior John P. Usher, also of Indiana.

Gideon Welles of Connecticut, appointed secretary of the navy, was an attorney and newspaperman who had served in the lower house of the Connecticut legislature and as state controller. Montgomery Blair, the postmaster general, like Welles had a less impressive resume than many of the others. He was, however, a scion of the Blair family, which bridged American political history from Andrew Jackson to Abraham Lincoln, and he represented the Anti-Nebraska Democrats who had joined the old Whigs and others in the coalition that became the Republican Party. The family's political influence also ran from Maryland, Blair's home state, to Missouri.

Like Blair, Attorney General Edward Bates represented the border slave states, in this case Missouri, where he had been a member of the state's constitutional convention and attorney general before his service in both the upper and lower houses of the legislature. A Whig, he had been asked to join Fillmore's cabinet as secretary of war, but had declined. He had been considered as a potential Republican candidate in 1860, but his associations with the Know-Nothing party made him anathema to immigrant voters, so he had been passed over. In a peculiar way, he symbolized the war in the cabinet. One of his sons was in the Union Army, one in the Confederate Army and a third at West Point.

Of the members of the cabinet – Bates, Cameron, Chase and Seward – all had been in the mix for the Republican nomination in 1860. Seward had been the favorite. In choosing men of that caliber, Lincoln knowingly risked being overshadowed by men, particularly Chase and Seward, who considered themselves better able to lead than he. Their appointments really signify Lincoln's self-confidence. He would run risks in order to surround himself with talent.

Lincoln worked well with his cabinet and, if necessary, around it. Lincoln's conduct during the Trent Affair, in which two Confederate diplomats were removed by the U. S. Navy from a British ship at sea, is just one example. Seward and Lincoln initially proved too truculent toward England. Lincoln gained information and insight from Senator Charles Sumner of Massachusetts, who had a substantial number of contacts in England. As a result, the President moderated the language of Secretary's Seward's communications, and tensions gradually eased. That was particularly true after the United States essentially, though discreetly, disavowed the actions that had created the crisis.

Before the 1860 Republican Convention, Seward was the best known

Republican in the country. He certainly expected, as secretary of state, to be at least the "power behind the throne" in the administration. Lincoln's gift for managing men and his willingness to compromise were well displayed in their relationship. Seward was brought fully into camp as one of the most talented and willing subordinates any President has ever had. Chase was equally talented, if a less selfless and cheerfully willing. His work at the treasury department contributed mightily to the strength and success of the administration.

Stanton had a rather jaundiced view of Lincoln when he agreed to replace Cameron, but he, too, would come to serve the President with intelligence, energy, diligence and even fervor. It would be Stanton who, immediately after Lincoln's last breath said, "Now he belongs to the ages."

Bates was one of the more conservative members of the cabinet, though he cooperated in most instances and rarely formally disagreed. Blair served into 1864 when, apparently for reasons of political expediency, Lincoln accepted his resignation. There was no ill will between the two, and Blair campaigned for Lincoln's reelection.

Gideon Welles did an outstanding job administering the navy department, overseeing the expansion of the peacetime navy to a wartime force nearly 10 times as large and the rather revolutionary alteration of a small, largely sail-driven, deep water navy to a mixed force of what now might be called a combination of a blue water and a brown water navy, as well as an enormous expansion of the use of steam power and armored vessels. In addition to war on the rivers and the seizure of New Orleans and Mobile Bay, the navy's blockade of Confederate ports was increasingly effective throughout the war. It deprived rebel forces of commerce and cash but also of access to strategic materials. Succinctly put, as a whole the Lincoln cabinet proved to be both talented and successful and was well utilized by the President.

It is probably in the areas of leadership that Lincoln's talents are most visible. Like his predecessors, he brought evidence of his talent and ability from the obvious success of his law practice, Further evidence of his gifts emanates from the confidence placed in him by his fellow legislators in Illinois and those in the inner circles of the Whig, and, later, Republican Parties. Much the same might be said of his predecessor as well, but, in the case of Buchanan the talents seem to have disappeared with the inauguration. In Lincoln's case, they not only remained; they grew and flourished.

It was not, of course, that he did not make errors; he did. But he seems to have recognized them and, when he did, then took steps to obviate them by taking counsel, as he had with Senator Sumner at the time of the Trent Affair. Lincoln would correct his mistakes and move on.

If Seward and Chase were innately distrustful, even jealous, of one another, Lincoln was not above turning their vanity to his purposes. In some cases, he would rather ostentatiously consult Chase, in Seward's absence, particularly in regard to issues of emancipation. Chase, more radical on the topic than Seward, offered Lincoln not only advice but also political "cover" against criticism from the Republican Party's radical wing. At the same time, barring obvious error or clear deviation from administration policy, each member of the cabinet was allowed to run his department with substantial independence, assuming always that he remembered who set administration policy.

The President often used his well-known penchant for storytelling and/ or humor to deflect, even to ignore, questions he did not wish to answer. In that way he was able to defer, if not always avoid, criticism.

Determination regarding first principles was a norm for Lincoln as well as a major strength. If deference to the Border States on the slavery issue was necessary during the early part of the war, then Horace Greeley and other radicals were free to stew about the President's "fickleness." When the time for emancipation arrived, moderates on the slavery question could fulminate to their heart's content, but the President would act. Consistency was not considered a major virtue in this administration, except in matters of principle.

Called upon to wage the largest war Americans had ever fought, Lincoln was blessed by the fact that, sharing the very Whig idea that a President need not initiate legislation, he could concentrate on military and strategic problems, such as what to do about slavery. Meanwhile, Congress moved forward on such issues as tariffs and transcontinental railroads and homestead acts and the other elements of the 1860 Republican platform.

Many of his generals, to whom he initially deferred upon the basis of their presumed expertise, were unwilling or unable to act decisively. Faced with that reality, he sought, like a good lawyer, to educate himself about his new case. He read books on military strategy and tactics, with mixed results. The passing of time and the removal of timid or incompetent generals ultimately would provide him with compliant commanders. If those commanders did not always completely agree with Lincoln, they did understand what the term "Commander-in-Chief" meant. It is interesting to note that while General McClellan was, and remained, beloved at least by the Army of the Potomac, even after his final relief, when he ran against Lincoln on the Democratic ticket in 1864 the soldier vote was overwhelmingly Lincoln's.

It may be safely said of Abraham Lincoln, that he discharged the duties of the presidency with humanity, with purpose, intelligence and grace. As

Lincoln has been lauded for his honesty, so he is recognized for the depth of his intellect, for the solidity of his integrity and for the breadth of his imagination. Those virtues are magnified when he is compared with his immediate predecessors.

When we read Lincoln's speeches today, nearly 150 years after his death, we are still struck not only by the grace and beauty of his use of the English language, long correlated with intelligence, but by his use of analogy, simile and metaphor. All are surely signs of the imaginative use of language.

Given these attributes and characteristics and the depth of humanity that characterizes his thought, his claim to high regard seems self-evident.

We would illustrate this conclusion by referencing the last paragraph of his First Inaugural, with which we began this chapter. Then we would cite the conclusion of the Gettysburg Address: "... we here highly resolve that these dead shall not have died in vain – that this nation, under God, shall have a new birth of freedom – and that government of the people, by the people and for the people, shall not perish from the earth." Finally, we would cite the conclusion of his Second Inaugural Address: "With malice toward none, with charity for all, with firmness in the right as God gives us to see the right, let us strive on to finish the work we are in, to bind up the nation's wounds, to care for him who shall have borne the battle and for his widow and his orphan, to do all which may achieve and cherish a just and lasting peace among ourselves and with all other nations."

In these we find three of the most literate, lyrical and moving passages in the English language.

The Republican platform of 1860 outlined the domestic policy agenda of the party and of the administration. An ambitious platform – driven by a victorious, dynamic and vigorous party – it sought to proscribe slavery in the territories. It advocated a transcontinental railway. It sought to make free farmland available to actual settlers and to establish a protective tariff. In the absence of southern representatives and senators, who had opposed these measures, they were all enacted.

The Lincoln administration, then in less than five years, fought and won a great war, preserved the Union and ended slavery. In addition, it passed the Homestead Act and established the land grant colleges. It passed protective tariff legislation, established the agriculture department, although not yet with cabinet status, and reformed and stabilized banking with the National Banking Act. Some of these actions caused tension between northeastern and western Republicans. Not all were happy with each result. Given the fact, though, that the administration was engaged in the Civil War at the same time, the sum total of domestic legislation, reform and innovation is highly impressive.

The abolition of slavery had not been a portion of the Republican Platform of 1860 and clearly was driven by events and by presidential decision and energy – though a good many members of Congress were cheerful accomplices in the task.

Foreign policy was not on holiday during the Civil War, but from 1861 to 1865 the war determined which foreign policy issues were to be most seriously addressed. Other than diplomatic notes, the French invasion of Mexico shortly after the Civil War began was pigeonholed until after America's war had ended. In Europe, the Russian Tsar found it politic to favor the Union, while Britain and France, at least until 1863, toyed with diplomatic recognition of the Confederacy. At the same time, those two nations considered pressuring for some sort of mediated settlement, which almost surely would have been to the South's advantage. British shipyards built or converted vessels as blockade runners and commerce raiders for the Confederate States.

Lincoln and Seward adhered to the principle of "one war at a time." They were aided by able work by Charles Francis Adams, the son of one President and the grandson of another, as minister to England. William L. Dayton, the minister to France, also aided the cause. They labored to solve problems by argument, sometimes to delay by discussion and to ease problems with Europe's major powers, while focusing on winning the war at home. By and large, the policy was successful, but there was little room at the time for boasting of American diplomacy. Today, the efforts may be seen as firm and genuine. At the time, they were of course contingent upon day-to-day events and figures, and, like all contingencies, seemed at times futile or ephemeral.

Probably the closest thing to a critical mistake during Lincoln's presidency was in foreign affairs. That was the Trent Affair. Without doubt, it had the potential to bring England into war with the United States, and there were important figures in England who would have wished it so. It began with the seizure of the British mail steamer Trent by the United States Navy. Aboard were James Murray Mason and John Slidell, Confederate diplomats en route to Europe as Jefferson Davis' emissaries to Britain and France. Brought to New York, they were incarcerated to great public acclaim. Both Seward and Lincoln were nearly as pleased as the public. However, the seizure was in violation of international law and longstanding U. S. policy extending back before the War of 1812.

An angry British government began shipping British soldiers to Canada. Fortunately, Prince Albert, Queen Victoria's Prince Consort, urged delay on the British government. Meanwhile, President Lincoln, advised by Senator Sumner, rethought the American position. Despite public opinion, Lincoln backed down.

Militarily, Lincoln's early proclamation of the blockade contained the possibility for considerable mischief. It came perilously close to granting recognition to the Confederacy, and, initially, the United States Navy could not physically maintain it. Jefferson Davis' embargo of cotton experts proved to be a useful balm.

Other matters with potential for significant error were recognized by Lincoln himself, as when General John C. Frémont and Secretary of War Cameron early in the Civil War unburdened themselves of pronouncements freeing the slaves. Lincoln, determined to keep the Border States in the Union, either caused the proclamations to be rescinded or, as in Frémont's case, revoked it himself.

To borrow Whitman's metaphor in mourning for Lincoln's death in O Captain, My Captain, overall, for the uncharted waters in which he was sailing, Lincoln proved to be agile and sagacious: an adept and astute helmsman.

As we mentioned at the conclusion of our discussion of Franklin Delano Roosevelt, our respondents placed Abraham Lincoln first when asked their present overall view of America's Presidents.

Chapter 11 - Theodore Roosevelt – September 14, 1901 – March 4, 1909

"There is a homely adage, which runs, 'Speak softly and carry a big stick: you will go far.'"
– West African adage, quoted by Theodore Roosevelt, Minnesota State Fair, 1901.

"We demand that big business give the people a square deal; in return we must insist that when any one engaged in big business honestly endeavors to do right he shall himself be given a square deal."
– (Theodore Roosevelt, An Autobiography, p. 822.)

In the election of 1900, William McKinley was elected President of the United States with Theodore Roosevelt of New York as his vice president. In the wake of McKinley's assassination on September 14, 1901, Roosevelt became President.

Born in 1858, so far the only President ever to have been born in New York City, his accession to office to office at 42 made him to date the youngest man ever to serve as President of the United States. (John F. Kennedy remains the youngest man ever elected President, at 43, in 1960.)

In the 2002 SRI tracking poll, the experts ranked Theodore Roosevelt in third place.

Theodore Roosevelt was, famously, a fragile child. He suffered from asthma and other infirmities. Intellectually precocious and encouraged by his father, he determined to overcome his physical problems and almost willed himself into improved health. A rigorous regime of physical conditioning and exercise – boxing, riding, hiking and camping – saw him emerge as a robustly healthy young man. As the ideal of his era would have put it, he personified a sound mind in a sound body.

He became an accomplished writer early in life, and his interests were wide-ranging. Few if any Presidents have been as frequently published or in as many areas of intellectual interest. He developed an early interest in nature, particularly in birds. His first two books were on ornithology and were published before his graduation from Harvard in 1880. He graduated magna cum laude and was elected to Phi Beta Kappa.

The years immediately following his college graduation were full of what seems almost frenzied activity. On October 27th, 1880, his birthday, he married his first wife, Alice Lee Roosevelt. In 1881, he was elected to the New York State Assembly as a Republican. He was its youngest member. In this period he briefly was enrolled in the law school of Columbia University. In 1882, he published his first work of history, The Naval War of 1812. It was very well received in academic circles, was required reading at the Naval War College, and, for a time, a copy of the book was placed aboard all vessels of the United States Navy. It remains an often reprinted and not infrequently cited standard work on the subject. In 1882 he was also commissioned as a second lieutenant in the New York National Guard and was promoted to captain in 1883.

In the assembly he was marked as a reformer, particularly regarding child labor. He also was interested in tenement housing conditions and other problems of New York City, which probably reinforced his tendency toward reform politics. In 1883, after his triumphant reelection by a 2-1 margin, he quickly became the minority leader of the assembly, though only barely 25.

In February of 1884, within a 72-hour period following the birth of his daughter Alice, he witnessed the deaths of his wife, Alice, and his mother. In the wake of his bereavement, he retreated to the far West, where he threw himself into the culture of the area and into ranching. During this period in the Dakota Territory, while emulating the life of a westerner of the period, he continued to write and publish.

Returning to New York City, he was an unsuccessful candidate for mayor in 1886. Roosevelt was badly defeated, finishing third. Shortly thereafter, in December of 1886, in London, he remarried. His new bride was his childhood friend, Edith Carew. The marriage would produce five additional children – Theodore, Jr.; Kermit; Ethel, Archibald and Quentin. Quite notably, all of his sons would serve in combat in World War I. Quentin, a pilot, was killed in action. Kermit, awaiting America's decision to enter the war, served with the British in modern day Iraq and later with the American Expeditionary Force. He also, like his surviving brothers, would serve in World War II. Archibald, like his oldest brother, would serve with the First Infantry Division in World War I. He was severely wounded, awarded the Croix de Guerre and retired from the service. In World War II he solicited the assistance of his distant cousin, President Franklin Roosevelt, returned to service and fought with the 41st Infantry Division in New Guinea. He was again severely wounded, in the same leg as World War I, and awarded the Silver Star. Theodore, Jr. rose to the rank of lieutenant colonel in World War I and won the Distinguished Service Cross. He also was wounded in action. He would become a general officer in World War II, assistant divisional commander of both the First Infantry Division in North Africa and Sicily and the Fourth Infantry Division on D-Day at Normandy, where he would win the Congressional Medal of Honor. When President

When President Theodore Roosevelt's Medal of Honor was awarded in 2001 (it had been recommended as a result of his exploits in Cuba in1898) they became only the second father and son combination awarded the medal. The first instance was that of the MacArthurs – Arthur in the Civil War and Douglas in World War II.

Between 1887 and 1899, Roosevelt published no fewer than nine books, one in collaboration with his longtime friend, Henry Cabot Lodge of Massachusetts. In 1889, President Benjamin Harrison appointed Roosevelt as a United States Civil Service commissioner, a position he held until his resignation in 1895. He then became president of the Board of Police Commissioners of New York City. His vigorous pursuit of police corruption garnered favorable personal publicity, as did his frequent forays onto the nighttime streets of New York in his efforts to examine the efficiency and effectiveness of the police department.

After McKinley was elected President in 1896, TR was named as assistant secretary of the navy. It was an appointment he relished, and in it he demonstrated energy and intelligence, ability and flair. With the outbreak of the Spanish American War, he resigned from the navy department. He then emerged as commander and principal recruiter for First United States Volunteer Cavalry Regiment, "Roosevelt's Rough Riders," serving first as a lieutenant colonel and later colonel.

The Rough Riders ranged from college boys to cowboys, a diverse and colorful group that attracted considerable attention from the press. His leadership was effective and, like the unit, was characterized by verve and valor. The so-called charge up San Juan Hill (Kettle Hill) was one of the most publicized events of the Cuban campaign. For it, he was nominated for the Medal of Honor.

Upon his return from Cuba, his heroism and reputation caused the New York State Republican Party to nominate him for governor. The election was closely contested, and Roosevelt won by fewer than 20,000 votes of more than 1.3 million cast. His two-year term saw his popularity grow. His reform tendencies, however, were not welcomed by the party's state leadership, so they maneuvered to nominate him as the national party's vice-presidential candidate on the McKinley ticket in 1900, effectively removing him from Albany.

Despite his comparative youth, Theodore Roosevelt presented a significant résumé. In addition to the precocity displayed in his early education, he brought to the table an outstanding undergraduate education and record of publication well before he attained his 25th birthday. That resume also included his election and reelection to the New York State Assembly and his selection as assembly minority leader.

By the time he was 40, he also had run for mayor of New York City, been a United States Civil Service commissioner, a New York City police commissioner, assistant secretary of the navy, a colonel commanding a combat regiment in Cuba and the governor of New York. He was entitled to claim military fame and wide ranging political experience as well as a significant record of publication on both academic and modern political topics, as well as on the American West.

As a party leader, as both governor and President, there were complexities, perhaps contradictions, in TR's political life. He was, without doubt, an immensely popular political leader. He was probably the most popular Republican chief executive between Lincoln and Reagan, certainly between Lincoln and Eisenhower. In practice, howeved – by the standards of his day, and, perhaps in particular, the standards of the GOP's Senate "Old Guard" – he was not a comfortable fit. He represented the party's progressive wing. Not infrequently, particularly in the Senate, he would find more support from congressional Democrats than from Republicans.

In his use of the presidency as the "bully pulpit," TR was drawing to a degree upon changes begun in the McKinley administration. By embracing them fully and welding them to his own personality, he further developed the concept of the White House as the center of the federal government and also made it a personal machine for influencing public opinion. That opinion, in turn, became a vehicle for influencing the development and course of political events. In personalizing the presidency, TR would alter or influence the Republican Party by attracting new voters to its banners and by swaying the opinion of loyal party members. He would be far less successful – indeed, on occasion counter-productive – when he tried to alter or reform the thought of Old Guard party nabobs like Senator Nelson Aldrich of Rhode Island.

Roosevelt became, almost surely unintentionally, the incarnation of the new ideas labeled as "Progressivism." He often sought to downplay that identity in a party that – in Washington, at least – was seeking ways to

270

oppose such reforms. For the Old Guard, the problem was that whether TR functioned as a preacher or an icon his message was virtually inescapable. It was always heard and very frequently greeted with at least some degree of approbation.

Certainly, he was a communicator of the first order. Whether as author or orator, he was one of the most successful and influential of all American Presidents. Author of nearly a score of books, he also served as editor of Outlook magazine and contributed numerous articles to a wide variety of magazines, periodicals and journals. He was fluent in several languages and it is claimed that he had a photographic memory. Some suggest, with little dissent, that no American President was ever more widely read than Theodore Roosevelt.

TR's relationship with Congress between 1901 and 1909 is probably best described as prickly. The post-Civil War period had seen an expansion of the authority and ascendancy of the legislative branch. By the time of McKinley, the executive branch had begun to push back. Roosevelt would push harder and less tactfully than McKinley. "Matchless in his day as a campaigner and popular politician, Roosevelt did not display comparable excellence in his relations with Congress and his party."

He seemed, at his accession, to have understood the likelihood of a problem. His decision to retain all the members of McKinley's cabinet has been seen by scholars as a bid to prove that he was conservative, not radical; that he was unlikely to throw out the baby with the bathwater. That caution waned as his self-confidence grew. His unguarded criticisms of members of Congress, or Congress in general, coupled with a tendency to prefer executive fiats, went down badly. In less than eight years he would send more than 400 presidential messages to the legislature, averaging more than four per month. By the start of his second term, the technique had become old hat, tedious and irksome to members who to a substantial degree were less well disposed to change than was the President.

In one area, he did seem to exercise some sensitivity to the Old Guard. That was in his deference to the protective tariff. High tariffs were, perhaps, the oldest of the party's shibboleths, reaching back to the days before the party's existence when it was a Whig idea. Stiff tariffs were central to the platforms of Henry Clay, who was Lincoln's ideal American politician. It was a plank that had stood McKinley in good stead in 1896 and 1900. While TR cheerfully would have signed a reduced tariff measure, and occasionally spoke to the topic, it was not really addressed until the presidency of William Howard Taft.

Nonetheless as he became surer of himself he sought to develop legislation designed to counter the activities of the trusts – unions of major companies designed to limit competition and restrain trade. TR always, however, drew a clear distinction between good trusts and bad trusts. If a trust controlled an entire industry but provided good service at reasonable rates, it was a "good" trust to be left alone. If it jacked up prices and exploited the public, then it was the public's enemy and his as well. As he applied more pressure, a breach developed between President Roosevelt and the Senate Republican leadership over these matters. Narrow at first, it widened.

As time passed and Roosevelt's activism in urging legislative action grew, so did the friction. Discomfort with House Republicans does not appear to be equivalent to that in the Senate, but certainly Speaker Joseph Cannon, who had entered the House when Roosevelt was 14, was often a reluctant ally, sometimes simply recalcitrant. The House, of course, had wider Republican majorities than the Senate. Perhaps presidential popularity (and coat tails) had greater impact there than in a Senate whose members were still chosen by state legislatures and not by popular vote.

Theodore Roosevelt appointed three men as associate justices of the Supreme Court. The first, Oliver Wendell Holmes, Jr., was both the most famous and the most influential. Holmes was, oddly enough, bracketed by the Roosevelts. Appointed in 1902 by Theodore, he resigned in 1932, the year in which Franklin was elected. The second justice was William Rufus Day of Ohio, who served from 1903 to 1922. Finally, in 1906, he nominated William Henry Moody, who, like Holmes, was from Massachusetts.

Holmes is regarded as one of the three or four most influential justices to serve in the 20th Century. As a general rule, he supported federal regulation to control big business, was a strong supporter of a broad interpretation of freedom of speech under the First Amendment – although not to include the right to shout fire in a crowded theater – and was a legal pragmatist. President Roosevelt was, however, disappointed when Holmes did not support the government in a crucial anti-trust matter, the Northern Securities Case.

Holmes had enlisted in the Union Army while in his senior year at Harvard, and saw extensive combat service from 1862-1865. At war's end he returned to Harvard for law school. As a practitioner, he edited the American Law Review, published frequent legal articles and, in 1881, wrote The Common Law. In 1882, he was appointed to the Supreme Judicial Court of Massachusetts and, in 1889, was elevated to chief justice. He served in that capacity until his appointment to the Supreme Court. Eminently well qualified, he is famed for his decisions and his judicial philosophy, as well as for the quality and clarity of the prose in which those decisions were couched.

William Rufus Day was a close friend of President McKinley and had served him as assistant secretary of state and secretary of state, signing the Peace of Paris that ended the Spanish-American War. McKinley then appointed him to the United States Court of Appeals in 1899. It was from that position that Theodore Roosevelt elevated him to the Supreme Court in January of 1903. He retired after 19 years of service. Day was a workhorse, the author of more than 400 opinions and fewer than 25 dissents. He was a reliable vote on the anti-trust side of the era, though skeptical of federal power. It was the expansion of state regulatory authority that made him most comfortable. To him, that posed fewer constitutional problems than did the expansion of federal authority.

Moody, the last appointment, was, like TR and Holmes, a Harvard alumnus. His resumé included service in the House of Representatives and as both assistant secretary of the navy and attorney general under Roosevelt. Appointed in late 1906, he served for only four years. Severe rheumatism shortened his career, and he never sat after the spring of 1909. While he may be said to have displayed a bent toward expanding federal power, the brevity of his service makes him difficult to define clearly.

Like his predecessors of the 1850s, Theodore Roosevelt may be said to have enjoyed good fortune with the economy in an era in which there was little federal intervention in economic affairs. The "full dinner pail" of the McKinley campaigns, associated with the gold standard and relatively high tariffs, generally continued throughout the Roosevelt years, with the exception of the brief bank crisis of 1907. Recovery from that event was evident as early as January of 1908.

Our scholars consider Theodore Roosevelt the luckiest of America's presidents. His leadership style was well attuned to the ambience of his era, and the problems and opportunities he faced coincided with realities that, by and large, worked to his advantage.

Thus, at a time when Britain felt isolated among the European powers and was increasingly concerned with the growth of German power, the United Kingdom was disposed to gratify the United States if possible when difficulties arose regarding the Alaska-Canadian boundary. The fact that TR was an anglophile did nothing to alter that disposition.

His basic tendency toward moderation and his search for a middle ground also were helpful. His perceived attacks on the trusts were neither universal nor unalloyed. The President sought to regulate, to control if necessary and to punish only what he perceived to be bad trusts. He recognized that some of the new, immense corporations were not malefactors at all, but benefactors. He had no desire to harm them or to litigate against their interests. In a similar fashion, while he thought that the protective tariff of his day was too high, he recognized its place in the pantheon of Republican Party principles and contented himself with occasional anti-tariff pronouncements. He never crusaded on the issue.

This element of his temperament undoubtedly stood him in good stead as he acted as a mediator between Japanese and Russian delegations and interests and demands, resulting in the Treaty of Portsmouth (New Hampshire) ending the Russo-Japanese War in 1905. Those efforts also brought TR the Nobel Peace Prize.

Certainly, the President was capable of bold and uncompromising action. That facet of his personality and policy was probably best seen in his orders and decisions in relation to creation of the Panama Canal. When the Columbian government proved reluctant to act in accordance with the wishes of the United States in regard to Panama, Roosevelt moved with alacrity and vigor. A revolution in the Columbian province of Panama created a Panamanian nation, with some assistance from the United States Navy. The necessary treaty with the new nation was speedily concluded, and the Canal was soon open for business.

For most of the years of Theodore Roosevelt's presidency, there were nine cabinet positions, including the postmaster general. The departments of agriculture and of commerce and labor had been created in 1901 and 1903, respectively. No fewer than 29 men occupied those positions. At the outset, all were McKinley holdovers who had been retained for the sake of continuity and to proclaim TR's moderate political stance to the Old Guard.

The President had no strong affinity for individuals and positions. He was prepared to "mix and match" as the moment seemed to require. Thus, when John Hay, the incumbent secretary of state died, he moved the incumbent secretary of war, Elihu Root, a sterling performer in both offices, from war to state. Charles Bonaparte and William Moody each would serve the administration as both attorney general and secretary of the navy. George B. Cortelyou, in his turn, would be secretary of commerce and labor and secretary of the treasury. Victor Metcalf would move from secretary of commerce and labor to secretary of the navy. Ultimately, TR would have no fewer than six secretaries of the Navy. This President also expected his cabinet appointees to lend their talents to the campaign trail when he deemed it useful. As a general rule, the members of his cabinet were diligent, efficient, intelligent and trustworthy.

Few men, if any, were as intelligent and as temperamentally suited to the office as Theodore Roosevelt. He, himself, remarked on how much he enjoyed it. The personalization of the office in the President and the expansion of the public relations aspects of the executive branch were his delight. He not only personified position and policy, he carried the task out with flair. It all seemed to many of his contemporaries very much in accord with the temper of the new century, and the man seemed almost to burst with vigor, imagination and zeal.

Any brief consideration of his administration would bring to mind a plethora of terms, ideas and policies. To mention a few:

(A) "Trustbusting." Though his successor, Taft, would prosecute more cases, TR's prosecution of the Northern Securities Case to its successful conclusion came to epitomize the concept.

(B) The Roosevelt Corollary to the Monroe Doctrine illustrated an exuberant, self-confident America, forbidding European intervention in the Western Hemisphere but itself willing to intervene to preclude such activity.

(C) Regulation of big business activity was a hallmark of the administration, as shown in the Hepburn Act (1906) or the Pure Food and Drug Act (1906). In the case of the latter, the President's enthusiastic support was bolstered by the publication of Upton Sinclair's novel, The Jungle, exposing horrendous conditions in the meat packing industry. Certainly too, TR's name is and undoubtedly always will be linked with

(D) the emergence of the conservation movement in the United States.

While he certainly faced difficulties, particularly in the Senate, in advancing portions of his agenda his messages to Congress and other uses of the bully pulpit were an important instrument in his success and an important fact of political life in the early years of the 20th Century.

He was also the first President to intervene actively in a labor dispute when problems arose in 1902 between miners and the owners of the anthracite coal mines. By 1903, the President, by sheer force of will and actions of dubious legality and constitutionality, had effected a solution favorable to the miners and which provided coal to heat American homes.

Probably no aspect of his presidency was nearer to his heart, or more evocative of his imagination, than his devotion to the conservation of natural resources and natural beauty. He began establishing natural parks in 1902 with Crater Lake in Oregon and four others. He also established the first federal bird reservation in 1903 and federal game reserves in 1905, when he also supported the creation of the National Forest Service. In 1906, he signed the National Monuments Act. By 1908, it included the Grand Canyon.

Regrettably, President Roosevelt had a rather checkered record in racial affairs. By the turn of the century, Americans in general and the Republican Party in particular had largely turned away from concern about the plight of black Americans. A new social emphasis on overcoming the pains of the Civil War and reaching a new accommodation with white southerners was the standard social construct of the period. Indeed, during the Spanish-American War, recruiting broadsides had been issued signed by surviving general officers from both the Union and Confederate sides of the Civil War. These publications clearly called men to the colors as an exercise in the final reconstitution of the Union. President Roosevelt, whose instincts may have been sound, nevertheless found himself in sympathy with that sentiment.

It is true that he was the first President ever to invite a black man to dinner in the White House. That was author/educator Booker T. Washington, who was himself an accommodationist. It is also true that Roosevelt then coped well with the anger of white southerners. However, it was also TR who in 1906 dealt poorly with the case of black soldiers of the segregated 25th Infantry Regiment when some of them were accused of rioting, resulting in a white death in Brownsville, Texas. The army essentially railroaded a dozen accused soldiers. They were not given counsel, and scholars have found little if any convincing evidence of due process. By the autumn of 1906, when no other black soldiers could be found willing to testify against the 12, the Army recommended that three companies of soldiers be dishonorably discharged and denied any future government employment. It was essentially a massive instance of guilt by association. Roosevelt ordered the discharges as recommended, though the men had not been indicted and had been convicted of no crime. They were offered no opportunity to defend themselves. The case seems particularly thoughtless and repugnant.

Nonetheless, his success as a leader is beyond argument. The 1906 congressional elections illustrated that. Most scholars agree that the Republican victories in that off-year election when the majority party normally loses seats owes much to TR even though the President, closing in on the end of his second term, was not even on the ballot. There is general agreement that credit for the triumph belongs to the person and policies of Theodore Roosevelt. Few, if any, scholars doubt that had he chosen to seek another term in 1908 he would have won handily. Of course, in his delight at winning the presidential election of 1904, he had said publically that serving the three and a half years of McKinley's term would constitute his first term and the electoral victory of 1904 initiated his second term. Therefore, in keeping with George Washington's two-term precedent, he would not run again. If, in 1908, he regretted those words, he never said.

Perhaps his Progressive Party campaign of 1912 against the incumbent President, Taft, and the Democratic candidate, Woodrow Wilson, may be said to speak to the issue of regret. TR's candidacy that year surely won the election for Wilson.

As chief executive, he seems to have displayed some of the same traits as his distant cousin, Franklin. He possessed a very high degree of self-confidence combined with almost boundless energy. He was decisive. He was committed to certain ideas, perhaps best identified as progressive, which he thought would serve the nation well. He labored and lobbied intensively for those ideas. In foreign policy, he, as well as events, moved the United States from triumph to triumph and from the realm of diplomatic near-obscurity to a growing role on the world stage.

In 1902, Venezuela was behind in its debts to and Britain and Germany. Ultimately, the dispute led to the bombardment of Venezuelan fortifications and to eventual arbitration. It prompted TR, by 1904, to shake the "Big Stick" as he enunciated the "Roosevelt Corollary to the Monroe Doctrine." It stipulated that European intervention in the Americas would not be permitted even if nations of the Americas were unable or unwilling to fulfill their obligations. Rather, the United States, as guarantor of the Monroe Doctrine, would exercise a sort of international police power in the hemisphere and would guarantee that the obligations would be fulfilled.

By the half-way mark of his first term, he successfully had concluded the dispute between Canada and the United States over the boundary between Alaska and British Columbia. It appeared that America had the better claim, and Roosevelt was not disposed to compromise, as he consistently informed Great Britain. The verdict, in October of 1903, was entirely satisfactory to the President. We have already mentioned the Panama Canal.

Similarly, whether negotiating the Treaty of Portsmouth in 1905 or attempting mediation between France and Germany in Algeciras, Spain, in 1906, the President of the United States definitely had become a figure of international stature in world affairs.

The President's personal style of foreign policy has also, recently, been suggested as having planted the seeds of the American/Japanese conflict in World War II. It is alleged that his tacit agreement to allow Japan to expand into Korea, which thereby began its military exploitation of mainland Asia, made future confrontation inevitable. (James Brady, The Imperial Cruise.) The facts alleged are not in dispute. The thesis, like most theories, will be subjected to argument.

Secretary of State Root provided excellent service in a diplomatic dance with Latin America. Due deference was paid to each government's sense of self-esteem. Even Columbia, still smarting from the loss of Panama, was more or less placated.

Britain was actively cultivated by the administration and, in return, cultivated the United States. Unfortunately, this left Germany neglected. Kaiser Wilhelm had nurtured hopes of an alliance with the United States. Circumstances, however – and President Roosevelt's lack of trust in Germany's Kaiser – made the relationship too tenuous even without taking into account President Washington's warning against entangling alliances.

In the last stages of the second term, tension mounted with Japan. The primary cause may be said to have been American racism. Japanese migration to California had produced unease. That, plus fear of the Chinese immigrants, resulted in both local and national decisions to limit or forbid Japanese and other Asian migrants from entering the United States. Starting in 1906, Japan and the United States, despite a number of setbacks and obstacles, worked out what would become the "Gentleman's Agreement." Secretary of war William Howard Taft went to Japan with the President's grown daughter, Alice, in tow to speed the process. In the end, Japan agreed to tighten its emigration policy. This at least gave the appearance that Japan was in charge of the process. In essence, Japan refused permits to migrate to members of the laboring class except those traveling to America to reunite with their families.

That tension certainly had some effect, though it was not the only cause for President Roosevelt's decision to send America's fleet of 16 battleships – the "Great White Fleet," plus their auxiliary vessels – on its famous cruise around the world from December, 1907, until February, 1909. TR also was also motivated by a desire for publicity for the navy. That, he hoped, might move Congress to increase appropriations for additional ships. He did in fact get authorization for two more battleships before the fleet completed its cruise.

While the fleet was visiting Japan in November, 1908, the Root-Takahira agreement was signed. It pledged both powers to a commercial open-door policy in China and to an agreement to at least consult one another if China's territorial integrity was threatened. Both provisions reflected policy positions important to the United States. Coupled with the administration's other foreign policy achievements between 1901 and 1909 Theodore Roosevelt is entitled to considerable praise in diplomacy and foreign policy.

Few people who have served at any level of government would be able to present better credentials attesting to their intelligence than TR. In addition to his education and his mastery of foreign languages, he established through his publications legitimate claims as a naturalist, ornithologist, political scientist and historian. No other President has published as many serious studies ranging as extensively over such a variety of fields. In addition, he was a prominent magazine editor. As editor of Outlook, he not only supervised and wrote, but he also personally reviewed the poetry of Edward Arlington Robinson, introducing the poet to a wide audience. He was also a substantive political reformer who, like many other Presidents, was able to attract other gifted intellectuals into his orbit. He devoted time and energy to insure that the wonderful Charles L. Freer art collection would come into possession of the United States government. It is likely that his precocious interest in ornithology and nature might well have formed the intellectual basis for his advanced and staunch conservationist principles.

It would be an inanity to suggest that no errors or miscalculations occurred in the seven-and-a-half years of Theodore Roosevelt's presidency. Race, as epitomized in the Brownsville, Texas, incident and its aftermath, would surely occupy a prominent place on a list of errors. The-wink-and-a-nudge agreement to Japan's expansion into Korea might be another. None of his errors, however, seems to have registered as such with any large portion of his constituency. Indeed, they probably reflected the prejudices and eccentricities of his people and his era.

It is possible, regardless of academic rankings, that no President, except Washington in his first term, was ever as popular in his own time as was Theodore Roosevelt. Among the five top-ranked American Presidents in SRI polling, most – Washington, Lincoln, FDR – saw administrations characterized by triumph over disaster or threatened disaster. Jefferson represented the then-astonishing fact of a peaceful transition of power from one faction or party to another without resort to violence or revolution. In addition, Jefferson's first term was characterized by the Louisiana Purchase and the dramatic physical expansion of the nation. His second was marked by the issues of the Anglo-French wars, impressment and the Embargo.

TR, of course, like Jefferson, led the United States both into a new century and a new era. The political changes in TR's America owed considerable debt to the McKinley administration but even more to the personality of the President. Nevertheless, as important as they were for the United States in the 20th Century, those changes were probably not very visible – certainly not earthshaking to the individual citizen of the day. What was visible, exciting and full of hope for the future was the persona of the President, whose total enjoyment of the experience was nearly tangible. It, and he, were "bully!"

The professors who have responded to the surveys over the years, always have placed Theodore Roosevelt among the top five. In the 2002 survey, in their present overall view, he was awarded fourth place.

Chapter 12 Ratings of Recent Presidents
– And the Nominees Are – Kennedy to Clinton

While not the main theme of this book, we are including the ratings of recent Presidents – those who have served in the recent past, the 40 years between the inauguration of John Kennedy and the end of President Clinton's term. As we have stipulated, the younger President Bush and President Obama lie outside the scope of this work. As a result of the interest shown by our colleagues and by readers of the various drafts of this book, we were persuaded to include these rankings of what would be best described as recent or modern Presidents. These results, like those which form the core of the book, are based on the responses to the SRI 2002 survey. The eight Presidents and their rankings in the poll are as follows. Interestingly enough, at this point they occupy the fundamental middle-ground. Thirteen presidents are ranked higher than they are collectively and 14 lower.

1. John Kennedy	14	5. G. H. W. Bush	22
2. Lyndon Johnson	15	6. Jimmy Carter	24
3. Ronald Reagan	16	7. Richard Nixon	25
4. William Clinton	18	8. Gerald Ford	27

Of the modern Presidents, the highest ranking in any category was second. That place was awarded to Lyndon Johnson in the category Relationship with Congress and to William Clinton for Handling of the U.S. Economy. The worst ranking, last place, was awarded to Richard Nixon for Integrity 41st, followed closely by Lyndon Johnson's 40th for Foreign Policy Accomplishments.

We will begin with a list of the eight, accompanied by the categories in which each finished best and worst.

	BEST		WORST	
Kennedy	Communication ability	5	Integrity	35
Johnson	Relationship with Congress	2	Foreign policy	40
Nixon	Willing to take risks	11	Integrity	41
	Foreign policy accomplishments	11		
Ford	Integrity	13	Communication ability	36
Carter	Integrity	5	Luck	36
Reagan	Luck	3	Background/Intelligence	38
Bush	Background	10	Handling of U.S. Economy	35
Clinton	Handling of U. S. economy	2	Avoid crucial mistakes	38

John F. Kennedy – January 20, 1961- November 22, 1963

Siena College Research Institute   Overall Ranking # 14

CATEGORY	RANK
1. Background [family, education, experience]	11
2. Party leadership [political]	16
3. Communication ability [speak, write]	5
4. Relationship with Congress	15
5. Court appointments	11
6. Handling of U. S. economy	8
7. Luck	21
8. Ability of compromise	11
9. Willing to take risks	11
10. Executive appointments	7
11. Overall ability	16
12. Imagination	6
13. Domestic accomplishments	15
14. Integrity	35
15. Executive ability	15
16. Foreign policy accomplishments	17
17. Leadership ability	9
18. Intelligence	11
19. Avoid crucial mistakes	18
20. Your present overall view	15

"Every nation knows, whether it wishes us well or ill, that we shall pay any price, bear any burden, meet any hardship … in order to insure the survival and the success of liberty."

Inaugural address, January 20th, 1961.

Lyndon B. Johnson – November 22, 1963- January 20, 1969

Siena College Research Institute   Overall Ranking # 15

CATEGORY	RANK
1. Background [family, education, experience]	16
2. Party leadership [political]	4
3. Communication ability [speak, write]	13
4. Relationship with Congress	2
5. Court appointments	10
6. Handling of U. S. economy	18
7. Luck	25
8. Ability of compromise	8
9. Willing to take risks	10
10. Executive appointments	9
11. Overall ability	12
12. Imagination	15
13. Domestic accomplishments	5
14. Integrity	37
15. Executive ability	11
16. Foreign policy accomplishments	40
17. Leadership ability	14
18. Intelligence	19
19. Avoid crucial mistakes	33
20. Your present overall view	16

"We have talked long enough ... about equal rights. We have talked for 100 years... It is time now to write the next chapter and to write it in the books of law."
November 27, 1963

Richard M. Nixon – January 20, 1969 – August 9, 1974

Siena College Research Institute   Overall Ranking #25

CATEGORY	RANK
1. Background [family, education, experience]	17
2. Party leadership [political]	19
3. Communication ability [speak, write]	19
4. Relationship with Congress	34
5. Court appointments	29
6. Handling of U. S. economy	21

7. Luck	33
8. Ability of compromise	30
9. Willing to take risks	11
10. Executive appointments	33
11. Overall ability	19
12. Imagination	18
13. Domestic accomplishments	22
14. Integrity	41
15. Executive ability	24
16. Foreign policy accomplishments	11
17. Leadership ability	25
18. Intelligence	16
19. Avoid crucial mistakes	40
20. Your present overall view	33

"I am not a crook."
Press conference, November 17, 1973

Gerald R. Ford - August 9, 1974 – January 20, 1977
Siena College Research Institute   Overall Ranking # 27

CATEGORY	RANK
1. Background [family, education, experience]	18
2. Party leadership [political]	26
3. Communication ability [speak, write]	36
4. Relationship with Congress	23
5. Court appointments	21
6. Handling of U. S. economy	37
7. Luck	26
8. Ability of compromise	17
9. Willing to take risks	31
10. Executive appointments	23
11. Overall ability	30
12. Imagination	31
13. Domestic accomplishments	30
14. Integrity	13
15. Executive ability	27
16. Foreign policy accomplishments	27
17. Leadership ability	32
18. Intelligence	33

19. Avoid crucial mistakes   23
20. Your present overall view   25

"My fellow Americans, our long national nightmare is over."
Gerald Ford on the day he succeeded Richard Nixon, August 9, 1974.

James E. Carter – January 20, 1977 – January 20, 1981
Siena College Research Institute   Overall Ranking # 24

CATEGORY	RANK
1. Background [family, education, experience]	27
2. Party leadership [political]	35
3. Communication ability [speak, write]	24
4. Relationship with Congress	35
5. Court appointments	17
6. Handling of U. S. economy	17
7. Luck	36
8. Ability of compromise	27
9. Willing to take risks	21
10. Executive appointments	22
11. Overall ability	26
12. Imagination	17
13. Domestic accomplishments	25
14. Integrity	5
15. Executive ability	31
16. Foreign policy accomplishments	24
17. Leadership ability	30
18. Intelligence	10
19. Avoid crucial mistakes	31
20. Your present overall view	23

"The love of liberty is a common blood that flows in our American veins."
Farewell Address, January 14, 1981.

Ronald W. Reagan – January 20, 1981 – January 20, 1989
Siena College Research Institute   Overall Ranking # 16

CATEGORY	RANK
1. Background [family, education, experience]	36
2. Party leadership [political]	5

3. Communication ability [speak, write]	7
4. Relationship with Congress	9
5. Court appointments	25
6. Handling of U. S. economy	20
7. Luck	3
8. Ability of compromise	15
9. Willing to take risks	15
10. Executive appointments	27
11. Overall ability	23
12. Imagination	19
13. Domestic accomplishments	17
14. Integrity	23
15. Executive ability	17
16. Foreign policy accomplishments	14
17. Leadership ability	9
18. Intelligence	36
19. Avoid crucial mistakes	10
20. Your present overall view	14

"Mr. Gorbachev, tear down this wall!"
Ronald Reagan, Berlin - June 12, 1987

George H. W. Bush – January 20, 1989 – January 20, 1993
Siena College Research Institute   Overall Ranking # 22

CATEGORY	RANK
1. Background [family, education, experience]	10
2. Party leadership [political]	22
3. Communication ability [speak, write]	28
4. Relationship with Congress	21
5. Court appointments	31
6. Handling of U. S. economy	35
7. Luck	20
8. Ability of compromise	13
9. Willing to take risks	24
10. Executive appointments	20
11. Overall ability	24
12. Imagination	25
13. Domestic accomplishments	27
14. Integrity	19

15. Executive ability	21
16. Foreign policy accomplishments	13
17. Leadership ability	20
18. Intelligence	23
19. Avoid crucial mistakes	21
20. Your present overall view	21

"My opponent won't rule out raising taxes. But I will. ... Read my lips, no new taxes."
Acceptance speech, Republican National Convention, August 18, 1988

William J. Clinton – January 20, 1993 – January 20, 2001
Siena College Research Institute   Overall Ranking # 18

CATEGORY	RANK
1. Background [family, education, experience]	30
2. Party leadership [political]	13
3. Communication ability [speak, write]	8
4. Relationship with Congress	28
5. Court appointments	15
6. Handling of U. S. economy	2
7. Luck	11
8. Ability of compromise	5
9. Willing to take risks	17
10. Executive appointments	19
11. Overall ability	14
12. Imagination	11
13. Domestic accomplishments	12
14. Integrity	40
15. Executive ability	18
16. Foreign policy accomplishments	21
17. Leadership ability	15
18. Intelligence	9
19. Avoid crucial mistakes	37
20. Your present overall view	20

"I'm going to say this again. I did not have sexual relations with that woman, Miss Lewinsky. ... And now I need to go back to work for the American people."
January 26, 1998.

Appendix A
Statistical Methodology

The ratings that lie at the core of this book are based on the Siena College Research Institute's 2002 survey sent to the history and political science departments at all four-year colleges and universities in the United States. That survey, representing both the end of the century and the end of the millennium, presents an historical and logical point from which to measure successful presidents and presidencies from George Washington to through Bill Clinton.

In 1980, the authors created a questionnaire, the result of which was a matrix, then 20 x 39, representing the Presidents who had served until that time. It had been created by the usual process of pilot tests and focus groups, and the 20 questions were designed to elicit judgments about significant questions relevant to presidential performance and to be as fair and equitable to all presidents as possible, considering that the period under discussion exceeded 200 years. Designed as a tracking study, we have administered the survey with each change of administration since that time.

The cover letter asked each department head to give the survey to the presidential scholar in residence. This accomplished two objectives: results would provide expert opinion and would also preclude the introduction of any bias on our part.

Respondents were asked to rate each President in each category on a scale of 1 (poor) to 5 (outstanding). Each category is assigned a weight of 5 per cent; therefore, no single category can dominate the result. We then multiply the average score of all 20 categories for each President by 20 (i.e. 3 x 20 = a rating of 60). The effect of this calculation is that 60 is an average score. As a result, we produce an overall numerical rating for each President, as well as a separate rating for each category.

We have been impressed with the consistency of the results of the polling. Changes have been few and minor. Thus, for example, the same five Presidents, with minor variations in place, have always constituted the top five Presidents. Similarly, the three lowest-ranked Presidents have also always been the same individuals.

Appendix B
The History of American Political Parties

A. During the debate over ratification of the Constitution, 1787-1788, there was a fundamental political divergence into Federalists, who favored the Constitution and a stronger central government, and the anti-Federalists, who opposed the Constitution and favored leaving power in the hands of the states and localities. Little or no significance of this division remained after ratification and the establishment of the new government.

B. Early national government 1789-1793. Most are Federalists, working to make the new system work. There is some disagreement but little organization.

C. Slow emergence of nascent political parties (1794-1800). Washington remains above the battle. Adams/Hamilton, etc., vie for leadership of an uneasy alliance of pro-nationalist, mercantile alliance, generally spoken of as Federalists. Jefferson/Madison, et al, more states rights-oriented, more agrarian in outlook, are base of emergence of what will become the modern Democratic Party. (Jeffersonian Republicans, Republican Democrat)

D. Triumph of the Democratic Party. (1800-1824) from Jefferson's electoral victory in 1800 to the "Era of Good Feelings," Federalist Party withers away. The "Era of Good Feelings" (Monroe's Presidency) is usually seen as the end of the somewhat amorphous First Party System.

E. The emergence of latent political parties from Democratic Party triumphalism, 1824-1832. Political coalitions within the Democratic Party lead to the emergence of a pro-nationalist party (National Republicans, then Whigs) while the states' rights, quasi-populist wing of the party becomes the Jacksonian Democrats. (The Democracy, as it was then known, real origin of the modern party system and the modern Democratic Party.

F. 1832-1854 – The Second Party System, dominated by Democrats and by Whigs. Introduction of party conventions and other techniques that indicated superior organization and much broader popular participation in politics. The era was also characterized by significant third-party activity

– the anti-Masonic Party, the Liberty Party (Abolitionists) and the Free Soil Party. Ends with turmoil over the Kansas-Nebraska Act and the disappearance of the Whigs and the emergence of the Republican Party.

G. 1854-1896 – The Third Party System. Dominated by Republican and Democratic Parties with Republicans usually in control of the presidency and Congress though, after Reconstruction (post-1876) Democrats did on occasion control the House of Representatives and usually made a decent showing.

H. 1896-1932 – The Fourth Party System. Dominated by the Republican Party which was, clearly, the majority party in the era. Absolute control of the presidency, other than Wilson's two terms. Political issues shifted from slavery, the Civil War and Reconstruction to the Panic of 1893, the Progressive Era, World War I, the New Immigration to the Crash of 1929 and the onset of the Great Depression.

I. The Fifth Party System 1933-1968 or later. Sometimes referred to as the New Deal Party System. There is disagreement as to whether the system continues, in some form, until today, or whether it ended sometime between 1960 and 1980. In any event, it was dominated for the earliest decades by a resounding Democratic vote. The New Deal coalition of urban bosses, the "Solid South", industrial unions and minority voters, certainly sustained itself well into the latter 1960s, or even the mid- '70s.

Endnotes

Bibliography

Primary Sources:
Theodore Roosevelt, Rough Riders/An Autobiography, New York, 2004.
Siena College Research Institute Polls, 1982, 1990, 1994, 2002.

Secondary Sources:
Appleby, Joyce, Thomas Jefferson, New York, 2003.
Brady, James, The Imperial Cruise: A Secret History of Empire and War, New York, 2009.
Burns, James McGregor, Roosevelt; The Lion and the Fox, New York, 1956.
Carter, Graydon (ed.) "Vanity Fair's" Presidential Profiles" New York, 2010.
Carwardine, Richard J. Lincoln, Harlow, Essex, U.K. 2003.
Chernow, Ron, Alexander Hamilton, New York, 2004.
Chernow, Ron, Washington: A Life, New York 2010.
deKay, James Tertius, Roosevelt's Navy, New York, 2012.
Donald, David Herbert Lincoln, New York, 1995.
Eisenhower, David, with Julie Nixon Eisenhower, Going Home to Glory: A Memoir of Life With Dwight D. Eisenhower, 1961-1969, New York, 2010.
Ellis, Joseph J., American Sphinx; The Character of Thomas Jefferson, New York, 1998.
Ellis, Joseph J., Founding Brothers; The Revolutionary Generation, New York, 2000.
Ellis, Joseph J., His Excellency, George Washington, New York, 2004.
Ferling, John, Setting the World Ablaze: Washington, Adams, Jefferson and the American Revolution, New York, 2000.
Folsom, Burton W., Jr., New Deal or Raw Deal: How FDR's Economic

Legacy Has Damaged America, New York, 2006.

Fondren Library, Rice University, Oveta Culp Hobby, Biographical Sketch, RiceUniversity.http//LibraryRice/edu/collections.

Goodwin, Doris Kearns, Team of Rivals: The Political Genius of Abraham Lincoln, New York, 2005.

Gould, Lewis L., The Presidency of Theodore Roosevelt, Lawrence, KS, 1991.

Hannaford, Peter (ed.), The Essential George Washington, Bennington, VT, 1999.

Johnson, Paul, George Washington; The Founding Father, New York, 2005.

Klein, Philip S., President James Buchanan; A Biography, Norwalk, CT, 1962.

Levy, Leonard, Jefferson and Civil Liberties: The Darker Side, Cambridge, MA, 1963.

Lonnstrom, Douglas A. and Kelly, Thomas O. II, Rating the Presidents: A Tracking Study, Presidential Studies Quarterly, v. XXVII, Number 3, Summer, 1997.

Lonnstrom, Douglas A. and Kelly, Thomas O. II, The Contemporary Presidency: Rating the Presidents: A Tracking Study Presidential Studies Quarterly, v. 33 Number 3, September, 2003.

Larson, Erik, In the Garden of the Beasts: Love, Terror and an American Family in Hitler's Germany, New York, 2011.

Matuz, Roger; ed. By Bill Harris, revised by Laura Ross, The President's Fact Book, New York, 2009.

McCullough, David, John Adams, New York, 2001.

McDonald, Forrest, The Presidency of Thomas Jefferson, Lawrence, KS, 1976.

McPherson, James M., Tried by War: Abraham Lincoln as Commander in Chief, New York, 2008.

Medhurst, Martin J. Dwight D. Eisenhower: Strategic Communicator, Westport, CT, 1993.

Medhurst, Martin J. Eisenhower's War of Words: Rhetoric and Leadership, East Lansing, MI, 1994.

Nevins, Allan, The Ordeal of the Union, 1847-1865 (8 v.) The Emergence of Lincoln: Douglas and Party Chaos, v. I, New York, 1959.

Powell, Jim, FDR's Folly: How Roosevelt and the New Deal Prolonged the Great Depression, New York, 2003.

Rayback, Robert J. Millard Fillmore, Newton, CT 1959.

Romano, Carlin, Chronicle of Higher Education, March 21, 2010, Does

One 'Compromise' Fit All.

Roosevelt, Theodore, The Rough Riders/An Autobiography, New York, 2004.

Salerian, Alen J. and Gregory H. Salerian, A Review of FDR's mental capacity during his fourth term and its impact on history, The Forensic Examiner, Spring, 2005 31+, Academic Onefile, Web 23 Nov. 2011.

Shales, Amity, The Forgotten Man: A New History of the Great Depression, New York, 2007.

Staloff, Darren, Hamilton, Adams, and Jefferson: The Politics of Enlightenment and the American Founding, New York, 2005.

Taranto, James and Leonard Leo, Presidential Profiles, New York, 2004.

Van Deusen, Glyndon G., Thurlow Weed: The Wizard of the Lobby, Boston, 1947.

Van Deusen, Glyndon G., William Henry Seward, New York, 1947.

Wallner, Peter A., Franklin Pierce, New Hampshire's Favorite Son, Concord, NH 2004.

Whitney, David C., (revised by Robin C. Whitney) 10th ed. The American Presidents, Garden City, NY, 2005.

Wilkerson, Isabel, The Warmth of Other Suns, New York, 2010.

CPSIA information can be obtained at www.ICGtesting.com
Printed in the USA
LVOW06s1659250815

451463LV00003B/445/P